YOU CAN'T KILL THE BOOGEYMAN

YOU CAN'T KILL THE BOOGEYMAN

The Ongoing Halloween Saga— 13 Movies and Counting

Wayne Byrne

Foreword by Tony Timpone

BLOOMSBURY ACADEMIC
NEW YORK • LONDON • OXFORD • NEW DELHI • SYDNEY

BLOOMSBURY ACADEMIC
Bloomsbury Publishing Inc
1385 Broadway, New York, NY 10018, USA
50 Bedford Square, London, WC1B 3DP, UK
29 Earlsfort Terrace, Dublin 2, Ireland

BLOOMSBURY, BLOOMSBURY ACADEMIC and the Diana logo are trademarks of Bloomsbury Publishing Plc

First published in the United States of America 2025

Copyright © Wayne Byrne, 2025

Cover design: Sally Rinehart
Cover images © iStock.com/Marc Dufresne; iStock.com/aetb; iStock.com/metapompa

All rights reserved. No part of this publication may be reproduced or transmitted in any form or by any means, electronic or mechanical, including photocopying, recording, or any information storage or retrieval system, without prior permission in writing from the publishers.

Bloomsbury Publishing Inc does not have any control over, or responsibility for, any third-party websites referred to or in this book. All internet addresses given in this book were correct at the time of going to press. The author and publisher regret any inconvenience caused if addresses have changed or sites have ceased to exist, but can accept no responsibility for any such changes.

Library of Congress Cataloging-in-Publication Data Available

ISBN: HB: 9781493079780
   ePDF: 9798765161241
   eBook: 9781493079797

Typeset by Deanta Global Publishing Services, Chennai, India
Printed and bound in the United States of America

To find out more about our authors and books visit www.bloomsbury.com and sign up for our newsletters.

For Jen

Contents

Acknowledgments ix

Introduction xi

"Halloween": No Slash in the Pan by Tony Timpone xiii

1 The Night Horror Came Home 1

2 Santa Mira, Silver Shamrocks, Samhain, and Stonehenge: We're Not in Haddonfield Anymore! 43

3 Severing Family Ties 59

4 A New Dimension 126

5 All in the Family 194

6 Evil Dies Tonight: *Halloween* Lives Forever 216

Index 235

Acknowledgments

First, I would like to thank my literary agent, Lee Sobel, for your interest in my work and for guiding me toward this project. Of the numerous horror film franchises that I could have written about, *Halloween* was the one that made me truly excited because I knew that the filmmakers involved in this series of films were artists that I wanted to examine and celebrate.

To all at Rowman & Littlefield and Bloomsbury for your assistance throughout this process. I greatly appreciate it.

Massive thanks to all those from the *Halloween* franchise who took the time to speak with me and share their experiences of making these films. Your contributions are invaluable. I am delighted to have met you all, and that includes Dean Cundey, Rob Draper, Dwight H. Little, Danny Lux, Peter Lyons Collister, Daniel Farrands, David Geddes, Gloria Gifford, Marianne Hagan, Alan Howarth, Brad Loree, Daryn Okada, Dominique Othenin-Girard, John Ottman, Phil Parmet, and Tommy Lee Wallace.

Special thanks to Tony Timpone for providing a wonderful foreword and for offering an expert view on the impact of the *Halloween* franchise on American Cinema as you professionally observed it. You helped connect the fans to the films through your brilliant coverage of them as editor of that most glorious horror bible, *Fangoria*.

To Mark Beer, Sean Clark, Lucinda Lewis, David McGiffert, Nick McLean, and Roy H. Wagner for your kind help in making introductions that were crucial to my crafting this book into what it is.

Deepest affection and gratitude to my dear friends Carolina Cioara and Amanda Kramer for your continued support.

To my wife, Jen, for being there always. I love you.

Introduction

This is not a definitive history of the *Halloween* franchise. This is a critical and cultural celebration of the artists involved in its creation and their art. The main players of this property (John Carpenter, Moustapha Akkad, Jamie Lee Curtis, etc.) have gone on the record numerous times over the years to tell their story of conceiving and contributing to what has become a legendary piece of American Cinema.

Among the myriad documentaries, books, and articles already available that have astutely detailed the production aspects of *Halloween* and its sequels, this book will stand alone in charting the careers of the filmmakers behind this most beloved horror franchise. Through exclusive conversations conducted with them, we examine and discuss their unique sensibilities that helped create such a rich and varied body of films that have remained relevant in pop culture and film history for the past 47 years. In speaking with these artists and discovering more about their background, influences, and techniques, we gain further insight into what makes their work a crucial element of what we love about these films. Some of the stories in here you will be familiar with. Other tales, you may not. Either way, I hope you enjoy my collection and presentation of such in this book, which is a paean to all the great artists whose vision made this franchise a special piece of film history.

"Halloween"
No Slash in the Pan
Foreword by Tony Timpone

"Who's the best slasher?"

Countless people asked me that question during my long editorial tenure at *Fangoria* (1987–2010). When the world's #1 horror magazine chronicled the original reign of the slashers, three frightful figures stood tallest above their bloody brethren. Back in the 1980s, I coined them the Titans of Terror, the Sultans of Slaughter. They were the unholy trinity of *Friday the 13th*'s Jason Voorhees; *A Nightmare on Elm Street*'s Freddy Krueger; and, of course, *Halloween*'s Michael Myers.

For a time, Jason held the title as the genre's quintessential, unstoppable killer, the one with the highest body count. Freddy then took slasherdom into a whole new realm, that of the dream world. You couldn't hide from Freddy because he stalked you in your nightmares.

But then there was Michael Myers (aka The Shape), the one who started the modern slasher without whom the others don't exist. In terms of body count alone, his carnage in just one film, 2021's *Halloween Kills*, surpasses multiple *Friday the 13th* and *Elm Street* entries combined, at 31 victims, give or take.

From my *Fangoria* desk, I noticed a curious phenomenon when, in 1988, a flood of iconic horror characters terrorized the screen like never before. These included Chucky in his first film, *Child's Play*; Pinhead in *Hellbound: Hellraiser II*; Freddy in *A Nightmare in Elm Street 4: The Dream Master*; and Jason in *Friday the 13th, Part VII: The New Blood*. However, the one that garnered the most *Fangoria* reader mail was *Halloween 4*, which brought back Michael after a seven-year cinematic sabbatical. Even though fans supported the other franchises, they held a more fervent interest in the less slick and more rudimentary *Halloween 4*. Could it be because Michael is the scariest of the slashers? Maybe so.

The huge success of John Carpenter's *Halloween* (1978)—with a $300,000 budget and a $70 million gross—would, surprisingly, be topped time and time again as the series progressed: $75 million for *Halloween H20: 20 Years Later* (1998); $80 million for Rob Zombie's *Halloween* remake (2007); and the jaw-dropping $255 million for David Gordon Green's *Halloween* reboot (2018).

After nearly $900 million and 12 films (excluding the Shapeless *Halloween III: Season of the Witch*), it's easy to crown Michael Myers King of the Slashers. But blood and guts are not the series' sole raison d'etre. To give Michael his due, we have to acknowledge that many of his adventures are not only Hitchcockian suspenseful but also just plain scary. Pretty impressive for a character who never utters a word, huh?

Think you can reason with Michael Myers? Not happening. Michael just wants to kill. He blows into Haddonfield like a human twister, and according to Carpenter, that's what makes the killer with "the devil's eyes" so darn scary.

"Michael Myers was an *absence* of character," Carpenter has said many times over the years. "You can't explain that. He's just pure evil, a force of nature. He's part person, part supernatural force."

In *You Can't Kill the Boogeyman: The Ongoing Halloween Saga— 13 Films and Counting*, author Wayne Byrne avoids any further highfalutin analysis on what makes Michael Myers tick, leaving that to the shrinks. What Byrne prefers to elucidate is what went into the making of the long-running franchise, uncovering nuggets of information that not even I came across when I covered the series for decades at *Fangoria*.

Instead of another interview with Carpenter or star Jamie Lee Curtis (at this point, we know their answers by heart), Byrne offers insights from less heralded behind-the-scenes personnel. We learn why executive producer Moustapha Akkad chose

Dwight Little and Dominique Othenin-Girard to direct *Halloween 4* and *5*, respectively, as well as what made Donald Pleasence so cranky on the sets of both those follow-ups. Byrne reveals more painful details of the *Halloween: The Curse of Michael Myers* reshoots and why fanboy-turned-screenwriter Daniel Farrands was barred from the set, as well as how the dreaded Weinsteins mangled composer John Ottman's *Halloween H20* score.

Yes, there's plenty of juicy gossip in the pages before you, all backed up by the likes of *Curse*'s Marianne Hagan (Kara Strode) and *Resurrection*'s Brad Loree (The Shape), to name a few. In addition, the series' great cinematographers all weigh in with fresh material, from the original film's Dean Cundey to part 5's Rob Draper, who wanted his installment to mirror the look of Orson Welles's *Touch of Evil*.

Of all the horror franchises, none has had as many sequels, remakes, and reboots as *Halloween*. At the end of the divisive *Halloween Ends* (2023), Laurie Strode and the survivors of the Haddonfield massacres carry the shot, stabbed, and mangled Michael Myers to a junkyard, where they ceremoniously drop his body into a giant industrial shredder, upon which what little blood he has left spews in all directions. But as author Wayne Byrne proves in this book, "You Can't Kill the Boogeyman."

Chapter One

The Night Horror Came Home

> "I realized that what was living behind that boy's eyes was purely and simply . . . evil." —Dr. Samuel Loomis

John Carpenter's *Halloween* is more than a movie: it's an emblem of the horror genre; the logo of myriad merchandise; and a symbol for successful, independent cinema that has crossed over into mainstream culture to become an industry unto itself. In the blank, expressionless face of Michael Myers, we see all these things. But *Halloween* did start out as just a movie, and a modest one at that. Budgeted at $300,000, the film is a deceptively simple but stunningly designed piece of art.

The story begins in the quiet suburban town of Haddonfield, Illinois, on Halloween night, 1963. Six-year-old Michael Myers slays his teenage sister in a brutal stabbing, which results in his being detained at Smith's Grove Sanitarium under the care of Dr. Samuel Loomis (Donald Pleasence) until 15 years later when, in anticipation of a court hearing, Michael escapes the night before Halloween. The following day, the killer returns to the streets of his youth and begins stalking local teenager Laurie Strode (Jamie Lee Curtis) and her two schoolmates, Annie and Lynda. Michael has come home, and on this Halloween night, he will wreak havoc on Haddonfield and its inhabitants. Only Dr. Loomis can help Laurie survive the man he describes as having "no reason, no conscience, no understanding in the most rudimentary sense of life or death, good or evil, right or wrong."

As terrifying and brutal as the film is, director Carpenter and his creative collaborators bring an aesthetic elegance and tastefulness not normally found in low-budget genre filmmaking, setting the bar high for horror movies to come, including its own sequels. There were hints of the director's carefully crafted minimalism in his previous film, *Assault on Precinct 13* (1976), and in many of the films to come in his career, but if there is such a thing as a director's "definitive film," it is arguably *Halloween* for John Carpenter. While filmmaking is a community effort (and this is a prime example of how working with the right collaborators results in the best work imaginable), *Halloween* is conversely an example of the auteur theory in practice. Carpenter not only directed but also cowrote the film (with producer Debra Hill) and provided the haunting and now iconic score. As if to hammer the point home, his name is placed above the title of the film in the opening credits. Aside from literally claiming authorship by declaring it *"John Carpenter's Halloween,"* his artistic signature is all over the film—panoramic photography, carefully composed framing, simple synthesizer scoring, slow-building tension, and precision editing. But it took others to help define those aesthetic elements, such as cinematographer Dean Cundey and production designer and editor Tommy Lee Wallace, both of whom have recurrently worked with Carpenter over the years and are just as responsible for some of the most acclaimable aspects of *Halloween*; they are just as crucial in helping it become celebrated as one of the best and most influential horror films of all time.

Horror has been an elemental force of cinema for as long as the artform has existed. Like some of its greatest monsters, its form has shifted and changed to appear more relevant to the times and to its audience. A good filmmaker can use horror to entertain us while also saying something about the world in which we live by slipping in subtle social commentary as we cower in the dark with our popcorn. Wes Craven did this best with *A Nightmare on Elm Street*, in which he introduced a character in Freddy Krueger who symbolized not only the immediate context of fear and malevolence but also metaphorically represented the breakdown of the traditionalist ideals of family, domesticity, and middle-class society. Indeed, the genre has produced works that are cerebral, conscientious, sometimes politically correct, and often subversive in their satirical subtexts. Not all horror films aim so high, though, with intellectual aspirations and esoteric sociopolitical subtexts; some are merely a meaningless exercise in terror that appeals to a base desire for the vicarious thrills of sex and violence that they present. John Carpenter's *Halloween* is a singular work of high art without making any grand allusions to abstract psychological or sociological concerns; nor does it merely offer cheap thrills and titillations. Its intelligence is not academic but rather, aesthetic. It is a towering achievement of film form and function, as were certain works before it, such as Orson Welles's *Citizen Kane* (1941), Frank Capra's *It's a Wonderful Life* (1946), John Ford's *The Searchers* (1956), and Don Siegel's *Dirty Harry* (1971), in which all the elements of production, from screenwriting to art direction, from scoring to cinematography, and from editing to direction, combine to illustrate that illusively achieved idea of cinematic perfection. Like those examples of high regard, *Halloween* is flawless in every respect.

If *Halloween* has ancestors in the history of Hollywood horror, then they can be traced back to the likes of Alfred Hitchcock's *Psycho* and Michael Powell's *Peeping Tom*. Both of those films from 1960 present their antagonists as damaged human beings who belong to the real world; they are not hideously scarred and disfigured, nor are they unusually sympathetic monsters, born on the Universal Studios backlot, from whom audiences can safely distance themselves. Michael Myers is, within the narrative of at least the first film, human and, therefore, terrifyingly relatable. In the opening moments, we meet him as a six-year-old boy, costumed in the fantastic garb of a clown just as any suburban child might be on Halloween night. Unlike Hitchcock's and Powell's films, Carpenter's psychosexual subtext is far more subtle, though no less troubling, when considered. In the opening moments, the viewer vicariously experiences teenager Judith Myers's massacre through her younger brother Michael's point of view. The act of sexual intercourse that Judith engages in with her boyfriend prior to her slaughter occurs off

The iconic original poster art for *Halloween*. Compass International Pictures/ Photofest ©Trancas International Films

camera, for the opening scene is viewed through Dean Cundey's expertly devised Panaglide photography, which places us in Michael's perspective: we see only what he sees. This subjective view of events implies an undercurrent of incestuous lasciviousness or curiosity. As Judith is voyeuristically stalked, she becomes sexually aroused and is subsequently murdered, her breasts featuring prominently within the subjective cinematic frame (Michael's and, thus, our eyes) as she lies slain on her bedroom floor. In an interesting camera move, Michael glances over to the postcoital bed before looking back to his nude sister and then stabbing her. The inherent intimacy of this opening, viewed from Michael's internal gaze, is what makes it so successfully disturbing and a moment of bravura filmmaking. From this scene, we can trust that we are in the hands of master filmmakers. Anyone who was familiar with Carpenter's previous film, *Assault on Precinct 13*, already knew that. But the aesthetic presentation of this scene—bold, daring, and original—heralds not only one of the great director–cinematographer relationships in American Cinema but is also a celebration of cinematic collaboration.

One of those who was there and contributed to this confluence of talent was production designer, editor, and Michael Myers mask maker, Tommy Lee Wallace. His association with John Carpenter goes back all the way to their days in Bowling Green, Kentucky, where both men grew up. He recalls those early days of being immersed in art and music:

"John and I grew up in this little college town in Southern Kentucky, and although we didn't really get close until we were teenagers, we knew of each other because we went to the same K through 12 school on campus. My knowledge of movies and my love of movies was not of the same ilk as someone like John,

Young Michael Myers commits his first act of terror. Author's Collection

who was just wild about them from a very early age, especially horror movies and sci-fi movies. I loved my share of them and had my favorites, such as *The Giant Gila Monster* and *Battle in Outer Space* [both 1959] and so forth. But I was just a typical kid going to the movies on a Saturday, whereas John already had figured out who and what a film director was and that he wanted to be one. This was by the time he was nine years old. I was more devoted to music, playing different instruments, and being interested in art."

Wallace and Carpenter got into rock and roll together and formed a band, a time that Wallace considers the pinnacle of their high school and early college years. Playing together in Kaleidoscope helped seal their friendship. Carpenter then left Kentucky for Southern California to enroll in film school, while Wallace went to Ohio University to study fine arts and graphic design. Upon graduating, he had to decide whether he was going to move to New York City to follow his dreams of being a graphic designer. "The design world was exploding," Wallace says. "There was Push Pin Studios and people like Milton Glaser, Peter Max . . . just a lot of great graphics around, especially album covers and posters. It really turned me on, so I seriously considered going to New York."

However, while in college, Wallace began taking cinema courses. This was the time of the revolutionary New Hollywood movement, when film was finally being considered worthy of academic study and taken seriously as "the art form of the century." This all got Wallace thinking, so he paid a visit to his friend Carpenter on the West Coast during spring break of his senior year, a trip that proved most fortuitous, as he recalls:

"I took my portfolio along with me, which was very strong in graphic design and illustration. Lo and behold, the faculty at USC liked what they saw, and I was accepted into their program. So that fall, after college graduation, I went off to California and was kind of entering film school as John and some of his contemporaries, like Dan O'Bannon, were exiting slowly but surely. At that time, Dan and John were taking their student film *Dark Star* and expanding it into a feature. The University of Southern California cinema department is well-known for being kind of a funnel into the Hollywood film industry. So I made use of that, and I helped John out on his early efforts. It felt like it was a natural progression. I didn't really feel like I turned left or right; I just kind of watched the doors open and walked through them."

Having been to an art school, Wallace was already familiar with the aesthetic side of things, so now it was time to learn the practical and logistical elements of filmmaking. USC was known as a premier training ground for future Hollywood professionals, and it was here that Wallace learned about the hands-on, everyday work involved in film production, from cameras to sound and everything in between. "USC was phenomenally good at being your trade school approach to making a movie and showing you how you do it. It was like, 'Here's how production works,' and they would have us pitch our story to faculty members. And those experiences imitated to some degree the professional world. It was fantastic training."

With the new wave of young American auteurs blazing a trail in Hollywood at the time, Wallace and his fellow students were inspired to follow in their footsteps, as he admits, "We were absolutely emboldened by that era of New Hollywood filmmaking. George Lucas was fresh out of our very film school about a year or two; one of my classmates was Bob Zemeckis; and, of course, there was John. And there were numerous others. When I became a TA [teaching assistant], one of the class members was Ron Howard! So this was all bubbling up. And I've just touched the surface; there were many others, a lot of talent. And it was clear that you could move from that experience into, if not a studio job, then into working on one of the many independent films that were going on out there for not much money, but which took a lot of ingenuity. If you went to film school, you were given the chance to make several films, and of course, every student filmmaker knows that you have got to do it with Scotch tape and chewing gum because you don't have big budgets. And so virtually everyone who went through USC was getting out there and getting involved, either originating some film idea of their own or getting connected in some way with a crew, even if it was in some lowly position like loading

Cokes into coolers. Just getting involved in it and starting to network with people. I don't think the term 'networking' was alive yet, but that's what we were doing. It was a very natural process, and it was very exciting because Lucas and Spielberg and Coppola were all basically kids who had just gone out there and been bold enough to start making movies. It was certainly a source of inspiration in that way."

Before *Halloween*, Wallace would work with Carpenter on his two earlier films, the first of which was *Dark Star*, which began life as a USC student film in 1972 but released as an independent feature in 1974. *Dark Star* is a satirical science fiction film that follows the absurd adventures in space of bored astronauts Lieutenant Doolittle (Brian Narelle), Sergeant Pinback (Dan O'Bannon), and others as they navigate their mission to destroy any unstable planets they come across.

"*Dark Star* was made out of the trunk of our cars and on the fly," Wallace recalls, "and we shot for a few days in an actual studio, a dusty, old, rickety studio up in Hollywood that had plenty of ghosts in there from filmmaking past. But we really felt like big shots, like, 'Gee, we're on an actual soundstage!' It was as moldy and oldie as it got, but it was a soundstage, an official soundstage with a sliding door and padding on the walls. So that was exciting. I was kind of Dan O'Bannon's right-hand man for the completion of the movie because Dan had a tremendous amount of talent and so he was very busy: he was serving as production designer, he was in the movie, he was the cowriter, and he was editing it, but he was only one man. He had his hands full. Then I came along, and I was knowledgeable about making believable pieces of graphics for the background, or things like a laser box, or a corridor that serves as an elevator shaft. I was the first person he'd run into that he could rely on to take his idea and run with it and do something respectable with it. So that was a fantastic experience."

Carpenter's following film, *Assault on Precinct 13*, is a violent, claustrophobic thriller set in a defunct police station under siege from Street Thunder gang members after they follow the traumatized father whose young daughter they shot in cold blood. Armed conflict ensues between the gang and those defending the precinct, among whom is highway patrol officer Lieutenant Ethan Bishop (Austin Stoker), criminal Napolean Wilson (Darwin Joston), and several others. The film was influenced by Howard Hawks's remarkable 1959 western *Rio Bravo*. But narrative similarities aside, Carpenter uses the setup to hone his own style in earnest. It is here where we see all the elements of Carpenter's distinctive aesthetic coming to fruition for the first time, though once again, the director would require the assistance of some friends to realize his vision.

"*Assault on Precinct 13* was a little bit more official than *Dark Star*," Wallace admits. "John got a couple of his friends from USC to put up some money, and they found another guy who was the son of a wealthy businessman from Philadelphia, I believe. And so it was shot on a shoestring budget that began with about $100,000, and we were back at that same rickety old lot. By then, it had been refurbished a bit and was called Producers Studio, and it now had several soundstages. We occupied one stage. And I had the good fortune of using a set-building team that was on the lot, and I learned so much from them about the official way to go about building and painting a set or aging down a set, all that sort of thing. So I was getting a fantastic education and getting paid for it, not much but a little bit. *Dark Star* and *Assault on Precinct 13* were sort of an extension of graduate school."

The practical experience obtained from those two films came in handy when Wallace became the production designer on *Halloween*, which meant accepting the major challenge of turning sunny Pasadena into the drab, leaf-strewn Illinois suburb of Haddonfield. Wallace recalls the effort:

"Los Angeles in the spring and Illinois in the fall are about as different as night and day. So we first had to give up the notion of a beautiful multicolored autumn setting. And we had to hide the palm trees. It was less refined kind of stuff; it was a case of 'What can we get away with here and still have a convincing movie?' The answer is 'leaves.' But autumn leaves were nearly impossible to come by. So I went down to a place where they sold dried flowers and pussy willows and things that decorators used in chic apartments. They had sprigs of oak branches with dried leaves on them, so I picked them up, pulled them off the stems, and gathered them into garbage bags until we had three or four full bags. Then before a shot, we would dump it out and get the fan going to blow them across the scene. Then after the shot, we would go rake them up, put them in the bag, and do it again. I didn't have pumpkins, not in the spring in Los Angeles. So we found some gourds from South America which were green. So what do you do? Spray-paint them Halloween pumpkin orange. Those are the kind of basics we were working with. John and I did not have the luxury of sitting down and going 'Let's choose our color palette' and so on because so much of it was having to go find the location and shoot it as close to the way it is when we walk in with only a little bit of leeway. Our set-decorating budget was something like 25 cents. So it all had to be done student-film style."

Wallace's contribution to the creation and culture of *Halloween* cannot be underestimated. As the production designer, he filled the frames of the film skillfully enough to make us believe that springtime in Pasadena could pass for an autumnal Midwest. But more than that, it was his design of the very logo of the franchise, Michael Myers's instantly recognizable mask (which he created out of both economical and legal necessity), that is his most significant contribution to the iconography of horror cinema. The script called for a mask, but there was neither time nor money to create one from scratch, which would have included designing, building, and molding it, among other things. Thinking practically, Wallace visited a novelty store on Hollywood Boulevard where he came across a rather bland and featureless mask that piqued his curiosity. In that inspired moment, Wallace made a purchase that would alter the face of horror cinema forever.

"That store had Frankenstein masks, Dracula masks, Richard Nixon masks, Gerald Ford masks, and maybe John Wayne. But all of them were sort of cartoony. And way down at the end of the store, I saw a Mr. Spock mask, and next to it was kind of a blank face. Well, it turned out it was supposed to be Captain Kirk, although it didn't look anything like William Shatner. It just looked like a blank guy. And I went, 'Aha! That might work.' So I bought that and bought a clown mask, which was an Emmett Kelly sad-sack clown mask. Funnily enough, clowns figured in a few movies later for me on *Stephen King's It*."

While the Captain Kirk mask was suitably expressionless, Wallace knew he had to alter it enough to evade copyright infringement or risk the wrath of Paramount lawyers, as he remembers distinctly that they needed to make it their own:

"We had to change it aesthetically, but John had warned me that maybe we ought to alter it in some other way because we had no idea what kind of trouble we could get into if it were revealed that we were using this mask from a famous TV show that was the property of Paramount. When I put the mask on, I found that it was very hard to see out of it, so I started by cutting the eyeholes to make them larger. And then I decided to pull the sideburns off. They looked kind of corny anyway. And when I pulled them off, holy moly, suddenly it was getting to be sort of a punky and strange new hairstyle. Then I darkened the hair with something called Streaks and Tips, which is a makeup department type spray, like temporary hair dye, and I added a few other odds and ends and details. I spray-painted the whole thing fish belly white, which was an appliance and refrigerator paint. I took those two masks to the studio, and we had somebody model them. First, they came out of the dressing room with the clown mask, and everybody agreed that was eerie and strange and could work. So it was like, 'Okay, we've got one in our pocket. Let's see what the other one is like.' And when the guy came out wearing that thing, it was just like, 'Oh, fuck me. That is scary. That's the scariest thing before we even get to the story and before we even get to the cinematography. Before anything! Just take a picture of that mask and it's scary.' And to this day, I don't quite understand the magic of that, although I wish I had a nickel for every mask that's been sold. But we knew then that we had a scary movie. And obviously we didn't just stop with a mask, but it was a powerful tool. We had a good script by John and Debra, and we had Dean Cundey. It all came together; it was a perfect storm after that."

Like Carpenter, Cundey came out of the low-budget independent world, having worked with the likes of Roger Corman,

Bruce Clark, and Jim McCullough Sr. Cundey's passion for film began early on when his mother would drop him off at the kids' matinee shows on the weekends. The eminent cinematographer recalls his fascination with the magic of movies:

"I was always intrigued by the fact that film could take you on this journey to somewhere impossible. But I also think that I was interested in how they did it as much as I was in the story. Sometimes the stories were compelling, but other times, they were not, as the weekend matinees would often have some cheap horror film about a giant bug or whatever. However, I was always interested in the fact that they could do it. So I began researching and reading about how they were made, and it grew from that. And there was a sense of magic about it. I always point to the fact that we go into a room—or we used to—where there is this big white wall with nothing on it. But then the projector comes on with these moving images, and we are sucked into the story and the characters as if we are there with them. We are there, but not like in the theater with a play where we are looking around the stage populated with real live people. In cinema, we are in the control of the director and cinematographer. So I got intrigued by films at a very early age."

Cundey put his passion into practice while enrolled at UCLA (University of California, Los Angeles) Film School. He did makeup on some student projects, something he had been interested in back in grammar and high school. Cundey was busy with this college work when, one day, Bruce Clark told him that he had talked the B-movie king himself, Roger Corman, into funding a low-budget movie. Cundey recalls immediately offering his services:

"I said, 'Oh, I'm interested in cinematography,' and they said, 'Well, we've already got Bob Eberlein,' who was one of my fellow students, 'and he's going to shoot it. But we need a makeup person. Are you interested?' And I said, 'Well, yeah, to work on a movie? Of course!' And so I did the makeup on *Naked Angels*, and then I got asked by Roger Corman to do a subsequent film that he was directing. He wanted me to do the makeup. It was serendipity I guess you could call it. I had always been interested in working in the camera department, but I realized it might be harder to just jump in there and get a job doing that. But I took anything I could get, so besides makeup I did a little bit of editing for a friend. I also worked as a lighting guy, and I was supposed to be the gaffer, the chief lighting guy, on a film called *Black Shampoo*. The day that movie was going to begin, the director, Greydon Clark, came to me on the stage where we were gathering and getting out the equipment, and he said, 'The cinematographer got in a car accident, and he won't be able to do the movie. Could you fill in for him until I get somebody?' And I said, 'Yeah, no problem!' He had seen some clips of stuff and a short that I'd done. Then at the end of the first day, I asked if he had found anybody to replace me, and he said, 'Well, it seems to be going okay. I'll keep looking, but don't worry about it.' So I just kept shooting and shooting and shooting, and at the end of the week, he came over and sat down on the dolly next to me and said, 'Well, you're not too bad at this. Maybe you should think about doing it.' I didn't want to say, 'Are you kidding? This is all I ever wanted to do!' What I did say was, 'Oh, thank you very much. What an excellent idea.' So I finished that film, and then I did four more with him. I was interested in trying to elevate the work, to elevate the movie. I was always thinking, 'Is there a better way to do this shot?' and 'Is there a better place to put the camera?' Greydon was very affable and good at taking suggestions. He wrote it and directed it, and he liked the fact that somebody else was interested enough in the movie to make it as good as it could be, that I was not just somebody putting the camera where he told them to. He was glad to have someone providing a different point of view and giving some input. That was the start of my career."

It was through his association with Greydon Clark that Cundey ended up in the *Halloween* camp as John Carpenter's cowriter, and producer Debra Hill was the script supervisor on some of Clark's films. Impressed with Cundey's work and with a desire to make her own movies, she took note of the budding cinematographer and called him when she was preparing to make a low-budget horror film about a babysitter's being stalked by a masked maniac. She informed him that the film would be directed by a guy who came out of USC, the rival film school to Cundey's UCLA alma mater.

"Debra said to me, 'It's going to be a suspense thriller and kind of a horror film.' I told her, 'That sounds visually interesting.' And she asked if I wanted to go meet this director, and I said, 'Of course!' So I went and met this USC guy, John Carpenter, and we watched a movie together. He owned a three-quarter-inch videotape machine and some movies, so we watched, ironically, the old black-and-white version of *The Thing* [1951]. He said, 'I've always loved this film; let's look at it.' And then we proceeded to talk all the way through it; we would point out and discuss some great shots. And then I told him that I would be delighted to work with him, and he said, 'Okay, let's give it a try.' So we went and started that movie, *Halloween*. It turned into a great adventure because there was very little money and it was a short schedule, I think three weeks."

Indeed, the collaboration turned out to be a great creative experience for Cundey. His task was to elevate the script and turn the film into something distinctive and polished. That he most certainly did. And he had the perfect partner in Carpenter to help craft what has become one of the most lauded works of cinematography in the horror genre. "John was a very good visualizer," Cundey applauds. "He understood the value of suggestions that I would make and suggestions that the actors would make. It became a great creative experience."

Cundey recalls the aesthetic and technical elements that went into devising and realizing the famous Steadicam shot of the opening scene. Camera operator and future cinematographer Raymond Stella was the man who carried the Panaglide in accomplishing Cundey's shot, the one that rivals in execution and invention the lengthy opening shot of Orson Welles's *Touch of Evil*.

"Ray and I first met when we were going to make a short film that his friend was directing," Cundey says. "That friend came to me and said, 'I've got this guy who wants to get into film and wants to be a camera assistant.' I said, 'Oh, perfect! We need one.' So I met Ray and showed him the camera equipment that I had. I said, 'Here's the camera and this is the magazine. The

Director John Carpenter (right) with *Halloween* producer and co-screenwriter Debra Hill on the set of their film following *Halloween*, *The Fog* (1980). AVCO EMBASSY PICTURES/EDI/RGR Collection/Alamy Stock Photo

lenses are all stored in here.' I asked him if he was familiar with the various lenses, and he confirmed that he was. So he seemed confident. Years later, he confessed that he had never seen any of that stuff before and said that he went to a rental house immediately after he left my house and asked them, 'What's an Arriflex, and how do we load the magazine?' So they showed him all this stuff, and he learned it all after he got the job. I always thought that was amusing. But I was impressed by his interest in doing it, and I hired him again for the next job and then again on the next job and so on. We worked together for many years."

One of the great things about the Panaglide work here is that unlike most filmmakers, who present first-person perspectives using handheld cameras with their nauseating shaking and juddering, Cundey had the good sense and taste to replicate as closely as possible the human field of vision. He gave the movie something that would resonate with audiences and feel more genuine when we are looking at the world through the eyes of Michael Myers, when most subjective camerawork in cinema does not at all represent how our movement and vision work in tandem.

"Yes," Cundey concurs, "I sometimes point that out about the use of handheld cameras. There are directors who demand, 'No, no, no! It's got to move more, more!' and I say, "Yeah, but as you walk, as you turn your head, as you sit up and down, your head, your eyes and brain are automatically compensating for the movement; they smooth it out. That is our experience. You're not used to seeing rough moving images. I think that was the intent of the Panaglide, to take the audience on this journey as if they were there or if they were seeing it, even if it's third person, seeing it in a way that is not distracting so that they can concentrate on the image, on the character, and on the situation. And so we tried something that was new for the time. The Panaglide and the Steadicam were not around very long, maybe a year or two, and they were only used for special-purpose shots; they were used for one-offs. But John and I said, 'Why don't we use it as part of the storytelling?' As a result, we learned quite a bit about how to tell a story with the moving camera."

Tommy Lee Wallace recalls the revolutionary device that made such intricate shots possible to effectively achieve: "John was working with a new toy which had just come into being, which was the Panaglide, which quickly became known as the Steadicam. And that was simply a brand-new thing. Previously, to get that point-of-view feel in horror movies, it had to be done handheld. But Steadicam replaced that, and its success really depended on the steadiness of your operator. If it was too shaky, it still kind of had a quality, but boy when you got it going on the Panaglide, it was like an eerie dream, like a floating sensation. *Halloween* proved that it could be terrifying. It could lend itself to suspense and generate real fear, and John exploited that to the max. He came up with one of the greatest single-shot scenes ever put on celluloid: the opening of the film when the camera approaches the house and you figure out that it's the point of view of young Michael Myers. From his perspective, the camera goes up through the house, and he kills the girl and then comes back down through the house, so simple and effective."

Wallace continues: "It was really something to be a part of. But we must give due credit to Ray Stella, who was the glide operator. He was the camera operator all the way through on both the dolly and the tripod but certainly on the glide camera. It was such a choreographed shot that it would be great to reproduce that and demonstrate how many people were involved around the camera. There was Ray Stella; there was the focus puller; and there was Dean, who had a light to fill in certain places; he'd turn up the handheld light so that the faces wouldn't go completely black. And I was there with a bucket of blood and a brush so that when we killed the girl, I'd start splashing. It was so choreographed that if you panned to the right or the left, you were looking at bare walls. We'd wallpapered right down to the precise camera angles that we were going to be filming. I walked the shot several times with John to know exactly what he was going to do. This is how you make a low-budget movie. That house was rickety and tumbling down, except for the parts that the camera saw. As we went through the house shooting the scene we could hear and see lighting guys jumping through windows and changing the lights around because we were going to come back down through the same territory and it had to be relit for that in real time while we were upstairs killing the girl. It was quite an adventure, and I'm deeply proud of it."

"After *Halloween*, a few more films began to use the Steadicam," Cundey says, "and I had a studio producer say to me, 'Let's use the Steadicam more, and we'll never have to use the dolly again. We can get rid of the dolly crew.' But the dolly is another tool, just as the Panaglide is a tool, the Steadicam is a tool, and each type of light is a tool. It's all about how you use these tools as opposed to just using them for economic purposes and for getting rid of other equipment and people."

Wallace says, "Dean was thoroughly instrumental in the look of *Halloween*. It has been wonderful to watch him move up in his career, because he had the talent all along. You only have to look at his work; even from the early days, it was just dazzling. So it was no surprise to me that every director in town came to a point where they wanted to work with Dean."

Indeed, it wouldn't be long before the man behind the stunning camerawork of *Halloween* would be sought out by the likes of Robert Zemeckis (for the *Back to the Future* trilogy), Steven Spielberg (for *Jurassic Park*), and Ron Howard (for *Apollo 13*), but in the interim years following *Halloween*, Cundey would bring his masterful photographic style to several more John Carpenter films. Whether it was low-budget genre works, such as *The Fog* (1980) and *Escape from New York* (1981), or bigger-budget studio productions such as *The Thing* (1982) and *Big Trouble in Little China* (1986), it seems that Cundey and Carpenter had the kind of collaborative chemistry that produces a wholly unique style and brings out the best in each artist. Cundey contemplates what it is about working with Carpenter that has resulted in a body of work as rich as theirs:

"John is very good at visual storytelling and not only in his own invention of shots and how he does it but in his understanding that I was interested in the same thing. I wasn't just lighting his movie and setting up a camera; I wanted to figure out how to engage the audience and tell the story in a visually interesting manner. He was great at the give-and-take of executing the shot. There were moments on the original *Halloween* when we were running out of time because of the night sequences and working with kids; they couldn't stay and shoot any longer than allowed so what we had planned to be a sequence in three or four shots would change when I suggested a more economical alternative. John would say, 'Oh, yeah, yeah. Let's do that.' He was able to understand it, as opposed to some directors I've worked with who wouldn't get what I was suggesting we do. I'd say, 'We pan over here and then over to here, and then we move in.' And they'd be like, 'Wait, wait, wait . . . move in?!' What I have had to do is record the shot with a little video camera and show them the idea; then they could see it and say, 'Oh, I see what you mean.' But John understood when I described things; he could visualize it, and he would say, 'That sounds good! How about we also do this . . .?' That was one of the things that was most enjoyable about working with John."

Director John Carpenter on the set of *Halloween* (1978). Compass International Pictures/Photofest ©Trancas International Films

"John was very self-assured," Wallace concurs. "He really analyzed how films were done, just the idea that you break a scene down into shots and you put it together like a puzzle. So he knew what he was doing. He had a great cinematic sense of how the correct attitude and approach for a director is: 'Okay, be expressive; tell the story. That's the whole point, but don't get too much in the way.' A lot of directors love to show off with bravado, with fancy shots that don't necessarily mean anything to the story. That was not John and is not John to this day. And I think that's the way to go. You don't have to be totally invisible; you can have some style, but at the same time, the point is to tell the story effectively. I think he would readily cop to the fact that *Assault on Precinct 13* was somewhat imitative of his favorite Howard Hawks movies. And so that assurance had something to do with those references, like 'Okay, I'm going to do what Hawks did in this scene from *To Have and Have Not* and what he did in this scene from *Rio Bravo*.' There was all of that at work. But I think John hit his stride on *Halloween*. He was no longer being derivative; he was doing something for himself creatively. I will also say that there was no time to fool around; it was unlike the previous movies, as this was a scheduled movie and there wasn't much money. I believe our budget was $300,000, but it was a TV movie type schedule. So I think part of John's style grew out of being in that hot seat and experiencing the sheer terror that you might not make your day, that you had better shoot all of this material and do it effectively because if you fall behind, you're dead. There's just no safety net. So I think part of his style grew out of having to be very simple, very straightforward, no fooling around."

With the film wrapped, postproduction work resumed, and once again, Wallace, he of many hats—and one mask—would step into his other crucial role on *Halloween*, that of editor. The precision editing of the film remains one of its fiercely underrated elements. The pace is as sharp as Michael Myers's knife, running not a frame too short nor too long, and it is thanks to Wallace and his assistant editor, Charles Bornstein, who had previously worked on a little picture called *Close Encounters of the Third Kind*.

"I was the designated editor on *Halloween*," Wallace affirms, "but I had no experience as a feature-film 35-millimeter editor at all. We desperately needed a well-organized cutting room. And Charles not only brought that, but he also brought good cutting instincts. By the time we were finished in the cutting room, I was so grateful for his contribution that I gave him coediting credit. I learned quite a bit in film school about editing, but I learned even more after *Assault on Precinct 13* wrapped photography and I went to visit John in the editing room; he was cutting his own material, which is a horrendously difficult task, especially for a full-length feature film and a director cutting his own stuff. It's very hard to be objective; you might come across a shot that you recall directing and sweating over on the set, and you suddenly realize it's not important to cut to this shot. You think, 'But I worked so hard to get this shot.' If you have those kinds of dialogues in your head, it makes the job of editing twice as hard. So John was grateful for a little company in the cutting room; he invited me to cut sound effects, and I just went, 'Sure!' So I learned that on the job too. Before it was all over, he gave me a crack at cutting the action sequences when the station is getting shot up and the people are diving for cover, all that material. That was my real introduction into cutting on a feature film for storytelling. So by the time *Halloween* came along, John felt confident that he could give me the nod. I felt very honored, and I felt totally ready to do that. A bit like I'm sure he felt totally ready to direct the movie, I felt totally ready to edit the thing. Those movies are finely cut; they were not sloppily put together. John and I sat together debating over one, two, three frame cuts where we were like, 'Is this better, or should I take another frame off?' I think John would agree with me that a few frames can make magic."

When *Halloween* was released in October 1978, little did Carpenter and Hill realize that their modest horror film would become one of the highest-grossing independent films of all time. Cundey recalls his surprise at the film's becoming as successful as it did after an inauspicious first week at the box office:

"When the film came out and was not successful in that first week, we all looked at each other and said, 'Well, it was a good experience.' Then in the second week, more people came out to see it, and soon it was a big hit. The rest is history. I think it is interesting that in the first week it came out, the audience wasn't expecting it, and they didn't go. It was like, 'What's this thing with the guy with a knife and the pumpkin?' And then word got out that you must go see this new movie called *Halloween*, and they started showing up. There's the uniqueness about it which took the audience a bit of time to comprehend. It has a dramatic, immersive style of storytelling that makes the viewer a part of it because you are there walking along smoothly behind Michael Myers as he walks across the street. And in that opening shot, you are the person moving throughout the house seeing and being involved. The most interesting part of working on it was the fact that we had that kind of freedom. It was not a studio production where some producer or executive would be saying, 'I don't get why we are using this new Steadicam thing. Why do we need that?'"

Aside from its significant financial and cultural impact, *Halloween* has also been credited with irrevocably altering the horror genre by kickstarting an entire industry of low-budget slasher films, of which the ripple effects have been felt to this day. In the film's wake followed imitators, some slick and well-made and others cheap and disposable. Regardless of production values, most of those films would rely on the cheap gag of gore to appeal to the youth audience, whereas Carpenter's film took the classier route of relying on suspense, rather than graphic violence, to unnerve its viewers. Tommy Lee Wallace has remained surprised over the years that *Halloween* has been credited with influencing such a horror subgenre, when clearly its aesthetic approach was far from the kind of macabre material that began to emerge from the margins of moviemaking under its influence.

"It's interesting to me that people call it a slasher movie," Wallace admits, "because I think in a way, they are correct, as it jet propelled the slasher film movement but it is a virtually bloodless movie. There's no gore to speak of in it, and I think that was its crowning achievement. It achieved what it did without excessive gore; it made itself one of the scariest movies ever with the pure tools of suspense and all that goes with it. It's also psychological: you tell the audience something, create an expectation, and then you play with that expectation. It's the difference between surprise and suspense. Surprise is when you come into a room and someone's sitting at a table and there's a box on the table and the box explodes. That's a surprise. But if you've been told ahead of time that the box has a ticking bomb in it and you come into the room, it's a whole different psychological effect—that is suspense."

Cundey concurs, "I often point out that the old horror films that Universal was famous for making, such as *Dracula* and *Frankenstein*, were also psychological, as there was no blood or gore in those either. You never see Dracula rip somebody's throat out; it was all in your imagination, created by this ominous figure.

The Night Horror Came Home / 23

Michael Myers in a still from *Halloween* (1978). Compass International Pictures/Photofest ©Trancas International Films

All that blood can be distracting, and it is gratuitous most of the time. Some filmmakers have this concept that it's going to make the audience more afraid, but to me, it feels like someone is saying that the simpler thing to do is to show more blood rather than building suspense and horror and terror, which *Halloween* does effectively."

One of the *Halloween* franchise's greatest champions and allies across the decades has been the legendary genre magazine *Fangoria*. Known for its coverage and celebration of all things within the world of horror cinema, it was, for a long time, the

Scream queen Jamie Lee Curtis stars as Laurie Strode in *Halloween* (1978). Compass International Pictures/Photofest ©Trancas International Films

only such publication devoted to what may have once been considered a niche interest. Only *Famous Monsters of Filmland* before it could have laid claim to being the definitive genre periodical, but with the horror boom of the 1980s, *Fangoria* took full advantage of the surfeit of product that was on offer from the mainstream Hollywood studios, the alternative independent world, and the straight-to-video industry. Since the publication's rise to prominence, numerous other titles have hit the newsstands, such as *The Dark Side* and *Rue Morgue*, but during that important period through the 1980s and 1990s, *Fangoria* was the market leader in the milieu, one that enjoyed often exclusive access to

Michael Myers lurks in the shadows behind Annie Brackett (Nancy Kyes/Loomis).
Compass International Pictures/Photofest ©Trancas International Films

films in production as well as to the filmmakers involved. With savvy producers' and unit publicists' knowing the value of being featured in the magazine, they were, throughout the decades, able to take full advantage of the mutually beneficial relationship that they had with *Fangoria* and its visionary editor, Tony Timpone. The first *Halloween* film to be covered during Timpone's tenure was *Halloween 4: The Return of Michael Myers*, which ushered in a whole new timeline and new era for the franchise, but Timpone had been paying attention to the films since their beginning when, as a high school student, he caught the original *Halloween* upon rerelease in New York City, as he remembers:

"I missed it the first time it came out in 1978, but I saw it when it was rereleased in 1979. When I became the editor of *Fangoria*, I was told what happened was the distributor pulled the movie after a few weeks, and so I had to wait a whole year to see it again. Reportedly this was because the New York City subdistributor, Aquarius Releasing, wanted to create a year's worth of demand. So just when the film was doing really well, that's when he pulled it out of theaters to create a demand to rerelease it the following year. That's when I caught it in Times Square in 1979 with a bunch of my high school buddies, and of course, we were blown away because it was just so suspenseful and scary. It's such a unique little movie. We were really caught up in the whole thing, but we never thought it would explode into the franchise that it became; that took me by surprise. And then I saw *Halloween II* and *Halloween III*, which I thought was a very fresh and totally off-the-wall approach to the franchise that works as a stand-alone movie."

Timpone continues, "I was a fan from the get-go. I got caught up in the virtuosity of John Carpenter. I could tell that this guy was trying to do something different. Another thing that really caught my attention the first time I saw it was the music; that relentless score really mirrored the relentless actions of Michael Myers. That really put the film on a whole new level. It is also beautifully shot by Dean Cundey. And then you have the performances, which are very likeable; I mean you have Donald Pleasence in there. This movie really gave new life to him and introduced him to a whole new audience. Seeing him in a movie like that just really elevated the material; he brought so much to the part. *Halloween* was the big bang when it came to the slasher movies. It really set the formula that became the standard, which was copied again and again and again. It created this whole subgenre that is still prevalent today, and launched the career of one of the great masters of horror, John Carpenter."

"Why me?" —Laurie Strode

Halloween II picks up immediately from the events of the first film. Dr. Loomis continues to trace Michael's whereabouts with the help of Sheriff Leigh Brackett (Charles Cyphers) on the streets of Haddonfield, where the death toll is rising fast as Michael evades the authorities while pursuing his intended target, Laurie Strode. The wounded teenager has been taken to Haddonfield Memorial Hospital, where Michael arrives and picks off the staff one by one as he stalks the dimly lit corridors of the wards. Dr. Loomis becomes increasingly anxious and unstable in his dogged pursuit of Michael, to the point that his paranoia causes the death of an innocent teenager, Ben Tramer (Laurie's secret crush), because the boy is seen trick or treating dressed in Halloween attire very similar to that of Michael. Loomis's state of mind is further agitated when he learns that Laurie is Michael's biological sister, a fact that officials at Smith's Grove Sanitarium kept from Loomis. Marion Chambers, a nurse, reveals that court orders dictated that Laurie Strode's real identity as a Myers' child be kept confidential following her parents' death, which occurred a couple of years after their son killed their older daughter, Judith, on Halloween night of 1963. The Strode family subsequently adopted Laurie, and as a means of protecting her, the administrators of Smith's Grove sealed all records alluding to her true familial background.

Since its release in October 1981, *Halloween II* has continued to divide opinion. The film tries its best to remain aesthetically and stylistically true to Carpenter's film, and for the most part, it does. Having been a crucial creative collaborator with Carpenter, as well as his close friend, and a cherished member of the *Halloween* family back in 1978, Tommy Lee Wallace was all set to direct the sequel. It seemed a logical choice, but it didn't work out as planned, as he recalls:

"When the idea of *Halloween II* first came up, nobody, including Debra, John, me, and other people around us, was that crazy about the notion of a sequel. We were all like, 'Well, wait a minute; we made the perfect horror movie. Why would we want to revisit that?' But I briefly became the director of *Halloween II*. It made sense in many ways, and it would have been fine. But the idea for a sequel didn't come immediately after the first one; a couple of years went by, and within that time, a sort of arms race occurred in terms of gore and violence in these kinds of movies. And I think *Halloween II* proves and disproves the point all

28 / You Can't Kill the Boogeyman

***Halloween II* (1981) poster art.** Universal Pictures/Photofest ©Universal Pictures

at once that more violence equates to success. It was a financial success, but the reason I didn't direct it was I hated the script. I felt like it did everything that the original *Halloween* didn't do. It just relied on gore and guts and didn't really have anything to say. It wasn't an actual story; it was just mayhem in a hospital. I think John was acutely aware of that when it was time to write *Halloween II*. I was stumping for a five-years-after kind of story, which could have been effective. I wanted the kind of story that wound up getting told in *H20*, with Laurie Strode having been away in trauma for five years and she finally ventured off to college in a really secure place, so secure that it could not only be a wall protecting you but a wall trapping you inside. That was my pitch. But John and Debra felt strongly that it would be better to go with a five-minutes-later approach, which was kind of a trap because what are you going to do with that five-minutes-later story that hasn't already been told in the first one? So I just didn't feel like that was the right way to start my career as a director because it would have been counterfeit. Hating the material is not a good place for a director to be. I could have faked it. I know I could have done a good job, but it would have been a lie. And, honestly, John and Debra deserved a director who was gung ho, someone who would just get in there and do it and really do it sincerely. I couldn't supply that. So I dropped out."

With Wallace out of the picture, Rick Rosenthal was hired, making *Halloween II* his feature debut as director. Actress Gloria Gifford, who plays Mrs. Alves, the head nurse at Haddonfield Memorial Hospital, recalls Rosenthal's approach to filmmaking as being particularly geared toward character development.

"Rick is a different kind of director because he studied acting, so he hired really good actors that he wanted for the parts. As a result of this, *Halloween II* is more character driven than the other movies. And that's part of why people like it and part of why people may not like it. This is one of the few movies where you get to know who everybody is before they die; you have a feeling about who, for example, Tawny's character is or who Pamela's character is. Rick was very innovative in his casting too. I think it was the first horror film outside of the movie *Blacula* which featured a black woman in a significant role. There were no black actors who were leading characters in horror movies, and that is another reason why *Halloween II* is a very different kind of thing. And this was, again, down to Rick because the role was written for a 55-year-old white woman.

That's what it said in the script. When he was bringing people to Debra Hill, he asked her if I could come in, and I did. But Debra was like, 'Well, she's too young!' And Rick said, 'No, no, no, she is an authority figure. You'll see. And then maybe I can make the other girls a little younger, and it'll work.' And then Debra said, 'Yep, okay, we'll go for it.' When I arrived at the set on the first day, I went down to hair and makeup, and they asked me what role I was playing. And I said, 'Mrs. Alves,' and they didn't believe me because they have the script, which does not say the character is black. I said, 'No, no, no, that's me.' And Rick was right. I've always played authority figures, so it worked. She is authoritative, and it's not stereotypical because it's not sassy and it's not Southern. We understand that she runs this place and she wants it to go well. I always must give Rick credit for that. He is always thinking ahead; he is a very smart guy."

With the limited locations and a tight-knit ensemble cast populating the hospital setting, it was crucial for the actors to believably create their own sense of drama between the carnage. It was director Rosenthal's experience in studying acting that led him to call some former classmates, as Gifford explains:

"Rick was in Milton Katselas's acting class, and Milton was one of the top acting teachers in the business; he was also a director. And Rick knew us from that acting class. He couldn't just give us the job, because this was his first movie; he didn't have that kind of clout. But he could bring us in and audition us, and he could root for us. And that is what happened. So Leo Rossi, Ana Alicia, and I were all in an acting class together, as were a few of the other people cast in smaller roles. It was a smart thing for Rick to do because this was his first movie and he was able to work with people who could speak his language."

Halloween II also marked the first time that Gifford worked with Jamie Lee Curtis, followed by appearing together in Gabrielle Beaumont's 1981 made-for-television film *Death of a Centerfold: The Dorothy Stratten Story*. "By the time we did the Dorothy Stratten thing, it was great because I had already worked with her. Jamie was extraordinarily easy to work with. By the time we were doing *Halloween II*, she was already the franchise; she was it. But she treated everybody the same way that she does today, and that is extremely respectfully. She gets along with everybody and causes no problems. And she's so smart. So I was really happy to work with her again on *The Dorothy Stratten Story* and have another chance to meet with her. She's amazing."

With Curtis and other important cast members returning, including Donald Pleasence as Dr. Loomis and Charles Cyphers as Sheriff Brackett, production was extra fortunate to have the original film's cinematographer, Dean Cundey, back behind the camera. So unique is Cundey's photographic style that no one else could have given the film the must-needed visual continuity nor its distinctive visual flair. Cundey recalls that retaining the look of the first film would be crucial in the believability factor that this is still the night that Michael came home:

"That was an interesting aspect of it because it was supposedly one continuous event across both films. John and Debra came to me and said, 'We don't know much about Rick [Rosenthal], but make sure that he understands that the style has to continue; it can't be something unusual.' And I said, 'Oh, obviously. That's quite reasonable.' So it was an interesting experience because I had to remember the style and remember the lighting, all of that. Then when I began working on the film and collaborating with Rick, he would say, 'Let's do this . . .,' and I would say, 'No, that doesn't fit within the style of the first film.' And he would reluctantly reply with, 'Fine, okay.' But he would go and try and do something different, and it was up to me to guide him down the same stylistic path as the original. After a while, Rick realized that was what had to happen, so he complied with my suggestions. I was surprised when I heard they were going to be making a sequel to that little movie we did because in those days, you usually did a one-off movie; nobody made sequels like they do now. And often the sequels made nowadays aren't as well-made or as successful. They are very derivative, and that was the fear with *Halloween II*, even back then, that it was going to be a derivative film. Nobody had ever expected that they would be making a sequel to John's film. This was my first sequel experience, because I had done all these things with Greydon Clark, which were low-budget drive-in movies with action and car racing, each one a stand-alone movie.

It was the same with the big studio releases; they weren't made anticipating that sequels would follow. So it was an intriguing thing trying to create a sequel to something that originally had no intention of being continued."

One of the notable aspects of *Halloween II* is that it functions very much in the tradition of haunted-house films, confined and claustrophobic. However, most haunted-house films tend toward the gothic, but nothing is gothic about a hospital with fluorescent lights; functional architecture; and a cold, clinical interior design. Cundey was tasked with creating something photographically stylish and aesthetically within the form of the first film but in the context of a hospital setting and working with the practical realities and obstacles of such a location.

"That was something I said before we started the film, that hospitals are classically brightly lit; people don't want to be scared in hospitals. I said that we must find a reason to alter the lighting. It was shot at night when all the bright lights are off, and you will notice that there are no other patients or nurses other than a few that are in the story. So I suggested, 'How about we make it so that the main lights go out at the dramatic part and only the emergency lights remain on so that we can have pools of darkness?' People agreed that this idea sounded good. So I had everyone place these small studio lights around the hospital that acted as the emergency lights, but we would have control over them; they weren't just regular fixtures. It was a very conscious effort to do that and to try to make it dark and spooky."

As with any picture that Cundey shoots, there are some memorable moments where the lighting is used to great effect as it cuts through the darkness. His use of lens flaring for deliberate effect is interesting and unusual. An example of Cundey's tasteful use of the technique occurs when Dr. Loomis and Sheriff Brackett are cruising in the patrol car and the roaming search light occasionally and blindingly points directly into the camera to create an intense flare. It's a jarring but aesthetically unique visual trick that essentially breaks the fourth wall because it acknowledges the fact there is a camera, the lens through which we the audience are viewing this fictional effort. Such formalist use of this certainly wasn't as common as in contemporary cinema, where the illusion-breaking effect is often overused for showy, stylistic purposes. Traditionally, studios did not want their cameraman catching flares because it was not only breaking the illusion and artifice of cinema but also suggested professional ineptitude and poor lighting design. Back in the days of the Old Hollywood studio system, cameramen could even be fined for being so careless as to capture a flare on film. It was only in the brave new cinema of the New Hollywood movement that filmmakers experimented with techniques that added to the photographic palette of their work. As such, László Kovács in *Easy Rider* (1969) deliberately and innovatively used lens flaring, as did Vilmos Zsigmond, daringly so in early Steven Spielberg films, such as *The Sugarland Express* (1974). Filmmakers influenced by this era were given license to break filmmaking conventions, and Cundey is one such artist who used unique and unconventional techniques as an expressive artistic signature.

"I was conscious of the idea that we wanted to do something that was edgy, that was different," Cundey admits. "I noticed that the perfection of Hollywood filmmaking, starting in the 1930s and going through the 1940s and 1950s, didn't ever allow for lens flares or focus problems or whatever, but that was starting to change. When that stuff started to be used, I said, 'It looks like it's going to be a new thing, where people are going to be more aware of something being captured in reality on a camera.' And it became a new style. But lens flaring is prevalent now to an extreme and can be very distracting. They deliberately put it in windows and behind people. It makes you question the reality of the scene. So I don't really agree with the style of some films now. To me, the audience should look and see what they are supposed to see that helps tell the story, but very often, the filmmakers will do strange things with the camera. For example, they will have a guy enter a room completely out of focus and then have him walk toward the camera and gradually come into focus. To me, that's not how we would see him if we were there in the room. So it becomes an artificial, distracting kind of thing. In the current effort to be new and edgy, the visuals are going away from what the audience should see and becoming what the filmmaker or cinematographer thinks is 'like totally cool, dude!'"

One of the key elements of the *Halloween* franchise is its instantly recognizable theme music. John Carpenter composed the score of the first film, but on many of the sequels, from the second film up to the sixth, Alan Howarth was the man on the keys. Born and raised in Cleveland, Ohio, Howarth's association with John Carpenter began on *Escape from New York*, when the synthesizer wizard contributed sound effects and music to that film. But being from Cleveland—the home of rock and roll, according to some—Alan went through the various stages of a budding rock star. His first contact with music occurred when he was a little kid with a fascination for his father's accordion, which had been sitting up in the attic. He pestered his mother for accordion lessons, which didn't last long, but he soon found a more agreeable instrument, as he recalls:

"In third grade, they gave us this aptitude test, and after completing mine, they sent a letter home to my parents saying, 'Oh, little Alan has an aptitude for music; he should be in the school band.' So I evaluated the instruments that were available with the school band, and there were no guitars or piano; the only cool instrument was the saxophone, so I took up alto sax in grade school and high school. But at that time, music was just a hobby. I wasn't into the whole situation of being a musician; it was just kind of there." Later, while Howarth was an art student, one of his classmates recommended that he join her boyfriend Dave's band because they needed a saxophonist to play at a sock hop happening at a girls' Catholic high school. As modest an event as it was, it gave Howarth a taste of what could be if he followed the more lucrative route of music instead of art. "I went to the gig," he says. "I read the charts, and I played dance music. Then at the end of the night, they paid me $80, and my eyes went wide, like, 'Whoa! Fuck art, I'm going into music!'"

When Dave's band decided to change direction by ditching the charts and turning it up to 11, they needed someone to provide the low end. So Howarth badgered his mother to get him a bass guitar from Sears and Roebuck. He quickly learned the bass, grew his hair, and hit the rock-and-roll scene on the west side of Cleveland. Throughout the 1960s, Howarth would join several groups, one of which was the Tree Stumps, who successfully won a Battle of the Bands competition and opened for Paul Revere & the Raiders in downtown Cleveland. Another band was Renaissance Faire, which was influenced by the psychedelic grooves of The Doors and Jefferson Airplane. That band then morphed into another group called Silk, who played for big audiences when they opened for The Who and Cream.

"At that stage, my hair was down to the middle of my back, and I thought I was cool. Then the usual band thing happened where you do the record, you end up resenting each other, and then the band breaks up. So I began working in a music store in Cleveland, and then I eventually opened my own music store called Pi Keyboards and Audio. We focused on synthesizers and tape recorders and were set up across from a nightclub called the Agora Ballroom, which was a great midweek stop for national touring acts like KISS, David Bowie, and U2."

A major step toward landing in Los Angeles came about when another Howarth group, Braino, became the house band in a small Cleveland nightclub called Smiling Dog Saloon. This venue was known for booking jazz acts, and one such band provided Howarth with the opportunity he needed to make his way out west. Weather Report was a jazz fusion band that featured some of the finest musicians in the genre, including saxophonist Wayne Shorter, bassist Jaco Pastorious, and keyboardist Joe Zawinul, among other notables. When they came to town for a show at the Saloon, the proprietor made a wise suggestion to the band after making a keen observation, as Howarth recalls:

"Weather Report came in to play, and the club owner says, 'You guys set up your own gear; you should bring these guys—meaning me and my sound guy, Brian Risner—along to do that.' I stayed to work in the store, but Brian did go out on the road with Weather Report and became not their first roadie but their first technical assistant to set up the gear and deal with all the sound stuff. Then about four years later, their album *Heavy Weather* came out, and they were going to go on a national tour with Return to Forever opening for them. By then, Joe Zawinul's rig had grown. He had the ARP 2600, an Oberheim Four-Voice, a Rhodes Chroma, and more, so it was Brian's job to take care of Joe's keyboards. And because they were going out on this big tour, they needed a stage crew, so I took the opportunity and went out with Weather Report from 1976 to 1980. The lineup was Joe Zawinul, Wayne Shorter, Jaco Pastorius, and Peter Erskine. They were all my buddies; I got to hang with them all the time, and I got to meet all the other jazz greats: Miles Davis, Herbie Hancock, Chick Corea."

Hitting the road with Weather Report brought Howarth to Hollywood. It was the right time and right place; his friend was working in the sound department at Paramount Pictures, where *Star Trek: The Motion Picture* was in postproduction. When that film's sound editors, Richard Anderson and Stephen Flick, ruminated aloud that they should find someone with knowledge of synthesizers to help with sound effects, Howarth's friend duly recommended him. "My buddy said, 'Oh man, you've got to talk to Alan. He knows all about synthesizers; he's with Weather Report.' And one of the guys looks at him and goes, 'Weather Report? Is that the one at eleven o'clock or seven o'clock?' But nonetheless, they got my number, and I went down to meet Richard and Stephen, both of whom went on to become Academy Award winners."

Anderson and Flick told Howarth to make an audition tape, and when he inquired about what exactly they were looking for, they said that the Starship Enterprise needed some effects as it went from warp one to warp seven. Howarth retreated to his modest dining-room studio, and with his Prophet-5 synthesizer and four-track tape recorder, he put a couple of tracks down that ultimately became the sound design of the Starship Enterprise going from warp one to warp seven. Suitably impressed, Anderson and Flick hired Howarth, and so began his career in film sound and music. "I turned in that tape, and I got the gig," Howarth says. "I was onboard with *Star Trek*, and it was exciting. I delivered the sound of the Enterprise, the transporters, lasers, the warp drives. It was all the stuff you can't record with a microphone; they had to be done in the studio. Remember, this was 1979, so editors were working with Moviolas and literally having to cut with razor blades. So the idea of having somebody who had a studio, had all the gear and could play it, really appealed to them. I could create original things for them when they needed it. All of a sudden, I was no longer struggling with the band business; I was working in a whole new industry."

Fate intervened once again because Todd Ramsay, the editor of *Star Trek: The Motion Picture*, was taking on another job of cutting a film called *Escape from New York*, which was directed by John Carpenter. With talent and equipment at his disposal, Ramsay felt Howarth would be an ideal hire to do the sound effects. Knowing that Carpenter was looking for a studio to work on the music for the film and with a hunch that the director would enjoy the company of Howarth, it made sense that Ramsay introduced the pair. It was the beginning of a great friendship and collaborative relationship.

"I invited John to my little studio in Glendale," Howarth recalls, "and we sat there for about three hours. And I played him some music and some sounds, and we talked. At the end of that, he goes, 'Yeah, let's do it!' So now I'm working with John Carpenter on *Escape from New York*. I had all this equipment, all those analogue synthesizers, tape recorders, so I made it easy for John to show up at my house and work. Our relationship was great because John is already a musician; his father was a professor of music and a concert violinist. John wanted to be a filmmaker, but music was in his blood. He was really gifted at making up themes, and they are very simple themes that work. That is really a lesson I learned from him because as a musician, you start getting more and more complicated to get your music to be cooler. You start doing these unnecessarily complicated pieces, but John would be like, 'No, no, no. This is movie music. It's background. It wants to stay simple and wants to be carpeting under the scene.' He doesn't want to draw attention to something; he just wants to support whatever's happening with the movie. So having John sitting in my studio hanging out all day, watching him do his thing, and having conversations felt like I went to the Music School of John Carpenter, and I graduated. Not many people get to do that. So we worked on *Escape from New York*. And when we were finishing up the mix, he said, 'Hey, I got my next movie assignment. It's called *The*

Thing [1982]; it's going to be a huge production. And they want to make another *Halloween*. But I can't do that, so you're going to have to do it.' So he kind of threw it over the fence to me, and that is how I ended up doing *Halloween II*."

Howarth continues, detailing his work on the sequel: "I was aware of *Halloween*, as I had seen it in the theater in 1978, but I wasn't totally into it. When I inherited *Halloween II*, I had John's iconic music from the first film to work with. I took the multitrack of that music and transferred into another multitrack, which had more tracks, and basically overdubbed my stuff onto John's music to support the action of *Halloween II*. By doing that, the texture changed; I took it from a lighter piano thing to this synth-driven score. Debra Hill was my main contact because she was running the show in John's absence, as he was busy on the other project. I had a meeting with Rick Rosenthal to talk about what I was going to do, but John had already established how you make a *Halloween* score: there's the main theme, there's what we called 'Laurie's Theme,' and then there's the attack theme. So the action on screen really dictated what part of that original *Halloween* score is used for that moment. There is some editorial work involved, but that was the core of how I approached it. I also got to do a couple of new music cues and scoring of my own, like the parking lot scene. It was fun from that standpoint too. But at the end of the day, it was the sequel. And it was supposed to be more of the same, literally taking place later that night, so I wanted the music to be quite like what had already been established."

Halloween II is a solid sequel. The film hits its generic horror-movie registers in a more routine manner than Carpenter's unique original does, but it successfully retains the essential elements of that first film—the returning cast members, Cundey's cinematography, Carpenter's music, the tension, and the tone—which allows for both works to function together as one long narrative. Perhaps more importantly, it gives viewers what they wanted, which was more Michael Myers. Of course, with added Michael comes more characters for him to pick off and to deliver sustained moments of blood and gore in contrast to Carpenter's restrained approach to such. The emphasis on visible violence here gives the film the feel of a straight slasher, but in fairness to Rosenthal, he wasn't just interested in merely offering more action-oriented fare because he does particularly well in presenting certain themes that have remained within the franchise for a long time. This film is where the idea of Michael Myers and Laurie Strode's being family is introduced, and such a revelation invites subtextual readings with which viewers could speculate upon incentive and provocation. The introduction of the familial connections between Michael and Laurie and, thus, the potential for intellectual discourse on themes could be seen to undermine John Carpenter's straightforward presentation of his killer as the blank embodiment of pure evil, unmotivated by anything so psychologically analytical as blood lust by blood ties. But for some, this thematic direction works well and has provided viewers with interesting and entertaining narrative arcs in the sequels to ruminate upon.

The revelation that Laurie is Michael's sister provides motivation for his obsessive pursuit but also adds to the psychosexual subtext, which can be noted throughout the franchise. Laurie is presented as something of a repressed character, bookish and unsocial, her intelligence apparently a repellent for any potential suitors. Her promiscuous friends drink beer and get laid as well as killed. Meanwhile, Laurie harbors a quiet crush on a local kid named Ben Tramer, but her longing is never fulfilled because Ben is killed in a case of mistaken identity after he attempts to flee a gun-toting Dr. Loomis while dressed in a similar mask and overalls to those of Michael Myers. In that moment, Laurie's romantic interest is immolated, denying her an opportunity to join her friends on the dating scene and further explore her sexuality, just as Michael denied Judith a life in the company of men. Even the potential for romantic interest in Jimmy, the ambulance driver, is thwarted as Michael rampages through Haddonfield Memorial Hospital.

The brother–sister thread weaves throughout the franchise but diverges into two alternating strands. From *Halloween 4: The Return of Michael Myers* to *Halloween: The Curse of Michael Myers*, the sixth film, Laurie is said to have been killed in an accident with her husband, leaving her daughter, Jamie Lloyd, orphaned

Jamie Lee Curtis (left) and Donald Pleasence film a scene from *Halloween II* (1981). Universal Pictures/Photofest ©Universal Pictures

and the new target for Michael. In the seventh film, *Halloween H20: 20 Years Later*, Laurie Strode is alive, if not very well. She is living under the assumed name of Keri Tate and is the headmistress of Hillcrest Academy, a private prep school. The biographical elements set up in the fourth, fifth, and sixth films are retconned. There is no mention of her having had a daughter, though she does have a son, John, with whom she has a strained relationship. John is the product of Laurie's failed marriage to an abusive addict, which no doubt added further to her traumatic life because we see her self-medicating with booze and prescription pills.

In an attempt to enjoy some semblance of a regular life and have companionship, she forms a clandestine relationship (another act of suppression) with Hillcrest guidance counselor, Will Brennan, but as long as Michael is on the prowl, Laurie can never fulfill her romantic destiny nor meet her sexual needs and desires. In one scene where she and Will are being intimate, when she reveals her identity and relationship to the infamous killer, the moment is cut short. Will asks, "What happened to the sister? She died, right?" before Laurie reveals that "she faked her death. And now she is the headmistress of a very posh, secluded private school in Northern California, hoping and praying every year that her brother won't find her." Naturally, this revelation kills the romantic mood before Michael kills Will later that evening. Once again, it becomes clear that the only man constant in her life will be Michael Myers. Filmmaker Rob Zombie ran with the brother–sister narrative and explored the familial themes in greater depth for his 2007 reboot and its 2009 sequel. However, David Gordon Green's 2018 film entirely ignores this theme and functions strictly as a direct sequel to John Carpenter's original film. Thus, there is no familial connection between Laurie and Michael, and accordingly, there is absolutely no psychosexual subtext to the last three films of the franchise.

Interestingly, two of the horror films that Jamie Lee Curtis starred in between *Halloween* and *Halloween II* feature themes that would become part of the Michael Myers and Laurie Strode mythology: family ties between killer and victim, sexual repression and frustration, and identity issues. In *Prom Night* (1980), the killer turns out to be the distraught twin brother of a young girl who, six years prior, was teased to her death after she attempted to join an unwelcoming group of kids playing hide-and-seek in an abandoned building. In *Terror Train* (also 1980), Curtis's character endures an awkward kiss with her potential killer, just as she does with Michael before she dies in *Halloween: Resurrection*; in both cases, the kiss ends with an act of violence. For the transvestite killer in *Terror Train*, the moment of intimacy instigates a flashback to the traumatic moment that inspired his descent into madness, thus triggering another mental breakdown. For Michael, his sister's kiss could be a final acknowledgment of their strangely intimate connection. Here, physically closer than they have ever been, Laurie clings to Michael, fatally wounded after his penetrative act of stabbing her. Now eye to eye and knowing her time has come, she seals her death with a kiss, or perhaps kiss-off: "I'll see you in hell." With that, she falls to her ultimate demise, all family ties literally severed.

While the Michael Myers–Laurie Strode familial narrative, founded in *Halloween II*, would continue to be utilized in various ways throughout the remainder of the series up to that opening scene of *Halloween: Resurrection*, there is one film that functions entirely without it. Indeed, not only is Laurie Strode absent from the third film but so, too, is—controversially and commercially detrimentally—Michael Myers. In fact, nothing at all from the diegetic world of the first two films made it into the next entry in the franchise: Tommy Lee Wallace's *Halloween III: Season of the Witch*.

Chapter Two

Santa Mira, Silver Shamrocks, Samhain, and Stonehenge
We're Not in Haddonfield Anymore!

"Irish Halloween masks?" —Ellie Grimbridge

Halloween is in the air once again, and children across the country are craving an exciting new trio of masks being sold by the Silver Shamrock Novelties company. On October 23, a man named Harry Grimbridge ends up in a hospital after being pursued by some well-dressed men intent on doing him harm. Dr. Dan Challis (Tom Atkins) is working the night shift and tends to the ailing man; Dan retrieves a jack-o'-lantern mask from Harry's grasp, one of those coveted items being advertised as the must-have novelty to be worn for a mysterious televised event heralded as the "Big Giveaway" that will be broadcast on Halloween night. It turns out that Harry is a store owner who was on a business trip to the Silver Shamrock factory in the Northern California town of Santa Mira, but for reasons of self-preservation, he needed to flee. Later that night in the hospital, he is attacked and killed by one of his besuited pursuers, who then immolates himself in the parking lot. When Harry's daughter Ellie (Stacey Nelkin) arrives and talks with Dan, the pair decide to investigate further, using what little information they have about Harry's business dealings with Silver Shamrock and traveling to the ominous company town of Santa Mira to follow up.

Santa Mira is an idyllic coastal enclave with dairy ranches and scenic rolling green hills, predominantly Irish in population.

44 / You Can't Kill the Boogeyman

Halloween III: Season of the Witch (1982) poster. Universal Pictures/Photofest ©Universal Pictures

The town's most prominent, and powerful, person is an industrialist toymaker by the name of Conal Cochran, an Irish gentleman on the surface but a scheming megalomaniac with plans for mass murder behind his charming façade. Dan and Ellie pose as commercial buyers and take a tour of the Silver Shamrock facility along with a genuine businessman named Buddy Kupfer, who is there with his family. Kupfer tells Dan and Ellie that Cochran is one of the richest men in the country, a toymaking tycoon and genius having invented such legendary prankster items as Sticky Toilet Paper, the Soft Chainsaw, and the Dead Dwarf Gag. With Cochran's credentials duly considered, Dan and Ellie infiltrate the factory and uncover the madman's dastardly plot to return Halloween to its Celtic origins and rituals, which include sacrificing children at Samhain, the Gaelic festival that marks the end of the harvest season and the coming of winter. Cochran explains to Dan, who is now a captive of the evil entrepreneur, the real meaning of Halloween, as opposed to the contemporary tradition of going door-to-door begging for candy:

"It was the start of the year in our old Celtic lands, and we'd be waiting in our houses of wattles and clay. The barriers would be down, you see, between the real and the unreal, and the dead might be looking in to sit by our fires of turf . . . Halloween: The Festival of Samhain. The last great one took place three thousand years ago when the hills ran red with the blood of animals and children."

This time, however, it won't be the hills of Ireland running red but rather, the living rooms of American households across the country, as Cochran has sinisterly planted a microchip on the logo medallion of each mask. The microchip contains a fragment of a stolen Stonehenge megalith that Cochran's androids have been chipping away at in the Silver Shamrock "final processing" plant. The theft of the Stonehenge rock occurred nine months previously and was one of 19 pieces that each represent the 19-year cycle of the moon.

And just how did Cochran steal a five-ton Stonehenge megalith from Southwest England and transport it to a rural Irish community in Northern California, USA?

"We had a time getting it here, you wouldn't believe!"

Okay, then. That's that explained.

In every horror franchise are outliers, those entries that for some reason deviate wildly from what has gone before. Sometimes it's the work of a visionary director who wants to put their own stamp on a property, sometimes it's the result of corporate meddling out of commercial concerns, or sometimes it's plain ineptitude at a creative or studio level—think, for example, *Hellraiser: Bloodline* (1996), *Freddy's Dead: The Final Nightmare* (1991), and *Texas Chainsaw Massacre: The Next Generation* (1995). *Halloween III: Season of the Witch*, however, is the outlier's outlier. Reviled upon release and making a heroic return only in recent years, the film is the most outrageously original sequel to appear in any already established franchise. But from the beginning, there was never any intention for there to be a continued story arc across a series of films, and if we look at *Halloween* and *Halloween II* as essentially a single story, then *Halloween III* begins to make more sense. As different and unique as it may be, there is a consistency of style—visually, tonally, sonically—and it fits perfectly within the aesthetic playground of John Carpenter, not to mention the fact that it is lensed by Dean Cundey, retained from the first two films; directed by erstwhile Carpenter collaborator and *Halloween* production designer and editor Tommy Lee Wallace; and scored by John Carpenter in collaboration with *Halloween II* music man Alan Howarth. So what's missing? Well, Michael Myers, of course. But this is not a slasher movie; it is a sci-fi paranoia pod movie and one of the best damn horror films of the 1980s.

To understand the origins of *Halloween III: Season of the Witch*, one must observe some details. The film was written by Nigel Kneale, the screenwriter of *Quatermass and the Pit* (1967), among other British cult films of the 1950s and 1960s. The town in which *Halloween III: Season of the Witch* is set is named Santa Mira, a direct lift from the small town taken over by incognito extraterrestrials in Don Siegel's *Invasion of the Body Snatchers* (1956). Indeed, reflecting that film's suggestive subtext in which the façade of middle-class conformity masks a malevolent conspiracy, the besuited minions of Conal Cochran are, on the surface, good compliant company men well-maintained and suitably groomed for a day's business, only Cochran's business is mass murder. Underneath the shirts and ties are mere mechanical droids on duty for death and destruction.

Bringing Nigel Kneale's story to the screen with singular artistic vision was Tommy Lee Wallace, finally making his directorial debut after bowing out of *Halloween II*. Despite the considerable production values onscreen and the ambitious scope of the story, Wallace was still working with the relatively low budget of $2.5 million. Crucially, for the director, he had the full backing of John Carpenter and Debra Hill behind him when adversity struck, especially in the form of other insidious company men: studio executives.

"The suits wanted us to change things," Wallace reveals, "but John and Debra were immensely supportive of me. John made a brave choice in letting me do the film the way I wanted to, and he saved me when we were told that I had to make those changes. *Halloween III* was my chance to set something straight for Don Siegel, because the ending of the movie was a tribute to Don and the original *Invasion of the Body Snatchers*. There's a bookend beginning and ending to that movie set in a hospital. Kevin McCarthy is telling the story of what happened, but that was added because originally, the movie was supposed to end with Kevin looking at the camera saying, 'You're next! You're next!' However, the studio wouldn't let Don Siegel end the movie there; they had to let the audience off the hook: 'Oh, it's going to be okay; those things are gone . . . ,' blah, blah, blah. I hated that."

Wallace continues, "So my ending for *Halloween III* was an homage to Don Siegel and to do what he couldn't. Sure enough, once we had put the film together, I got a call from John, and he said, 'The studio thinks the ending is too much of a downer, and they want us to do something about it. How do you feel about that?' And John had the power; he had final cut on this movie as the reason the whole thing came together. And I said, 'Gee, John, how about you?' He said, 'It's your movie; you decide.' And I said, 'Let's leave it the way it is.' And he said, 'You got it.' Now think about that; that's unheard of. I'm a first-time director, and he handed me final cut. It was the right choice. It's the right ending for the movie. But it doesn't happen that way very often. I think I made a bold choice. One of the questions usually asked at these conventions where there's some sort of panel is, 'Do you think all the kids died?' And I say, 'No, I don't. We're still here, aren't we? It didn't end the world. It massacred a whole bunch of kids, but it didn't get them all, just the ones stupid enough to sit in front of the TV with a mask on.' At that time, there were three major networks, and they shut down two of them. But we don't know whether they got the last one or not. So I think some kids got massacred, sure. One of the things I love about storytelling is it doesn't have to be cut and dried; you can be ambiguous. But audiences in the United States *really* want that confirmation and conclusion. And I just say, 'Well, fuck you. You don't get that. It's going to be ambiguous. Just live with it.'"

"Tommy was great to work with as a director," applauds cinematographer Dean Cundey. "Because he knew the history, he knew that all of us had come from the same place, that we had the same intention and respect for the subject matter. He was particularly good because he had been an editor on the first film, so he knew what pieces needed to be made to put the story together. That was always my big thing—still is—that what the audience should see at any moment tells them the story, tells them where they are, what the characters are doing, and so on. So that has always been my focus . . . no pun intended . . . well, maybe. But Tommy understood that you needed pieces that told the story, and that's what we shot. So he was a very good collaborator."

Former *Fangoria* editor Tony Timpone recalls his excitement upon reading that the next *Halloween* sequel would come with some serious pedigree from the horror and sci-fi world: "I had been reading the articles in *Fangoria* about *Halloween III* before I worked there, and I loved the approach that John Carpenter initially had, which was just going to be that the title 'Halloween' was going to be an anthology movie moniker and that each movie would be something different. I thought that was a fun idea. But from a financial standpoint and a business standpoint, it wasn't a very good idea. I was always a fan of the screenwriter, Nigel Kneale, because I used to love the British *Quatermass* movies that he wrote. Seeing someone of his stature doing a low-budget American horror film was pretty eye-opening at the time. And it's a shame that the film really didn't quite live up to his vision and his original screenplay."

Halloween III: Season of the Witch is quietly subversive in its depiction of good and bad and in its presentation of a leading man of questionable morality, he who is traditionally unquestionably noble in all intent. The hero of the piece, Dr. Dan Challis, brilliantly played by Tom Atkins, who had appeared in the John Carpenter films *The Fog* (1980) and *Escape from New York* (1981), brings an everyman quality to the role that belies his profession as a physician. Everything about his character is far from the squeaky clean, politically correct leading men of today, whom you will not find smoking cigarettes, swigging six packs of beer, and seducing their deceased patient's grieving (and much younger) daughter any chance they get while performing their heroic duties. Director Wallace acknowledges the rarity of such a cinematic lionheart:

"He's a pathetic father, he has no relationship with his ex-wife, and he drinks. He's a rogue. I liked that part of it. And he's a little older; he's not a pretty boy. We talked about all those things at length because there were several other casting possibilities. But it was Debra [Hill] who thought that Tommy would be about right for the part. And, boy, when she mentioned him . . . I already knew him as we had worked together on *The Fog*. And we also ran in the same social circles, so casting him just struck me as right."

And, of course, the great Irish actor Dan O'Herlihy renders Conal Cochran as one of the truly great villainous characters of 1980's horror cinema. Warm, welcoming, and witty, O'Herlihy's Cochran carries the kind of Irish charm that makes him everyone's friend. Handsome, debonair, and devilishly brilliant in business, he is the kind of individual whom people admire, but this is his game: to welcome all with a smile and a handshake while he deceives and dominates.

O'Herlihy had developed his career as an actor on the stages of Dublin's famed Abbey Theatre and Gate Theatre, where he performed the works of eminent Irish playwrights, such as Seán O'Casey. He was later cast in Carol Reed's Belfast-set film noir *Odd Man Out* (1947), Orson Welles's *Macbeth* (1948), and Luis

Dr. Dan Challis (Tom Atkins) comforts Ellie Grimbridge (Stacey Nelkin) in *Halloween III: Season of the Witch* (1982). Universal Pictures/Photofest ©Universal Pictures

Buñuel's *Robinson Crusoe* (1954). Indeed, much work throughout the Golden Age of Hollywood ensued before Wallace hired him in the twilight of his career, which also included memorable roles in Paul Verhoeven's *RoboCop* (1987); John Huston's *The Dead* (1987); and David Lynch's television phenomenon, *Twin*

Peaks (1990). As well as bringing some Old Hollywood gravitas to the proceedings, O'Herlihy harnesses a sense of authenticity and relish to the role of Conal Cochran. Hailing from County Wexford on the coast of Southeast Ireland, one does see (from an Irish writer's perspective) a sense of playfulness along with the wickedness and a satirical invocation of the clichés of the charming Irish rogue caricature.

"Dan brought quite a bit of respect for Irish mythology," Wallace says. "When I wrote Cochran's long speeches toward the end about the history of Halloween, he added bits that made it more authentic and truer to his heritage. He didn't sound like a bad guy who just wanted to make mischief or to be horrible to children. It was a kind of tribal imperative, the way he delivers it: this had to happen, the planets are aligned, blah, blah, blah. 'It's time again.' That line rang truest to me: 'It's time again.' Oh, shit. Look out! There's something more at work here than just one guy. He's got the force of his own personal reading of history behind him. Dan had been a legitimate star but was more or less forgotten by the time 1982 rolled around, but boy, we caught him just as he was getting sort of forgetful. He didn't live all that

Evil Irish toymaker, Conal Cochran, counts down to the Silver Shamrock Big Giveaway, which is designed to wipe out the nation's population of children. Author's Collection

long past that movie, but he gave his very best with those long speeches. He was right on."

Interestingly, before O'Herlihy was cast as Cochran, Wallace had his eyes on another iconic figure of classic Hollywood cinema, as he reveals:

"I tried to get Fred MacMurray to play the role. A lot of people only know Fred MacMurray because of his fatherly avuncular-type roles in Disney movies and on the TV show called *My Three Sons*, this sort of pipe-smoking uncle guy over in the corner, spouting little bits of wisdom from time to time. But anybody who has seen Billy Wilder's *Double Indemnity* knows what an evil son of a bitch he could play. He was fabulous in that film, but in a way I'm glad it didn't happen. I mean it would have been fun. And I know he would have been a great version of Conal Cochran, but Dan nailed it so well. He brought the idea that great villains don't think of themselves as villainous."

"Dan O'Herlihy certainly came with a presence," affirms cinematographer Dean Cundey. "He was an established old-time actor, and so there was a lot of respect for him on the set. He seemed to appreciate that and almost relished it. His opinion was always valued. Here he was, this famous, classic Hollywood guy in the small environment of this low-budget horror film. He was wonderful."

With its depiction of the Irish as a malevolent sort, working their farmlands in ignorance and toiling in the factories in servitude of their rich, old countryman who intends on ridding the world of its children and thus future populations, it could be interpreted that the film (written by an Englishman at a time when The Troubles in Northern Ireland raged) as anti-Irish in sentiment. With Anglo-Irish relations in as contentious a state as they were, it is not surprising that Kneale's work may have been underscored by genuine xenophobia, as Wallace attests:

"I think the script that Nigel Kneale wrote was a bit hostile to the Irish. His biographer, Andy Murray, told me that he thought he meant that as satire and that he thought Nigel was being funny. But I detected a little bit more hostility than I was comfortable with, so I rewrote some sequences. The way that script worked is that Nigel wrote the original script, John rewrote

Nigel, and I rewrote John. John took no credit for his work, and Nigel took his name off it, which meant I wound up with a very dubious sole-writer credit on a movie that I did work on but certainly wasn't the originator of. So much of Nigel's original script is still in there; I'd say 50 to 60%. The other thing that Andy told me was that by the time he wrote that script in 1982, Nigel had experienced a lot of disappointments, especially throughout the '60s and '70s. Like many other writers, the scripts that he poured himself into maybe didn't get made. Or maybe they got made in a way that he didn't like, which is not unusual for a writer to see some director take his work and do something that just doesn't feel authentic to him. He experienced a lot of that. Andy said that by the end of the '70s, Nigel didn't much like anybody, so he felt like it wasn't personal to the Irish. He was just kind of nasty about everybody."

Despite having no narrative link to any other film in the franchise, there are several winks to viewers to acknowledge their awareness of its being a sequel, even if only in name. For example, as Dan enjoys his early-morning drink at a bar, he sees a televised trailer that is for an upcoming broadcast of John Carpenter's original film, and Jamie Lee Curtis provides the voice for the Santa Mira announcer informing residents of an imminent curfew. Elsewhere, *Halloween* cast member Nancy Kyes (Annie Brackett from the first film) plays the deserted Challis wife, while Dick Warlock (Michael Myers from *Halloween II*) plays one of Cochran's androids. But what truly places the film in the realm of the *Halloween* franchise is the return of cinematographer Dean Cundey and the music of Alan Howarth in collaboration with Carpenter himself.

Emerging from the suburban shadows of *Halloween* and the coldly lit hospital corridors of *Halloween II*, Cundey returns for *Halloween III: Season of the Witch* with an unusually warm and colorful palette for a horror film but one that works exquisitely within the context of its setting in a Northern California Irish farming community in the fall. The film was shot in the very striking setting of Loleta, California, an eerily remote and distinctive-looking factory town. Cundey's unique photographic eye for composition and color adds a sense of the surreal; the absurd; and, of course, the Irish, taking full advantage of the town's vibrant and verdant color scheme. The lush greens of the landscape and deep browns of the factory complement the vibrant blues of the sky, all of which are captured exquisitely with Cundey's wide Panavision lens in his richly composed exteriors. Indeed, the film looks bigger and markedly different in tone to all the other *Halloween* films, and with good reason. Initially, the films were to be anthological, featuring a stand-alone story with each release. Therefore, there was no need for visual continuity in this film as there was on the first sequel. As far as all were concerned, there would be no return of Michael Myers.

"That was all conceived in the conversations with John and Debra," Cundey confirms. "They said, 'With *Halloween III*, it's going to be different because we want to see if we can make a series of films about Halloween, but each one is going to be a stand-alone story.' I said that was reasonable. And then I read the script, and sure enough, there's no Michael Myers in it. It's all about Samhain . . . or 'Sam-Hain' as they originally thought it was supposed to be pronounced. Therefore, the idea was always to make it a unique, stand-alone experience for the audience, so we went for a more colorful, crisper look. You might say we used a more conventional style of filmmaking and storytelling. I think shooting it in Loleta was one very wise choice. It was good that they didn't try to set it in Los Angeles because it really opened the visuals. It was a very different look not just for us but to the audience. That's an important aspect of storytelling, that the audience be taken somewhere that's appropriate for the story and not necessarily convenient for the production. That setting was one of the things that was unique about it and unexpected by the audience, being that it was Irish in its milieu as opposed to just another horror film shot in Pasadena or set in some anonymous California suburb. The fact that it is set somewhere different was one of the things that set it apart, both good and bad. It helps it stand alone for a reason other than being an unsuccessful third entry."

Setting the mood exquisitely from beginning to end, Alan Howarth and John Carpenter's entirely electronic score is one of

"Welcome to Santa Mira." Author's Collection

the standout elements of the film. While Dean Cundey's visuals capture the rustic rural landscape and aestheticizes even further its natural beauty with his anamorphic framing and heightened color scheme, Howarth and Carpenter's score contrasts such warmth with their coldly synthetic music. Their clinically processed tone and inorganic blips and beeps imbue the film with an edgy technological awareness and underscore the themes of artificial intelligence in the film. As soon as the Universal logo fades to give way to the digital pumpkin assembling to the chilling score, we are immediately unnerved and enthralled. Alan Howarth recalls the score and its lasting impact:

"The music over the opening credits is called "Chariots of Pumpkins," and that is one of the most popular pieces on my Spotify. John wanted to do the music for *Halloween III*, so he was pretty much driving the score. I did all that sequencing work on it, but he was in the room with me. Before the movie, we sat down, and he pulled out the latest Tangerine Dream record so we could hear their latest synth work. And he said, 'Alan, this is going to be really easy; let's just rip ourselves off,' which was his way of saying, 'Hey, I really love what we did on *Escape from New York*.' And because it is an entirely different story, we were not married to the *Halloween* theme music anymore, so we did something completely different. It was a case of 'Let's do something new. Let's just create.' The *Halloween III* score really touches on a lot of different stuff. I particularly like the music that we did when the characters were driving into Santa Mira. I think that whole score came out really good and it actually helped establish me as a composer."

While *Halloween III: Season of the Witch* has finally been embraced by the horror community and fans of the franchise, it was a long, lonely road of obscurity before it reached this point. For much of the four decades since its release, the film's exposure to audiences had been limited to sometimes-shoddy home video transfers and sporadic late-night television scheduling. Despite being part of a legendary franchise, it felt like a cult film waiting to find its cult that could appreciate it appropriately, and at long last, it seems that it has. In the past decade, it has begun to be honored as being worthy of having a place in the pantheon of horror cinema, with documentaries; a book published detailing its production (written by Wallace); and retrospective theatrical screenings, such as the one observed by yours truly in, appropriately enough, Ireland. It has received respectable treatments on DVD and Blu-ray, with various companies around the world releasing it in worthy special editions that celebrate the film for what it is: a brilliantly unique horror picture that was unfortunate to have been labeled as a sequel to a classic film that had a well-established formula and iconic antagonist.

"What does a dodgy Irish businessman have to do with the boogeyman?" one could imagine fans lamenting at the time of its initial release.

"I think that had there not been a Roman numeral II after the title of the sequel, we would have been fine," Wallace ruminates, "but putting a Roman numeral III after our film *Season of the Witch* was a desperate mistake because it implied a true sequel, which it was not and never was meant to be. The idea of an anthology Halloween franchise year after year was brilliant; it still appalls me that we didn't get to do that because there are endless stories that could be told about the season. As happens, whether we did it or not, there are plenty of movies on the subject still being made to this day. But the film was in need of a better ad campaign. If only I'd been thinking at the time, I could have come up with something to put in an advertisement that would have set the table so that all the *Halloween* fans could see that so they were ready for something different. But instead, we got a lot of 'Where the hell is Michael Myers?' which is the subtitle of my book on the movie. It was sort of an unfortunate circumstance. It was crushing, because I was proud of the movie."

"The film was a disappointment to the audience," Cundey says, "and that is because they wanted Michael Myers, as we know now, because every *Halloween* film is about this guy who can't seem to die. *Halloween III* was so completely different, intentionally, that the audience was like, 'Whoa! Wait . . . where's Michael Myers?' I've worked on several films which were ahead of their time, whether they were visually different or whatever, and it was sad to me that the audience didn't get what *Halloween III* was about because they were too busy wondering where Michael Myers was. But now I think, with that separation of time, people might approach it differently. Sadly, the fact that it was named 'Halloween III' meant people expected a standard sequel to the first two films as opposed to what was intended and what was delivered."

"*Halloween III* really holds up," composer Howarth applauds. "The fact that they put the number on it meant people mistook it for another Michael Myers movie. If they had just left it as *Season of the Witch*, it wouldn't have received such a bad rap. But everybody comes to a *Halloween* movie expecting to see Michael Myers, and he wasn't in it. Originally, we were going to break it up into a *Halloween* anthology; every year, there would have been a different movie that went to another place and another story. But the dynamics around *Halloween III* when it came out meant they couldn't continue with that idea because it was evident that audiences wanted Michael Myers. At that point, John and Debra said to Moustapha Akkad, Irwin Yablans, and Joe Wolf, 'We've done all we can do with this. You guys were the producers; you own the title and the images. Just send me a check every time you do another one.'"

"I thought that the film itself turned out to be a lot of fun," Tony Timpone says. "It has very good performances. Dan O'Herlihy is terrific as the villain. Tom Atkins is a great two-fisted action hero. I was always a fan of his work, and he really carried the movie. And the music, that crazy little commercial jingle that you can't get out of your head. The score by John Carpenter and Alan Howarth is great too; it gives it the feel of an early-'80s Carpenter film. The masks that were created for the film by Don Post studios were very creepy and effective. It all adds up to a good little movie. It's a B movie that has a lot of heart and imagination. And, again, it's something different, and that's what I really appreciate about it. It deserves all the reappraisal it receives these days. It's great that Tommy Lee Wallace is finally kind of getting some satisfaction from that end."

"Ironically, the movie didn't do that badly," Wallace reveals. "It was perceived at the time as an utter failure; it didn't deserve that. It didn't perform as well at the box office as *Halloween II*, but it did okay. And so it's taken this long for it to spawn into something else. The fact that its popularity has grown in the last five years has been unbelievable. There are all sorts of memorabilia available to do with *Halloween III* now—you can get bags, action figures, a metal sign, a Ouija board, a wallet . . . I've even got *Halloween III* wrapping paper! They are tearing down that old factory that we shot at in Loleta; it's finally being demolished. And I have had fans showing up at conventions with a framed photograph of the factory, and underneath is a little chip of a brick from the factory. I mean, they're selling everything! But I'm very proud of the film. Every autumn season tells me that because people come up and say it has become part of their yearly ritual. They watch this movie because unlike *Halloween* 1, 2, 4, 5, 6, 7, 14, 27 . . . however many *Halloween* movies there are now, it's actually about Halloween. I think that's part of the secret as to why it has endured, because it is about the season. It is very gratifying that it's finally gotten the love that I feel it deserved. People used to come up to me at these conventions, and they would say, 'I don't care what people say; I think it's a great movie!' But they don't have to apologize anymore. There are more fans than there are naysayers now. It's finally found its audience."

Chapter Three

Severing Family Ties

"You're huntin' it, ain't ya? Yeah, you're huntin' it, all right. Just like me." —Jack Sayer

With Halloween III: Season of the Witch having disappointed fans who were expecting another Michael Myers killing spree, the franchise went into hiatus for several years. Released in 1988, *Halloween 4: The Return of Michael Myers* breathed new life into the franchise in bringing back its old villain. Set 10 years after the first film, Michael Myers has been in a coma at Ridgemont Federal Sanitarium since his and Dr. Loomis's explosive showdown at the end of *Halloween II*, but he awakens upon hearing that he has a young niece, Jamie Lloyd (Danielle Harris), living in Haddonfield with her foster family after her mother, Laurie Strode, was killed in a car accident. Now, with another familial link to sever, Michael escapes on Halloween Eve while being transferred to Smith's Grove Sanitarium and returns home to Haddonfield to eliminate Jamie, but not if Dr. Loomis has anything to do with it. Despite being disfigured from his last dance with Michael, Loomis travels to Haddonfield to save innocent Jamie and the town from a commemorative slaughter 10 years after Michael first came home.

As the third sequel to a 10-year-old property, this film is far better than it had any right to be. In the mid- to late 1980s, horror sequels weren't known for their aesthetic or storytelling qualities. It took visionary directors combined with quality

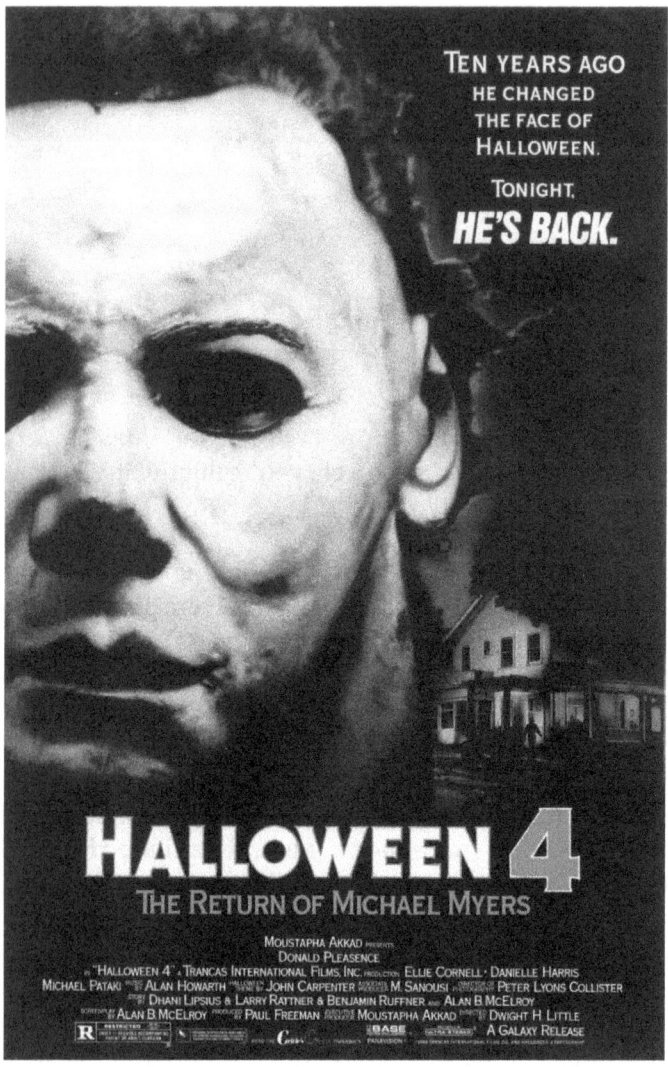

Halloween 4: The Return of Michael Myers **(1988) poster art.** Trancas International Films/Photofest ©Trancas International Films

collaborators to make notable films in a crowded genre marketplace. Richard Franklin's *Psycho II* (1983), Tom McLoughlin's *Friday the 13th Part VI: Jason Lives* (1986), and Chuck Russell's *A Nightmare on Elm Street 3: Dream Warriors* (1987) are some of the best examples of how to do a horror sequel right in that decade, and one would certainly add Dwight H. Little's *Halloween 4: The Return of Michael Myers* to that esteemed lineup.

Tommy Lee Wallace offered something completely fresh and unique with *Halloween III*, as per John Carpenter's initial vision for an anthology series based around the Halloween season, and it was appreciated by neither critics nor the core audience. With producer Moustapha Akkad's wanting to exploit his cash cow properly, he needed to bring the franchise back to its lucrative stalk-and-slash formula, which *Halloween II* proved was what audiences craved, and to do so, required the return of its familiar logo, the mask of Michael Myers. *Halloween 4* could easily have been a quick and cheap cash grab, but Akkad wisely brought in a director who highly respected the original film and could work well within the confines of a limited budget and tight schedule to deliver a quality product. Dwight H. Little was the man for the job; he brings just enough of an outsider influence and distinct style of his own while acknowledging and adhering to the expectations of the *Halloween* constituency. It is this approach, along with some stellar collaborators, especially cinematographer Peter Lyons Collister, that makes *Halloween 4* stand head and shoulders above most horror sequels in the 1980s.

Little found his passion for filmmaking in his early years after his father gifted him a Super 8 camera one Christmas. It was at that moment he discovered the magic of movies, as he recalls:

"Back then, those things were cheap. They just had one lens, and you put a little cartridge in it. You could shoot around with it, take it to the drugstore, and they'd send it out for development. Then you would get a little reel back with your 50 feet of film. Then you could either watch it on an editing machine, or if you had a projector, you could screen it on the wall. I got hooked very early on this magic trick, and it feels like magic because you're pointing the camera at life—the dog, the backyard, the car, whatever it is—and then you see it as completely different when photographed and projected on the wall. And when you discover what editing is, the whole thing goes upside down and becomes something else entirely."

This enthusiasm saw Little win a couple of local student film festivals, including one supported by the Ohio Arts Council. These accolades helped him to be accepted to study film at USC after he was turned down by several other universities around the country. At the time Little enrolled in USC, the New Hollywood era was in full flight, and many of the movement's prominent filmmakers were associated with the school, as he recalls:

"It was John Milius; Randal Kleiser; John Carpenter; Robert Zemeckis; and, of course, George Lucas. And then, incidentally, Spielberg kind of associated himself with USC, although he hadn't ever really gone there. These guys all belonged to a generation just ahead of us in film school, so we felt the wave of that movement because they were making it in Hollywood. We looked up to all these amazing mid-'70s auteur filmmakers who were actively making movies in this period: Scorsese, Mazursky, and Coppola. Sidney Lumet was making movie after movie after movie at the time. I was especially influenced by Sydney Pollack, a more commercial director who was never the darling of the film critics, but he made a lot of hit movies that I thought were very interesting. There was a sudden jolt of realism to these Hollywood movies, such as *Dog Day Afternoon, Serpico, Three Days of the Condor, The Parallax View,* and *Cinderella Liberty.* These were films that my group was interested in and influenced by, especially the work of John Carpenter; he was one of those filmmakers who made it feel that everything was possible."

Growing up in the Midwest meant limited opportunities for young film enthusiasts, such as Little, to experience the exotic cultural imports of the French New Wave or Italian neorealism, so another benefit of his move to California was exposure to the films of European auteurs, such as Bernardo Bertolucci, François Truffaut, and Luis Buñuel. And while these filmmakers and their avant-garde tendencies were greatly influential to Little, they were not represented at USC, which wasn't an avenue for indulgences of artistic impressions. Indeed, the curriculum was firmly focused on narrative-driven storytelling and practical approaches to cinema technique, which is to say students were there to learn mainstream Hollywood filmmaking.

"They weren't an art film school," Little affirms. "We weren't studying the experimental filmmakers or looking at San Francisco avant-garde cinema. We were learning how to tell narrative stories. They were very much about structure, about script, about three acts. On one hand, it was about drama, about writing heroes and villains and structure, and on the other hand, it was about editing. One of the first real classes I took was one where they would give us dailies for this American TV show called *Gunsmoke*, which was a TV western. But they gave us the dailies in black-and-white 16-millimeter and access to a Moviola, which was an editing machine. And then each of us would cut our own version of that scene from those dailies. And it was so interesting to see each student interpreted those dailies in a very different way. It was actually a fascinating class. And that's where I learned not only the expression but the technique of 'cut to the dog,' because there was this fight between the cowboy James Arness and the bad guys on a porch and there's all kinds of matching and continuity problems. So every time you'd get in trouble, they had a cutaway of this dog on the porch. You would literally cut to the dog, and that expression is common now. And then when you come back from the dog, you can sort of restart, so it was practical. And that comes back to a narrative point of view."

Comfortable in the knowledge of how to not only make movies but also fix them when needed, Little was poised to make a professional life for himself in the film industry. He would begin making important allies immediately. His USC student film called *Americana* was well received and won some awards, leading to his meeting a famous, flamboyant impresario named Allan Carr, who struck gold when he produced *Grease* in 1978. Carr then went on to make *Can't Stop the Music* in 1980, a badly received loose biography of Village People, starring that pop group. Little remembers working on the film with no little bemusement:

"I was basically a driver and a documentary behind-the-scenes guy. I was the driver for the Village People for about three days. This is the oddest job you can imagine. They were this very gay '70s disco band, who were just the nicest guys, and they were kind of overwhelmed to be in Hollywood. I also worked very closely with [Caitlyn] Jenner . . . before [she] became Caitlyn. It was a wild, wild experience. But I got noticed around Hollywood because of it." (Names and pronouns have been appropriately changed to more accurately depict Jenner's identity.)

When word began to spread that this hotshot USC graduate had something to offer other than good transportation skills, Little began to receive calls of further film work. One of those who sought him out was a film and television producer named Sandy Howard, who had made some genre films of varying quality, including *Man in the Wilderness* (1971), *The Neptune Factor* (1973), *The Devil's Rain* (1975), and *The Island of Dr. Moreau* (1977). Howard exploited his hit 1970 western, *A Man Called Horse*, which starred Richard Harris, by following it with two sequels: *The Return of a Man Called Horse* (1976) and *Triumphs of a Man Called Horse* (1983). It was on the latter film that Little would be brought in to help save the day when Howard realized he didn't have enough of a film to deliver to his foreign buyers.

"*Triumphs of a Man Called Horse* was unbelievably bad. And Sandy had to cut some stuff out, but that meant it was coming in short. He only had 82 minutes of movie, and he couldn't get his money if he didn't deliver the full-length film. So he didn't know what to do, but he had heard about me as this student filmmaker who was getting a little bit of attention. So he called me in, and he said, 'I got $5,000; I need eight minutes of movie.' He had the hat and the boots of Michael Beck's lead cowboy character, so we came up with this scheme where we'd have Michael Beck ride from right to left from Boston out to the American West for four minutes. And Sandy had a song that he had cleared for another movie. And he put this song over it, and he put titles over it. So there was a four-minute title sequence. And then at the end of the movie, Michael Beck rides his horse from left to right back to Boston, over end credits for four minutes to this Rita Coolidge theme song, "He's Coming Back." So, anyway, this DP [director of photography] friend [Peter Lyons Collister] and I went to Outwest and rented a horse. We rented a stable hand; we put them in the character's hat. We found a horse that had a white stripe, so we matched the horse. And then we just shot in pretty locations. Every time we would do a shot, we then changed the angle and the lighting. And he'd go right to left and then go left to right. And we kept doing it. And we gave this film to Sandy Howard. And he loved it and cut it into the movie, and he was able to collect his money."

Grateful to his young protégé, and with the VHS boom on the horizon, Sandy Howard offered Little a budget of $300,000 to make a little spy movie called *KGB: The Secret War*. This low-budget B movie was an opportunity for Little to cut his teeth making a feature film, the practicalities of which proved as much of a film school as USC did. Little's coproducer and cinematographer was Peter Lyons Collister, the man who would shoot *Halloween 4*. However, Collister and Little's association goes back before *KGB: The Secret War* to their time growing up together in Cleveland, Ohio, and attending the same private boys' school. While Little was getting into making films in the fifth grade, Collister was focused on still photography, harboring ambitions to work for *National Geographic*. However, Collister got a taste for film photography when Little asked him to help with one of his Super 8 movies. With his father's station wagon and a ladder at their disposal, their criteria were met, and the youngsters kept making Super 8 movies. In their senior year, they received a grant to make a documentary about alternative education for a school for wayward boys in Cleveland. The pair spent three months filming and editing their documentary, which ended up playing at various film festivals. Like Little, Collister enrolled at USC to pursue his filmmaking studies, where, from 1974 to 1979, they would continue to work and learn together.

"It wasn't like we said, 'Let's both go to USC together,'" Collister says. "Dwight got in after being turned down from his first choice, which was probably NYU. That's how we ended up going to USC together. We were roommates in our junior and senior year, and we made films pretty much either through the school or independently with each other. We made our senior thesis film together, and that won awards; Dwight won a car because the award was sponsored by Nissan."

"Peter and I literally grew up with each other," Little affirms. "We went to high school together; he was in college with me at USC, so he shot my student film; and he shot that title sequence for *Triumphs of a Man Called Horse* for Sandy Howard. Then he did *KGB: The Secret War* and *Getting Even*, and then we worked together again on *Halloween 4*."

"When Dwight and I grew up in Cleveland, we only had three TV channels," Collister recalls. "There were no old movie channels, and we didn't have rental tapes. We didn't get to see a lot of old movies, though I was lucky enough to have seen *Citizen Kane* when I was still in high school. But when we came up to USC, we would see 20 movies a week in our classes; it was just constant because we had to take a lot of film history. Our first two years, half of the curriculum for the film school was film history, so it might be history of the musicals from 1930 to 1950 or might be film noir, and then it would be French films. I would see so many movies at USC, and seeing old movies is very important to any aspiring filmmaker."

Once out of university, Collister found work as an assistant on USC alumnus Randal Kleiser's *The Blue Lagoon* (1980), which was photographed by one of the finest cinematographers of the era, Néstor Almendros, who had stunningly shot Terrence Malick's *Days of Heaven* (1978), Jack Nicholson's *Goin' South* (1978), and Robert Benton's *Kramer vs. Kramer* (1979).

"Néstor became a big influence on me," Collister admits, "and we made great friends until he passed really early on. But that era was a really good time for the indie world. We had hope. People weren't hiring USC film school graduates the way they did later in the '80s and '90s and at the turn of the century. It didn't have that cachet just yet. My dream in going to film school was to shoot one feature film on 35-millimeter, but I was very, very fortunate to be able to go on to become a professional filmmaker. We try not to use the word 'lucky' in the film business because I think luck is what you make it. Dwight and I never thought we would make a living out of this. But we have made a good living, and we still eke out a living out of doing what we love. We've been really close friends. I was best man at his wedding; he was best man at my first wedding. And even though we live kind of far from each other in terms of LA geography, we still see each other like four or five times a year; we'll meet for lunch and talk. The first feature film that we made together was *KGB: The Secret War*. Dwight cowrote a script that was okay, wasn't great, but we raised the money and got it done. But then it just got caught up in a bankruptcy of the company that made it. And the copyright wasn't done correctly, so it never really saw much of the light of day."

Despite the film's eventual obscurity, it did lead to another opportunity for both Collister and Little: a low-budget action film called *Getting Even*, starring Joe Don Baker. A B movie with a capital B, the film was shot in Texas, where production afforded Little the opportunity to work with more extravagance than he had been used to thus far, with the action-packed film incorporating helicopters, explosions, and fistfights. Collister recalls the proliferation of productions that kept nonunion filmmakers, such as he and Little, employed in those heady early days:

"It was impossible to get into the union at that time, but back then, there were all these independent companies. In that world, you're not making a lot of money, and so you've got to do four low-budget exploitation films a year to sort of eke out a living. So you do stuff like *Avenging Angel* and *Can't Buy Me Love* until you sort of get a break that can get you into the union. I worked with John Singleton on his Michael Jackson music video called "Remember the Time," which has Michael and Eddie Murphy in it. I got hired by Propaganda Films for that. John didn't have anything to do with it. When I met him, I had already been hired. And then John hired me on *Poetic Justice* and later *Higher Learning*. I was in the union at that point, but my crew wasn't. So a lot of them couldn't work on the film. But back in the late '70s and early '80s, you had the likes of Sandy Howard Productions, American International, and New Line Cinema was just starting out. So you had 15 or 20 companies that presold overseas, and they made low-budget horror, teen comedies, and action. So there was a group of us who would go back and forth on these things, on films like *Getting Even*."

When B-movie producer Nico Mastorakis saw *Getting Even*, he was impressed enough with Little's work to ask him to go to India to direct a movie that he had initially wanted to direct himself. Because Mastorakis could not travel to India to make the film, Little took the reins on what would be released in 1988 as *Bloodstone*. Surviving the production of *Bloodstone* and with the experience of filming in India, Little was approached by *Halloween* godfather Moustapha Akkad, who was interested in hearing what it was like shooting there. Knowing Akkad was preparing to bring Michael Myers back for a third *Halloween* sequel, Little took the opportunity to offer his services.

"Being that I was in the room with Moustapha, I was able to sell myself because I knew they were looking for somebody for *Halloween 4*. My writing partner, Alan B. McElroy, and I wanted to pitch an escaped-killer movie. I didn't want to do a horror movie. I mean, I knew it was a horror movie, but I didn't want to do a routine 'teenagers getting slaughtered right after sex' kind of thing, the whole *Friday the 13th* template. They had a treatment for *Halloween 4*, which was exactly that: kids running around partying and fooling around and getting killed. It was pretty standard fare. I don't know who developed it, but it was not very interesting to me. So I pitched Moustapha this escaped-killer movie; I was thinking more *Silence of the Lambs* than I was thinking of a horror movie. The first questions were, 'How do you establish that Michael is alive? How do you get him to escape back into the world? How do you turn him back into Michael Myers?' So everything in our script was very calculated. Alan [B. McElroy] and I allowed ourselves one elevator ride to do the whole backstory."

In doing so, the pair conceived what would prove the commercial resurrection of Michael Myers and the *Halloween* brand, as Little remembers: "We came up with the idea that we would find him in the burn unit 10 years later, burned beyond recognition and in a coma ever since the events of *Halloween II*, and they are preparing to transfer him to this other place. We have this guy getting into the elevator with these two hapless attendants, and he says, 'We're happy to get rid of him. Good riddance to Michael Myers.' And these two hapless attendants are just there to help. But of course, that gives us a chance to establish that he's been barely alive, that he was badly burned, and now they're going to move him. And this is Michael's chance to break out of the ambulance and kill the attendants. Now we've got to rebuild

Michael Myers. So the first thing he does is go to the gas station and kill the mechanic to take the overalls."

Step one sorted. What next?

"Then he destroys the gas station and blows up the telephone lines so that we shut down communication with Haddonfield. Then he goes into the variety store, and he takes a mask from the display of Halloween costumes. This is why the mask is so different in *Halloween 4*, because it wasn't something *he* designed; it was a commercially produced Halloween mask that you could buy off the rack. And there's been so much talk about the mask, like, 'Why didn't it look like every other mask?' Well, because of that! Now he's got overalls, and he's got the mask. And then there's another scene where he throws Bucky into the power grid and that shuts down the power. And then he goes to Jamie Lloyd's house and kills the dog. And now we have a serial killer on the loose, and I turned Donald Pleasence's character, Dr. Loomis, into a detective. I mean, he's a doctor, but in my mind, he was a detective. So here's the raincoat and here's the gun. He catches up with Michael in the gas station because he is just on the hunt. One of the things that Alan brought to the table that I just loved was the very first time Dr. Loomis is picked up, when he's trying to get ahead in the field. And he's picked up by this kind of crazy reverend who talks about hunting evil. And that was our chance to kind of define Michael a little bit without the audience feeling like they were being preached to, but we were telling him that he's evil on two legs. He's biblical, he's an avenger, and this guy is hunting him. He's been hunting him his whole life. And he recognizes a kindred spirit in Dr. Loomis. So I was really bringing that '70's influence to the film. Even though it is complete fantasy, I wanted it to have that sense of realism. That was my pitch to Moustapha."

Despite bringing this fresh angle to the well-established horror-genre tropes on which *Halloween* functions, the core of Little's approach remained to honor what made the franchise notable and successful to begin with. To take advantage of cheaper production costs, *Halloween 4* was filmed in Salt Lake City, Utah, which not only had economic benefits but also had the advantage of surface similarities to the Midwest. Wanting to pay homage to John Carpenter's original film, Little scouted suburban locations and picked a neighborhood that felt similar enough to the Pasadena one that Carpenter had used as his Haddonfield, Illinois, stand-in while having a Midwestern flavor to its architecture. Tapping into his own Ohio upbringing and years as a trick-or-treater, Little knew how the setting should look to feel authentically middle American:

"We had to be very careful with how we framed it because there's no mountains in Haddonfield, Illinois, but Salt Lake City is surrounded by mountains. So as long as we avoided that, we were able to recreate what I wanted, which was a Midwestern town. But I knew how to do that. Growing up in the Midwest, I knew every piece of architecture, so it was sort of second nature. And I knew enough about the imagery of the first film: the streets and the hedges and the neighborhood. And those neighborhoods, those little houses, to me it is all spiritually with the first *Halloween*."

To further evoke the true spirit of the Halloween season, Little decided to break away from the formula of the previous films' established opening credit style, which had each feature the image of a pumpkin behind the credits. Here, the director begins the film with a brilliantly atmospheric and beautifully photographed sequence of shots that refer to the agrarian origins of All Hallows Eve. The opening frames of the film set a wonderfully ominous tone along with the hauntingly minimalist score and static shots of a barren farmland adorned with seasonal icons: pumpkins, skeleton decals, a decorated scarecrow, all intercut with farm implements and machinery (something used gruesomely, and somewhat symbolically, in Dominique Othenin-Girard's *Halloween 5: The Revenge of Michael Myers*). It immediately feels like we are in the hands of filmmakers who not only know how to expertly evoke the right mood and tone but are also willing to subvert expectations. Gone is the traditional John Carpenter theme (for now) over the pumpkin and black backdrop, which means we're dealing with filmmakers who are willing to offer something new. Little explains why he boldly broke with franchise tradition:

"I thought, 'Why do we have to do this pumpkin again? Let's, let's give people what Halloween really was about, which is to ward off the darkness of the coming of winter, the dark days of winter. I just thought to myself one day, 'What is Halloween? I've grown up with it. I know it's a big commercial holiday now, but what is it really about?' And then I went to the library, and I started pulling up some agrarian books which had some history on Halloween and how it related to agriculture. I guess it is really about sort of a death, the end of the harvest season and coming of winter, and there's some Scottish ritual in there. And I started seeing these pictures in these books, of scarecrows. And I spent some of my childhood out in the farm country, so I kind of got it. So out of all that, we drove outside of Salt Lake City and found these fields and farms and created that opening, and it is evocative. But by the time we go into the mental ward, the credits are still going, so people know they are in a *Halloween* movie."

To help realize his vision, Little once again brought in his friend and fellow Midwesterner, Peter Lyons Collister, who came armed with a keen eye for stylish shadows and darkness as well as a familiarity with the seemingly safe seasonal suburban setting of middle America. The cinematographer recalls receiving the call from his old friend:

"I was thrilled when Dwight asked me to do *Halloween 4* because I didn't want to do too many comedies because a lot of them have a really bad look, and with this film, I knew that Dwight cared about the visuals. So that meant we could have some fun with it, even though it was really hard to do. I was not a giant horror fan. They scare me. But Dwight and I had always tried to raise money to make a horror film because he wanted to make one. He wrote the script for a film called *Scissors* where the crazy person kills everybody with these big scissors. And we tried to sell it overseas, but we didn't have any knowledge. But we did have a poster! Dwight reacts to horror films in a different way to me; he's always liked that genre maybe a little more than I have. I've only done two horror films, *Halloween 4* and *The Amityville Horror*, so it's not like I gravitate to the genre."

"Peter and I worked together on bringing something visually unique to the film," Little says, "so we did odd little flourishes that we thought we could get away with without people noticing. For example, there's a scene where the sheriff drives Michael up alongside the house and we let the audience know Michael is in the back of that police car. But the driver doesn't know Michael is in there, and the people in the house don't know he's in there. I had seen this successful French film where all the cars, for some reason, had yellow headlights, and I don't know why. But I said, 'Pete, let's put yellow gel in all the headlights with these cars at night.' Now, you don't notice that anything is different, but you *feel* that something is off. And then we did that scene in the diner, which is just the *Vertigo* shot or the *Jaws* shot depending on who you ask. It's the shot of Michael just standing there, and it was achieved by the camera moving back while the lens zooms in; it creates this odd visual change so that while you are looking at Michael, there is something weird about this. He remains the same in the frame, but the background is growing around him. It makes it supernatural. I did a lot of little tricks like that, but they were organic, not CGI [computer-generated imagery] or special effects. Choosing to be out at the long end of the lens was very hard at night because you need more light. Those lenses are slower, and you have depth of field problems. It's very hard to keep things sharp. After *Halloween 4* did so well, Pete went off and had a nice little career. For my next film after this, I had to go to Budapest and use somebody else from there. Pete is very gifted, but we were basically pals from childhood making these movies."

After Dean Cundey's splendorous 2.35:1 anamorphic widescreen cinematography on the first three films, *Halloween 4* was framed differently and was the first film to use the 1.85:1 aspect ratio. Collister discusses the practical, financial, and aesthetic reasons for such: "That was all Dwight. At the time, we could have gone Super 35, which would have created a 2.35 image by cropping it to make it look wider, but because we had so much nighttime photography, I was really worried about it looking too grainy. We couldn't afford to shoot anamorphic; there's no way we could have shot it that way. We were just feeling lucky that we were not shooting on 16-millimeter. We did have a Steadicam most of the time. And there was one week when our Steadicam operator, Alan Caso, had to go back for another job in Los Angeles, but he left all his gear on the camera truck. Dwight designed the shot running with Danielle down the sidewalk as she runs away from Michael, and I said, 'Okay, you know what; I know my camera operator—who was Paul Babin, who went on to become Allen Daviau's operator—can do it.' And he said, 'I can do it!' even though he had never done Steadicam in his life. So he puts on the Steadicam rig, and he does a rehearsal running with Danielle. And then he has to come to a stop because Danielle comes to a stop, and the camera looks around while he comes to a stop. So then it just pendulums; he's doing a side shot. So take two, and then take three. Not happening. So Dwight said, 'Okay, let's modify the shot here.'"

Collister continues, revealing some of the advantages of shooting on location in Salt Lake City as well as his own thoughts about his work on the film:

"Dwight and I talked about what we wanted to do a lot because we didn't have egos; if he saw me going in a direction that was not right or if I thought that something could be done better, then we could talk about it. We have certainly had arguments in the past on the set, especially on our first film because it was so low budget and I owned all the camera equipment, so I was like, 'I'm not putting the camera there!' But as far as the tonality and everything like that, one of the things that was nice about shooting in Salt Lake City was that it has a sort of Midwestern architecture there. And for some reason, the population was down at that point. So many of the homes were for sale or rent, and we got great ones for very little money as well as some great streets for her to run down. That was advantageous. We spent a lot of time picking locations, and things like the diner worked out well because we had the mechanic bay attached to it so we didn't have to go to separate places. It worked out in terms of the art direction because we didn't end up spending a lot of money doing anything else to it.

"We had a very good crew there. My key grip was great. And the guy brought a gaffer from Los Angeles, and then we fired him because he was argumentative and mean to the local crew. So I used a local little old guy who lived in Park City, and he was great. He was great because we didn't have a lot of resources and we certainly didn't have a lot of time; Dwight is my best friend, so I didn't want to keep him waiting. Somebody once said that a cinematographer could give 100% of the shooting day to the director, that's what we should be going for. But unfortunately, there are all these technical things that get in the way. As regards the look of the film, I'm not in love with some of my night lighting because I sort of fell back on old techniques; I think some of it might be too blue. If I was to do it all over again, I would add some green to it. But we wanted to make Danielle's house as warm and inviting as possible so then when she must escape and climb up on the roof, the tone gets colder. It takes on some very typical cinematography tropes, but it worked well. We built a little section of roof for Danielle to climb on, and that made it easier for us to work. But I cringe at certain things now. I think any cinematographer would tell you that if they could do any given shot differently, they would, or a little differently. There's some lighting in the high school I don't like, some night exteriors I'm not in love with, and some of the sheriff's office I'm not the happiest with. I do like how all the scenes in the house look; all the daytime scenes I really love. I like the daytime exteriors and some of the daytime interiors; I think that is really where we set the mood and not just the lighting but even the choice of camera angles. *The Exorcist* influenced me in so many ways. And I'm not saying that was a particular influence on what I did with *Halloween 4*, but when I was a projectionist at USC, I showed it on campus; I showed it two times on Friday night and two times on Saturday night. Boy, that was tough just listening to it in the projection booth, but it influenced me in several ways about lighting and the construction of horror. It's a whole different world when you're trying to scare people, and then you've got other stuff that you're not trying to scare people with."

A new *Halloween* film needed a new heroine for Michael to stalk. Jamie Lee Curtis was busy following in her parents' footsteps in becoming part of the Hollywood establishment as her star rose throughout the 1980s, after having served her time in the horror trenches with not only the first two *Halloween* films but also with *The Fog*, *Prom Night*, and *Terror Train* (all 1980). "We wanted Jamie Lee [Curtis] for a cameo," Collister recalls, "but she was over it by that point and said, 'No, I won't do it.' And then of course, she changed her mind and came back several times later. I know Jamie and am good friends with her, and I have criticized her for turning us down on *Halloween 4* because she has certainly done well with the franchise since then."

Enter Danielle Harris, playing the daughter of Curtis's now-deceased character Laurie Strode. Little Jamie Lloyd is brilliantly rendered with pathos and sweetness by 10-year-old New York native Harris. Little was suitably impressed by the precocious performer at a casting session for the film in Los Angeles, as he recalls:

"I did a big casting session in LA, maybe a hundred girls, and they were young, between 7 and 11 years of age. And the thing is that at that age, they're all trained to do commercials, so all their instincts are to be big and broad and not believable. And I said to Moustapha, 'I can't find anybody.' And he said, 'What? With everybody in Los Angeles, you can't find anybody?' I said, 'Let me look in New York.' And amazingly, he paid for the trip to New York and gave us a casting agent. So we set up a session in New York, and the third girl who came in was Danielle. Now, she was very young looking, but she was older than her character, which was helpful because it made her very precocious and very worldly beyond her age; she was around nine years old playing six or seven. I read her, of course, but when she came into the room, I just knew that it was her; there was something to her eyes. I went to Moustapha, and I said we really need to hire this girl. It's going to make all the difference. And he was just so wise, because most producers are constantly fighting you and second-guessing you. And he was like, 'Okay, that's the one. Let's figure it out.' That was amazing."

The next crucial role to be cast was that of Jamie's foster sister and best friend, Rachel Carruthers, and though an actress was already lined up for the role, Little had reservations about the choice and duly reconsidered. "With Rachel, we had a girl in

Jamie sees a vision of her Uncle Michael while shopping for a Halloween costume. Author's Collection

Los Angeles that everybody loved," the director recalls, "but my concern with her was she felt like what I would call an 'LA girl.' I mean, she was urban, she was sophisticated, and she was very sexy. And I thought, if you put her down in the middle of Haddonfield, Illinois, she couldn't make sense there. So we had come across Ellie back East, and I asked Moustapha to do a screen test with that LA girl and Ellie Cornell. We did it on 35-millimeter film, and we projected the screen test in a theater. We did it old school. We looked at both these actresses up on the screen. And it was clear that the other girl was fine, but Ellie was pretty; she wasn't a model, but she was very believable. And I thought that if you saw her in that world of Haddonfield, Illinois, you would think she fits in, so we cast Ellie."

With the new heroines and Haddonfield screen queens now in place, a familiar face would also be cast because *Halloween 4* would not only see the return of Michael Myers but also the return of his archnemesis, Dr. Loomis, and with that, the casting of Donald Pleasence. Pleasence's presence not only anchors the film in *Halloween* lore but also brings the required gravitas and screen history to raise the film above the average horror sequel. The veteran actor gave one of his best performances in the franchise as a man on the cusp of losing his own mind in his dogged pursuit of the patient whom he failed to heal. However, to remind audiences of the narrative continuity from the fiery finale of *Halloween II*, Pleasence was required to apply prosthetics to his face, the scars of his last battle with Michael Myers. Uncomfortable and potentially distracting, the actor was initially uneasy about of the appliance that would mark half of his face.

"Donald was self-conscious about the makeup at first," Little affirms, "but he got over it and was very committed. I was surprised at how intuitive he was, because he could have just taken the check and walked through it. His only thing was, as he was an older man by then, I noticed after about six or seven hours he got tired. And as he got tired, he would get a little cranky. Also, he liked a little nip later in the day. And so I just started to schedule him for six good hours and then let him go. And we'll do other things if we can afford it that way. I felt like if he did six good hours, it would be super easy. He's not an 11- or 12-hour guy. You're just not going to get that from him. He was in his early 70s by then. I was a fan of his, and I was kind of starstruck with him having done *The Great Escape* and the James Bond movies. But I also needed to just dig in and work with him. I told him that I didn't want him to play a doctor; I wanted him to play a police detective. And he looked at me like I've lost my mind. And I said, 'Think about it. You're not a doctor; you're not taking anybody's pulse or their blood pressure. You're tracking down a psychotic serial killer. You're a cop. You're a detective. And when he accepted that, he was off to the races."

"Donald Pleasence was not always that pleasant," Collister confides, "but he was a great actor. There was an issue with the makeup appliance that he was wearing, and it was the most bizarre thing. I guess we didn't notice it on the day we shot it. But one night at dailies, we noticed it was on the wrong side, and that was because Donald decided it should be on the other side. Here's some trivia: my second AC [assistant camera], or my trainee, was Mike Lookinland, who was the youngest brother on *The Brady Bunch*. I made him the projectionist for dailies because I could teach him how to project and he was free. And we were watching dailies in the hotel one night; we had wine and all this.

And then it gets quiet, and Dwight goes, 'Wait, the scar is on the wrong side!' And then Donald spoke up and said, 'Yeah, I thought it should be on the other side.' And we couldn't reshoot it, so there is one scene where he goes down in the gully and it is on the wrong side."

Little continues, "Another thing about Donald is that he was very good to Danielle and Ellie, as was George Wilbur, who played Michael Myers. George made sure that right after we'd say cut, he'd rip the mask off and he would give her a hug, making her feel relaxed. He'd say, 'Danielle, it's just me.' We were very careful with her, and he couldn't have been a better choice because he was a very gentle person. He was a very experienced stuntman. He had been in the movies for a long time, but he was the right personality to keep Danielle feeling okay. But we started with a different stuntman to play Michael. There was a conflict with him and the producers, and I won't detail it because I don't know all the facts. But we had to switch gears after maybe a little less than a week of shooting. And that's when I looked at a bunch of tapes of different stuntmen. I picked George just because of the way he moved, because I thought he moved like a shark. He was like Jaws; it was slow and slightly lumbering. He was a big man, but it was relentless, like that scene with the girls escaping out on the roof and they're putting stuff down the stairs trying to block him, and then he just keeps coming and coming and coming. They finally escaped and got on to the roof, and then he's up on the roof. And he had this bulk. So I picked him for his body language, and I liked how calm he was as a person."

Halloween 4 marked something of a new beginning for the franchise, taking off as it did in a whole new narrative direction with the introduction of Jamie Lloyd and her story as well as bringing in a new cinematographer and director not previously associated with the property. However, it did wisely retain two key elements of the earlier films, those being the reprisal of John Carpenter's original theme music and the return of composer Alan Howarth, who brought his distinct sound and style so brilliantly to *Halloween II* and *Halloween III: Season of the Witch*.

Howarth recalls receiving the call from Moustapha Akkad to return, along with Michael Myers, to the fold for the fourth film:

"John and I were busy scoring *Big Trouble in Little China* when I got a call from Moustapha Akkad," Howarth affirms, "and he asked me if I would want to do the music for *Halloween 4*. The thing is, John was my buddy, and I didn't want to do something like that without him knowing. So I talked to John, and he said, 'Do whatever you want.' So I got his blessing, and that set me on the path to being the composer on *Halloween 4, 5, and 6*. For each of those, I was bringing the original theme from *Halloween* because they go with Michael Myers. When you see Michael Myers, you're going to hear that theme, but it was the Alan Howarth version of *Halloween*. I kind of broke out on *Halloween 4*; it was sort of Alan Howarth does *Halloween* via Pink Floyd. I got to do my own thing. I didn't want to just bang out the *Halloween* theme straightaway at the start. I wanted to match the atmosphere of the setup. The whole thing here is we're back in Haddonfield, and we're going to have to deal with the Halloween season. So I did that eerie effect over the shots of the farmyard, which is a loop of a sampled cymbal. It doesn't have a beginning and end; it's just got great textures."

Indeed, it was the state-of-the-art technology of new synthesizers that appeared throughout the 1980s that influenced what Howarth was composing, as he remembers: "There was literally a new keyboard for every year that came around. So on each movie, I had new instruments, and that was inspirational in its own way. First we had was the Prophet 5, then there was the Prophet 10, then we had the Emulator I, and we got the Emulator II. And then we got the LinnDrum, which I had used on *Escape from New York*, so that was already in the bag. Then they released the ARP Avatars and the Kurzweil K250, which was finally a real sampler. It sounded good, especially the piano sample. It sounded quite authentically like an acoustic piano, but it was all sampled. One of the apexes of all that was scoring *Big Trouble in Little China* because on that, I had all these samplers, and I had all these analogue synths, and we put MIDI on the whole studio. That meant we could play the keyboard on one sampler and play nine other synthesizers at the same time. We had what we called MIDI stacks, where the electronic production got nicely thick and rich texturally; it wasn't just playing synthesizers. On an analogue 24-track machine, I started printing a stereo recording of nine synthesizers, with reverb and everything, all rich and chocolatey, and printed it right to tape. So it sort of amplifies the kind of quality of the production. In 1987, I got the Synclavier. They were the big dogs of digital synthesizer sampler machines, and that really put me over the top, as I had like 64 voices in it and all kinds of extra digital dimensions. On *Halloween 4*, they just let me do what I wanted, and with the technology available to me, I really got to stretch out on that one, especially with the stuff in the opening scene. I sustained the original theme for scenes like when they are on the roof of the house trying to escape from Michael, and it was a challenge because it was 18 minutes of tension. Eighteen minutes of the same thing on repeat becomes dull, so it was a challenge to keep it fresh."

With the film poised for release, it was time to spread the word that Michael Myers was back in town, and the man who would herald his return to Haddonfield and rally the horror community was Tony Timpone, then-editor of the legendary *Fangoria* magazine. Being the only horror specialist magazine on the block at the time, Timpone enjoyed a good relationship with the studios when it came time to market their product, and the people behind the *Halloween* films were no exception—until the Weinsteins took control of the franchise, but more on that later. *Halloween 4* would be the first film of the franchise to be released under his watch, and he did everything in his power to promote the film, with a full cover and multipage spread.

"The producers of *Halloween 4* were very savvy," Timpone recalls. "They approached me fairly early on. They were making that movie very cheaply and shooting in Utah, but we didn't have a correspondent in Utah at the time. But they really wanted *Fangoria* onboard right from the start. So they agreed to fly my writer Marc Shapiro to the set from Los Angeles to Utah, and they wanted to make sure they got the *Fangoria* cover at the time. I remember that they sent me their initial photography from the set, and the photos were just awful. They had a really bad unit photographer. The pictures were just terrible, so there was just no way I could get a cover story. And so they said, 'What can we do to get you a cover?' And I said, 'Well, maybe we could do a special shoot with your actor in costume as Michael Myers.' And that's what they did. When they were back in Los Angeles after wrapping the film, they hired a photographer, and they did a special shoot just to get that *Fangoria* cover. And it was the first time Michael Myers was ever on the cover of *Fangoria*, and it was from this special shoot that they did. But when they went into a photography studio and did this series of images for us, it was probably the best that Michael had ever looked because he was so well lit and had the knife with the blood on it. They captured the perfect shot for me, and it was one of my favorite covers. But the unit photography that they offered was terrible. It made the film look much worse than it was; it made the film just look cheap. Some of these things transferred into the movie itself. I mean Donald Pleasance's makeup was very cheesy looking, and some of the gore effects created by John Carl Buechler weren't the greatest. But luckily, they did this special shoot for me, and we landed a great cover. And then they wound up doing the same thing for *Halloween 5* because again, they had photos, but they didn't have that perfect cover image that we needed. So they made sure again to set up a special photo shoot, but this time, they actually shot on the set rather than go into a photo studio to do it. There was a lot of competition for the *Fangoria* cover back in those days."

With an appropriate October release date in place to coincide with the season in which the film is set, Little and all concerned had to work fast, and early good word from test audiences gave the filmmaker and his producers the confidence that they had a hit on their hands. However, time was of the essence, and postproduction following the principal photography needed to happen posthaste:

"We really had to hurry," Little says. "We shot it in April, and we had to be in theaters in October. We showed a rough cut to a very small, recruited audience in the basement of the old MGM Studios. And it was all temp music; there were no effects in it or anything. Rough cuts are really versions of the film which are not ready to show people, and yet we did screen it.

People were screaming, and because of that, the producers were over the moon. So then they spent a little bit more money, and we rushed to postproduction. Alan Howarth was able to recapture the original feel of the music, so that was a huge thing. They were thrilled when it opened at number one at the box office, and the next weekend, it was number one again. The third weekend, it wasn't number one, but it continued to do well. Then it went to VHS, and that sold, and then on DVD. It just kept going, so the producers were very happy with it."

The film even had an unlikely admirer in action star Steven Seagal, who wanted Little for his next film based on what he had seen. "That was the first call I got; it was Steven. He loved it. He thought it was a very interesting movie, and he wanted me to direct his next picture, which was *Hard to Kill*, which would have been his second film following his debut in *Above the Law*. He told Warner Brothers that he really wanted me to do that, but the people at Warner Brothers said, 'No, no, no, we're not giving this movie to a guy who did the fourth movie in a slasher series. It's not going to happen.' So Steven didn't have the power to overrule them, and they brought in Bruce Malmuth, who had directed *Nighthawks* with Sylvester Stallone. So he had a legitimate big-budget studio credit, and they gave the movie to him."

While Little's inexperience on studio fare made executives wary to hand over expensive star vehicles to him, the ever-frugal Menahem Golan, one half of Cannon Films, was keeping a watchful eye on anyone who could deliver a number one movie on the cheap and on schedule.

"Menahem called me and tells me three things," Little remembers. "One, that he read in the newspaper that the rights to Gaston Leroux's *The Phantom of the Opera* had become public domain so he said, 'Aha! I can make a version of *The Phantom of the Opera* for nothing!' Number two, that the Broadway play was still doing huge business in New York and he can make a deal with Robert Englund, who at that time, was quite a big deal from playing Freddy Krueger. And three, he said all he needs is a director and when he looked in the trade papers, he saw that the number one horror movie was *Halloween 4* and he called me. So that came together very quickly. *Phantom of the Opera* had to shoot right away because the opera house we would be shooting in over in Budapest was going to go back to its regular business of putting on operas. So it was all a rush, but it was all because of the success of *Halloween 4*."

Once Little was back in Los Angeles for postproduction on *The Phantom of the Opera*, Seagal was in touch once again. He informed Little that he hated the experience of making *Hard to Kill* because he had not gotten along with Bruce Malmuth. With an option to make one film with another studio outside of his Warner Brothers contract, he planned to make a film at 20th Century Fox. With the studio desperate to work with Seagal, the star had his choice of directors, so he named Little. With Fox's approval, Little and Seagal would make the brilliant 1990 action film *Marked for Death*.

The success of *Halloween 4* surprised even seasoned admirers of the franchise, including Tony Timpone. Being something of a conduit between the fans and the films through his leadership of *Fangoria* magazine, he recalls the impressed reaction from the ever-discriminating horror community:

"I didn't realize what a fanbase the *Halloween* movies had until *Halloween 4* came out. Out of all the slasher icons of the time—Leatherface, Freddy, Jason—I would really get the most mail from the *Halloween* fans. You would think it would have been *Friday the 13th* fans. And I did get a ton of mail from them, and our circulation went through the roof whenever we had any of the *A Nightmare on Elm Street* films on the cover. But the dedication of the *Halloween* fans was pretty much unrivaled. I was really surprised by that. So they were in 100% when they knew that there was going to be a *Halloween 4*, and when the film came out, the majority of the letters were pretty positive from the readers who wrote in. They really supported the film in a big way. They wanted that character back on the screen, and for the most part, they felt *Halloween 4* delivered. And I thought it was a pretty good film. I haven't seen it since it first came out, but I liked the fact that it followed a lot of the suspenseful tropes of Carpenter's film. It wasn't just a gore fest, and it wasn't a *Friday the 13th* knockoff; they tried to do a good job following in Carpenter's footsteps. Of course, it helped by paying Carpenter a nice fee so they could use his score again and by bringing back Donald Pleasence, even though it made no logical sense to have him in the movie; but there he was. It was much better than it had any right to be. I think it's one of the closest to the original in terms of getting the tone and the feel, and the cinematography really captures the time of year perfectly. Dwight Little did a good job, especially when you consider the quality of the films that came after it."

"I am very proud of it," Peter Lyons Collister says, "but I am prouder of Dwight than certainly me. I really loved that he introduced the twist at the end with Danielle holding the knife; she was such a talent and brought so much to the table. A lot of us didn't consider *Halloween III* as part of the franchise. I know people do now, but it was such a sort of a departure we felt that we brought it back to its origins with *Halloween 4*. And then it did really well. I remember Moustapha's son Malek, who produces them now; he was a production assistant on *Halloween 4* and lived in the hotel room across the hall from me with another PA [production assistant]. Their door would be open, and you saw just dozens of empty pizza boxes and a lava lamp; they were such kids. And it's great to see that he has taken over his dad's mantle. It is amazing how certain franchises hit, and I'm happy about that and happy that our one did well. I used to have the poster up in my house here, and people would go, 'Oh wow, that was so seminal to my childhood, or my high school years, my college years,' something like that, which is nice to see. It's funny because my father is still alive and living in Ohio, and he never sees any of my movies. A couple years after we made *Halloween 4*, my stepbrothers made him rent the VHS tape, and after the first scene in the ambulance, when Michael puts his thumb through the ambulance guy's forehead, my father walked across the room, hit stop and eject, and that was it. He said, 'That's it!' and he's never seen it. A friend of mine produced one of *The Avengers* movies, or *Captain America*, in Cleveland, and they had a chairback made with his name on it so he could go down and visit the set. But he was like, 'No, I don't want to go downtown and sit in a chair.' He doesn't care about the movies."

Halloween 4 has long enjoyed its placement high among the fan favorites of the franchise. Although Little certainly feels the nostalgic feedback for the film since Blumhouse revived the franchise with their recent trilogy, the director recalls a chillier reception upon its initial release in 1988 because despite the contemporary acclaim, audiences were critical:

"We did well with ticket sales; we made money. But we did not get well received; people had complaints about the movie in one way or another. It is a favorite now, but it really wasn't back then—the perception of it being that it was another slasher movie, was just another sequel, and it was a number four. So it's hard for a critic to embrace. No matter what sequel comes along, it will always be judged in comparison to John Carpenter's original, and rightly so. But I felt like we really tried to be very respectful of that film, and I think in many ways, we achieved that because it has a similar feel. But it has really taken these last 35 years, multiple home video releases, two Blu-rays, and annual screening on television to get to this point of acceptance. But it's really found itself over the years. I'm so thrilled that it's on television every year because it's almost like it's always alive. With *Halloween 4*, I was able to express something about the Midwestern farmlands, the moodiness of fall, the anticipation of the winter when things begin to turn dark and a little scary. And I also love the romantic frustration of Rachel and her boyfriend, who runs off with the pretty girl and she is left stranded with her foster sister. And he redeems himself in the end. And I think it makes the story not just about teenagers getting on in the boathouse; she's in love with this boy. And he dismisses her and runs off with this other girl, and she's heartbroken about it. And I think that Ellie played that really well. And so here's a movie that is ostensibly the fourth film of a franchise, a slasher sequel, but these characters are very rich. And I think that's why people come back to it."

With a hit *Halloween* movie on his hands, Little had to make a choice between staying in the world of Haddonfield and elaborating on the shock ending of *Halloween 4*, or moving into the world of major studio films. He chose the latter: "Alan and I talked about doing *Halloween 5* and would have loved to have made it because Alan and I think we would've killed it.

But I was afraid that if I did another one, it would take another year and a half of my life. And I would miss a window of a hit because it is so rare to have a hit movie; I've only had two. And it is really rare, so you want to act while it's happening. If I had taken that year and a half after *Halloween 4* and spent it on *Halloween 5*, I think we would have made a great movie. But whether it would have been, that is very hard to say. In the end, I didn't do it, but I was able to do *Phantom of the Opera*, *Marked for Death*, and *Rapid Fire*. But we did set it up for *Halloween 5* perfectly for whomever was going to make it, though they ended up doing things that were just not what I would have done."

"You're just like me." —Jamie Lloyd

With the financial and aesthetic success of *Halloween 4*, which as its title suggested was very much a "return" of Michael Myers, it was inevitable that Michael would seek his "revenge" for the delight of horror audiences and *Halloween* fans. The film opens with a recap of the climactic scenes of *Halloween 4*, in which Rachel Carruthers (Ellie Cornell) and Michael's young niece Jamie Lloyd (Danielle Harris) are chased by Michael until he is gunned down into a mine shaft by Sheriff Ben Meeker (Beau Starr) with the help of some gun-toting local barflies. For good measure, the sheriff's men drop dynamite down the shaft to make sure Michael is gone for good, but the wily villain finds his way out into a river that takes him downstream where he seeks refuge in an old hermit's shack. Michael's inclination is to kill the kindly mountain man that he meets there, but he is too weakened by the multiple shotgun blows to his body (naturally!), and he faints upon confrontation.

Cut to Halloween Eve one year later, and we see how Jamie is hospitalized in a children's clinic and living with the trauma of her uncle's reign of terror. At the close of the previous film, Jamie, clothed in a clown costume, attacked her mother with a knife in a moment that suggested the spirit of evil had left Michael and been transferred to her: the Myers curse passed on to the next generation. But a year after those events shows us a badly traumatized and mute Jamie experiencing a telepathic vision of her uncle's coming back to life after having been cared for by the hermit, whom Michael duly dispatches without mercy despite the old man's hospitality and care. While in her trance-like state, she scrawls "He's coming for me" on a chalkboard, heralding what will, indeed, be Michael's revenge as he returns to the suburban streets of Haddonfield once again to try to claim the life of his last living relative. Michael's former psychiatrist and archnemesis, Dr. Loomis (Donald Pleasence), is keeping a close eye on Jamie, more than aware that as long as she is alive, there is a chance that Michael could return to wreak havoc on the town in his murderous quest.

The franchise is now at the point of having Michael presented as an immortal figure of evil rather than simply a psychologically deranged man hell-bent on killing his family, and it is *Halloween 5: The Revenge of Michael Myers* that introduces an intriguing additional motivation behind Michael's bloodthirsty pursuit. Early in the film, as he returns to life in the shack, Michael is shown to have a tattoo of a runic symbol on his wrist that is later revealed to be the Mark of Thorn, a symbol of the Cult of Thorn, which is further explored in the sixth film, *Halloween: The Curse of Michael Myers*.

For this rushed sequel, Moustapha Akkad brought in a director of such unique, nay European, sensibilities that it would result in one of the most quirky, idiosyncratic, and indeed stylish films in the *Halloween* franchise. Enter Dominique Othenin-Girard, a Swiss-French filmmaker whose work was noticed by Debra Hill after they met at the Sundance Film Festival and who was subsequently introduced to Moustapha Akkad as a candidate for the director who could keep the *Halloween* franchise visible and viable. Little did Akkad and his associates realize they were in for meeting with a man of maverick sensibilities who would bring a distinct flavor to the franchise that not everyone would immediately recognize as something that the brand needed.

88 / You Can't Kill the Boogeyman

Halloween 5: The Revenge of Michael Myers (1989) poster art. Magnum Pictures, Inc./Photofest ©Trancas International Films

Othenin-Girard candidly reveals a history of mendacious behavior as having helped his embrace of storytelling, as he recalls: "I came to storytelling because I lied as a child, and I realized that if I want to be credible, then my lie must anchor itself in realism, into something that is true, something about me. That way I could get away, away from beatings at home, away from unhappy moments at school, and so on. But then it became a ritual to lie; I would lie about anything, little things, stupid things. It would become a game for me, and it took me a long time to get away from that because I created distance from people. I created an untrust. People couldn't trust me because I would joke or lie. And my lie would be obvious, but I would get them; I would fool them for a second. And then they say, 'Who are you? You fool me so well. What do you want?' Nevertheless, the trust was broken, and it gave me a lot of pain. As a child, I was physically beaten by my parents. This happened in Europe more frequently than in the States. I know that today, it's something unknown, but at the time, it was pretty regular. So I'm not putting blame on my parents specifically. That is not my point; my point is just fact. For many years, I sabotaged my own successes, and I realized I was functioning like this because as a child, I was beaten by this father that I loved so much and beaten by this mother who is the world to me, and I thought I was the problem. I felt that I was not good enough. I thought that if I got beaten by him and she was not saying anything, then the problem is me. My lack of confidence made me work hard to obtain some kind of approval from someone. So I became a jewelry maker at 16 years old. I worked hard to draw attention to myself, 'Look what I did! Do you like me? Do you love me?' And the other thing I learned was to seduce, to charm people. And these were ersatz, just unfulfilling, because if I had success with what I did, a film, for example, and people liked it, I would say, 'Don't you see I'm not good enough, asshole?' Or I would say to someone, 'You like me? You're a fool. You like someone who is not good enough.' Completely twisted. And *Halloween 5* came out of that; it was my sort of healing journey. It offered me the opportunity to work freely."

Othenin-Girard was not new to horror by the time *Halloween 5* was on the cards. He had made the haunting thriller *After Darkness* (1985) and the erotic horror film *Night Angel* (released in 1990), but it was when he showed Debra Hill his feature-length episode of the French television series *Série noire*, called

Cop Trap, that she facilitated a meeting between the director and Moustapha Akkad. "I made my first feature film when I was 23 years old," Othenin-Girard affirms. "It starred John Hurt and Julian Sands, and it went to the Berlin Film Festival and competition and so on. At that age it was all way beyond me; I didn't know what it meant really, and I didn't care. *Cop Trap* was my second feature film and sort of an outrageous thriller. I did it when I was 25 years old. It was a film that sort of shocked everybody. Debra saw it and said, 'Wow, there's a gem of a director here because the characters are fucking crazy. Moustapha, you have to see him!' So Moustapha sent me a script before our meeting, and I didn't know how to read that script because it was a mess. It took me more than a day to get through it."

Unfamiliar with the Hollywood horror franchises that were ruling the box office throughout the 1980s, Othenin-Girard went to Blockbuster and rented VHS tapes of *A Nightmare on Elm Street*, *Friday the 13th*, and *Halloween 4* and spent the night viewing them to gain some insight into what kind of business he may be getting into. The following day, he attended his appointment with Moustapha Akkad and met with several others already associated with a prospective fifth *Halloween* film. What followed was a most unorthodox meeting, as he recalls:

"I arrived at Moustapha's office, and there were two other screenwriters there, Shem Bitterman and Ramsey Thomas, who was also the producer, and two other people. They're all on my right, and Moustapha was in front of me. And I couldn't stare at them because I felt a little shame. Moustapha said, 'Okay, Dominique, what do you think of the script?' And I said, 'Do you want to do *Halloween 6*?' And he says, 'What the fuck! Who are you to ask me? This is none of your business.' I said, 'Yes, it is. Because if you want to ruin *Halloween 6*, then make this version of *Halloween 5*.' And he just looked at me and asked me what I thought of the script, so I said, 'Moustapha, may I be frank?' He said, 'Of course. I have no time to waste.' Moustapha could be a bit frank also, and rude. So I picked up the script, very politely went around his desk, saw where his trash can was, and put the script gently in the trash can and went back to my seat. My face was burning because these guys were hating me in that moment.

Nobody said a word. It was an outrageous thing to do, but it was time for me as a man to tell the truth. That's why I was so daring. I didn't care if I did it or not. I wasn't looking for a job; I was looking to be who I really was."

Staggeringly, Othenin-Girard managed to survive what could have been the moment that he committed career suicide. The charming filmmaker turned the meeting around by projecting an intellectual authority on the subject at hand, displaying his knowledge of Akkad's fiercest commercial rivals and the crucial, and sellable, elements of the horror genre. The director recalls:

"I said, 'Moustapha, on the market you've got three big horror series. You've got the surreal one where the killing happens in the weird world of the dreams by Freddy Krueger. That's *A Nightmare on Elm Street*, and that is suspenseful, kind of romantic, and very weird. You've got the body count one, which is *Friday the 13th*. That one shows gore and has a lot of fun showing killing and so on. And then you've got *Halloween*, and that is the one with the Hitchcockian suspense. The boogeyman is coming after you, and the kill is quick. And he kills the character that you love, not the 10 kids that you don't care about. If you respect that, then you have got a number six because then your series is really going straight to how John Carpenter did it. Moustapha, this is the key to your film,' I spoke frankly."

Rather than be irritated by his potential director's forthrightness, it seemed as though Akkad appreciated the outsider insight that Othenin-Girard projected.

"Dominique, how do you want to do it?" the producer asked. "The prep starts in six weeks, so you have six weeks to write it." As expected, Othenin-Girard stumped Akkad by saying no. "What do you mean no?" Akkad asked incredulously. "May I?" Othenin-Girard rhetorically queried.

He proceeded to open the door to the office and usher in an accompanying friend. Screenwriter Robert Harders (Brian De Palma's *Home Movies* [1979]) entered the room. "Who the fuck is this guy?" asked Akkad. "Moustapha, this is Bob Harders," Othenin-Girard replied. "Give us five minutes, and we will work on our idea." Othenin-Girard and Harders then workshopped their idea for the film in front of everyone in attendance, as the director recalls, "I explained to Bob that we have got a character who is a young girl who maybe has dreamed of killing her mother, or has killed her mother, and I want to start with this character. This is my character for *Halloween 5*, but I don't want to make her evil. I said to Bob that this is not allowed. She's innocent; she's a child. It was a good end for *Halloween 4*, but it cannot continue because the evil has to be Michael Myers. I want to stay on track of what John Carpenter set up. So what can we do? How do we do it?"

For the ensuing 15 minutes, Othenin-Girard and Harders discussed their ideas until Akkad had enough. "That's it. Everyone out of my office!" Akkad needed time to consider the pitch alone, while Othenin-Girard and Harders exited the office before they received any ire for their brashly presented proposal. "We got out very fast," the director says, "because we didn't want the other guys to run after us and kill us. And then Bob said to me, 'You're crazy. It'll never happen. Too bad. It was fun to do this with you. Ciao. Goodbye.'"

Prior to this endeavor, Othenin-Girard and Harders had been due to work together on a project titled "Burned Hills," which they were developing with Raffaella De Laurentiis before the mammoth production of David Lynch's *Dune* consumed her and everyone else involved.

"Bob is a brilliant writer and a brilliant mind," Othenin-Girard applauds. "I really love him. He has written many theatrical plays. And I still regret that we were never able to make 'Burned Hills.' This was right before *Dune*, and Raffaella got so involved in technicalities of making *Dune* that she didn't have any more time for our project." Despite the inauspicious pitch and Harders's assumption that they had blown their chance, an offer came through from Akkad, though the lowball remuneration immediately put Harders off the project, if not Othenin-Girard. "We got an offer from Moustapha after that meeting, but Bob said, 'Dominique, I can't accept it. They are making me eat dirt with the salaries they are offering. Good luck.' I said, 'Bob, I do understand. But I will accept dirt because I want to work.' And the offer they made was indeed terrible."

Regardless, Othenin-Girard went back to Akkad's office the next day and accepted the offer, upon which the producer demanded his newly hired director go and write with Shem Bitterman. And then, a familiar scene: "May I?" Othenin-Girard said as he went to open the door. "Michael, come in!" And in walked screenwriter Michael Jacobs. "Michael had a great instinct as a writer. We wanted to have the little girl, Jamie, be the central character, and he brought the *Eyes of Laura Mars* thing in the sense that she has a telepathic link to Michael Myers. And with that ingredient, we started to play, and that meant we could allow the character to go crazy. She gets to experience how he feels when he is close to having the joy of killing. When he kills, he is in ecstasy; it gives him some kind of rage. Dr. Loomis speaks about rage, and she feels his rage. They are family, so they are connected like this. Dwight Little did a very nice job with *Halloween 4*; I don't want to be severe, but it was a bit banal, a bit pedestrian. I wanted to update it, and I wanted it to be more memorable.

"Moustapha trusted me in my talk about providing him with a film on which he could continue to make the series with number six and that I would respect Carpenter's film. I told him that *Halloween 4* was very honorable, but I would never say more what I was really thinking about it other than that I was going to expand the situations of the characters. Michael Jacobs and I really worked on that script so fast together. We are best friends still today. And Debra Hill helped us a lot; I went back to her with the first draft, and she said, 'Are you crazy?! Telepathy? This is not Halloween. This is not Carpenter.' I said, 'Yeah, but I've got something: I don't want to make the girl evil!' And everyone said, 'Okay, you're right. You can't make the girl evil. You're right by wanting to have only Michael as the arch evil guy.' I said I want to handicap the girl, make her deaf and mute at the beginning because that will shock everybody, because she was traumatized killing her mother or wanting to kill her mother. That event shocked her into becoming deaf and mute. Moustapha said, 'You're crazy. Why deaf and mute?' 'Because it's got to be fun!' 'Are you sure?' Also, I wanted Michael to be naked at some point, to uncover his face, and that is breaking the rules. I'm a gangster, I know that; I break the rules."

94 / You Can't Kill the Boogeyman

And break the rules he did, as Othenin-Girard defied several tenets of the *Halloween* code, which is to say he brought in elements of comedy (the bumbling cops accompanied by clown music) and humanity to the proceedings (revealing, partially at least, Michael's face and having him show vulnerable emotions by crying). Another way the director shook things up was by bringing in a more deliberately artful style of filming. Dwight

Dominique Othenin-Girard, director of *Halloween 5: The Revenge of Michael Myers.* Courtesy Dominique Othenin-Girard

H. Little's work on *Halloween 4* was excellently executed in his direct, economical aesthetic, but Othenin-Girard would collaborate with Australian cinematographer Robert Draper to bring a rich expressionist look to the franchise. This director–cinematographer duo would enrich *Halloween 5* by taking what are traditionally banal safe spaces—a suburban home, a clinic, a barn—and turning them into Gothic forbidden zones. Draper's lighting infuses the photography of these spaces with a sense of the danger and darkness. For Othenin-Girard, scouting the locations would very much influence how he wrote and executed the material. "I wrote stuff based on what the locations offered me, such as the house which had the laundry chute. I realized that the laundry chute was a world inside of another world: the tube. I thought that the character could get trapped into the tube. And then I had to work with the barn and the forest, which was difficult because the pine trees are so hard to shoot. But the barn had to be something totally different. As you said, I'm an expressionist film director; I have this tendency of involving the camera with the characters, giving the audience an emotion not only by what is happening inside the page with the characters but with how it is seen, how it is sounding, and how it is lit."

Rob Draper has, against his initial wishes, become an established cinematographer in the world of horror, having worked on television horror anthology shows such as *Monsters*, *Tales from the Darkside*, *Tales from the Crypt*, and more recently, *Creepshow*, not to mention numerous feature films in the horror genre, such as *Dr. Giggles*, *Tales from the Darkside: The Movie*, and of course, *Halloween 5: The Revenge of Michael Myers*. But it's not like he didn't do everything in his power to avoid becoming a stalwart of such cinema.

"Here's the funny thing," Draper admits. "When I came over here to the US, I had an agent, and I said to them, 'The one thing I don't want to do is horror films because that's how everyone gets started.' I just didn't want to be classified as a guy doing horror films. And they said, 'Yeah, yeah, no problem.' And then the very first narrative film work that I ever did was the *Tales from the Darkside* television series. Up until then, I'd been only really shooting commercials. And then *Tales from the Darkside* came up, and that's how it started. And it went from *Tales from the Darkside* TV show to *Tales from the Darkside: The Movie*, *Halloween 5*, *Dr. Giggles*, and then *Tales from the Crypt*. But how I got into filmmaking was also completely by accident. I was working in a pathology lab running the biochemistry and hematology department. And my wife was a top three-day eventer, so she wanted me to film her riding the horses so she can learn from the mistakes and stuff. And so I ordered a Canon Scoopic 8-millimeter camera. And the day I went in to buy it, there was a guy there from the local TV station news, a cameraman who had retired, and he said, 'Look, I've got a camera I'm selling for half the price of what you're paying for this. For 350 bucks you will get a camera with a three-lens turret. And you can go out to the TV station and tell them you shoot part-time news; they'll give you free film and processing.' I thought, 'What a deal!' And so I bought a Bolex windup camera, and I thought I was going to look pretty slick running around the countryside with that. And basically, that's how it started. I knew nothing about photography. But I started doing it, and I just absolutely loved it. And back when I started, no one thought about getting into the film industry; there were no film schools, so it was something that never crossed my mind."

Draper did take the guy's advice and go to the news station, soon becoming a part-time stringer for a TV station. It was while working that job that he realized what he needed to know about editing to be able to shoot the good stuff, so he started teaching himself editing, working with the material that he shot that day that was to be ready to be broadcast that evening. He was eventually offered a full-time job as the senior cameraman and remained in that position for four years while also taking on documentary and commercial work until greener pastures called him over. "I came over to the United States in 1980," Draper recalls, "and I went to a place called the Maine Photographic Workshops, which was way up in New England. I just wanted to come over and see where I fitted into the global scheme of things, and then I moved here full-time in 1983. The idea was we'd come here for five years, but we've been here ever since. It started with a fluke, meeting that guy who was selling a Bolex camera. If he hadn't been there, I probably would never have gotten into the film industry. But the more I did it, the more I just absolutely loved it, and it was one of those things where a light bulb went off and you go, 'Holy cow, this is what I was supposed to be doing.'"

And it was the anthology horror shows of the 1980s that offered Draper a way into the industry and to make crucial connections, beginning with George Romero's *Tales from the Darkside*. Incorporating elements of horror, science fiction, and fantasy, *Tales from the Darkside* proved the perfect vehicle for Draper to hone his skills within the constraints of a packed schedule, a limited budget, and strict aesthetic boundaries within which to develop his style.

"Quite honestly, I couldn't have asked for a better way to get into narrative filmmaking than working on *Tales from the Darkside*," Draper says, "because they had a very strict set of rules. First off, we shot 16-millimeter, and you had to shoot at an f4. You were not allowed to use soft light; you could only use hard light. You had one day to prelight and four days to shoot the episode. Each director was allowed a hundred shots to tell the story, and we had Monday and Tuesday for the director and the DP [director of photography] to work out the shot list. Then on Wednesday afternoon, we had to meet with the AD [assistant director] and the UPM [unit production manager] to talk through the entire shot list, of what the shots were, how we were going to do them, and how it was going to cut together. I had to have a lighting plot done for all the sets to show them how I was going to light it. And then on Friday, we would prelight, and then Monday, we'd come in and start shooting. Also, we could only shoot on 100 ASA film; we weren't allowed to use high-speed film stock, which meant you had to use a lot of light, and it was all hard light. So you had to really learn; you have to light like the old Hollywood movies, which was fantastic for me because I loved it. I was a real film noir fan by that time, and that was a good thing when it came to *Tales from the Darkside*. John Harrison was the director of a lot of the episodes, and he went to do *Tales from the Darkside: The Movie*. I've worked with him a lot over the years, and we became really good friends. But the first time he was doing an episode of *Tales from the Darkside*, he called me up and said, 'Look, I've just got one question. Do you like film noir?' And I was like, 'Oh, man, you're talking to the right guy.' And we hit it off with that one comment. And so the first thing we did was shoot in a typical film style; we wanted to shoot it in black and white, but they wouldn't let us. So we had all the wardrobe done in shades of gray and had all the sets painted in shades of gray. And then I lit it with hard light, so it looked black and white anyway."

When Draper became aware that his eye was being sought to lens *Halloween 5*, he initially refused, and for understandably personal reasons. In 1985, he and his wife were living in New York City when he was asked by a filmmaker friend to shoot a documentary series on the apostle Paul, a job that would require Draper to leave home for six months for filming in Europe and the Middle East. "I didn't want to turn it down," Draper admits, "but the documentary came up right at the time my wife was going to have our first son. So she flew back to Australia, and I went off to Europe. She had the baby and had a terrible time giving birth, but everyone survived. When I went back to Australia, I had a three-month-old son, but I promised her I would never do that again." That promise was tested when Moustapha Akkad did everything at his disposal to convince Draper to accept the job as cinematographer for *Halloween 5*. In 1989, just as the film was about to go into preproduction, Draper's wife was pregnant once again, but he told his agent that there was no way he was going to be away when his wife gives birth to their second son. Despite his agent's pleas for his career, reiterating that this would be his client's first Hollywood film, first real feature, and the fact that it is a franchise, which almost means a guaranteed audience, Draper reiterated, 'No, I'm not doing it.' Deflated, for now, Draper's agent said he would return to the producers with the unfortunate news, saying that in doing so, he would be greatly disappointing director Othenin-Girard. Satisfied that he had stood his ground and that he would be available to his wife when the time came to deliver their next child, a call then came from Moustapha Akkad, who flexed his powerful position to appeal to Draper's needs, as the cinematographer recalls:

"Moustapha said, 'Look, we would love you to shoot this film. Dominique wants you to shoot it. What's the problem?' And after explaining my position to Moustapha, he said, 'Here's what I'll do. I'll fly you, your wife, and your son out to Salt Lake City. I'll get you a really nice apartment. And I'll fly your mother over from Australia so she can be with you. I'll make sure that you get the best gynecologist and obstetrician in Salt Lake City. If I do all of that, will you shoot the film for us?'" With Akkad providing such luxuries not only for Draper but also for his family, it took all of a fleeting moment to consider the offer. "I told Moustapha to hang on a minute, and then I said, 'Screw it. Yeah, let's do it!' I was right on the verge of saying, 'No, I can't do it,' but we did it. Moustapha was awesome, the loveliest guy. I've worked with a lot of producers over the years, and he was the main guy here, but he was all about family. He was just incredible and remained true to his word; he made sure my wife was well looked after, he did fly my mum over from Australia to be with us, and he got us an awesome apartment at the base of the road going up to Snowbird. So it was a damn good deal."

With Draper now onboard, Othenin-Girard had his man, and the two collaborated to create a distinctive style that helps the film stand out among others in the franchise. There are many moments in the film that evoke the styles of expressionist cinema developed by German auteur pioneers of the early-20th century, such as Robert Wiene (*The Cabinet of Dr. Caligari* [1920]), Fritz Lang (*Metropolis* [1927]), and F. W. Murnau (*Nosferatu* [1922]), and later imported into Hollywood to use in defining the aesthetic of film noir pictures during Hollywood's Golden Age. The influence of this style, which is informed by gothic sensibilities, high-contrast lighting, artistic use of darkness, atmospheric use of shadows, and unusual camera angles, was something both Othenin-Girard and Draper brought to the table. A striking example is the moment in the first act in which Michael chases Jamie through the clinic. The scene begins in the bright, friendly environment of a children's ward, but as Jamie flees her room to descend into the bowels of the building and through its steam-filled laundry room, the photography deftly allows the film to switch from suburban comfort to gothic nightmare in the space of a couple of minutes. It is an ingenious use of direction and cinematography that doesn't get nearly enough credit in the critical notices of the film.

"Your reference is a good one, Wayne," Othenin-Girard offers, "though I am not a director who is a cinephile, who has a reference to the history of film to help me to choose how to direct a scene; I am an animal. I work with my instinct, and it serves a purpose. I see and I create. It was Rob, more than me, who was always able to say, 'Ah, that's like this movie' or 'that is an impression of that movie.' In the scene with the drapes inside the laundry room, where she's running away from the gardener who she thinks to be the boogeyman who is trying to grab her and so on, that's a scene that I created on the spot by just saying, 'I want drapes, and I want to play with Chinese shadows and feelings.' And when I was there, I said, 'Rob, make the light flicker, please,' because I thought I needed to up it a notch and to really go crazy handheld with her. I had an easy concept; I said to myself, 'Okay, this is *Halloween*, so I need the top crisis to be Loomis against Michael; it must be the epitome of this film. I want this to be black and white. I want no shade; I just want hard contrast. And instead of white, I want gold. So I got this. And then in order to get the sense of contrast, I want to start the journey going in daylight with really soft light pastel colors and so on. Rob got the idea very well. And at the beginning, I need jokes. I need lightness with some little scares so that people start to enjoy the ride. You take off very gently. So the further we went with the film, the higher the stakes; we have Michael kill some very close friends of Jamie, all the while he is getting closer to her. So it's like a roller-coaster ride. With each killing, he gets a little bit closer to Jamie, and you have that stomach-in-your-mouth kind of feeling."

Draper elaborates on the aesthetic approach to the film, noting the influence of one of the inveterate film noir classics: "As soon as I got *Halloween 5*, I thought I had better watch parts one through four, which I did. I watched part four with Dominique, and all the way through, he just kept saying, 'I don't want it to look like that. I don't want it to look like that. I don't want it to look like that.' We tried to keep the main core elements of the *Halloween* franchise in there while straying as much as we could to the sensibility that Dominique wanted to bring to it. His big thing was that he didn't want it to just be like the other *Halloween* films. He said, 'I want it to be different and to feel different.' He wanted it to have a European flavor, and so we had to figure out how to do that and stay true to the franchise while pushing it far enough that he felt satisfied that we have made a difference. Dominique and I talked a lot about *Touch of Evil*, which is one of my favorite films of all time. Orson Welles used a lot of wide-angle lenses in close and down low."

The cinematographer continues, "Our biggest talking point through all of it was the use of wide-angle lenses. Dominique wanted to use the wide-angle lenses and create a lot of stuff moving through the edges of the frame to give it more of an explosive feel, but to do that on location was a real challenge because there's nowhere to put the lights. With most of the wide shots, Dominique wanted the camera way across the room jammed down on the floor in a corner so that when you put an 18-millimeter lens on, you saw everything. I had to come up with a way of lighting that avoided having lights in the shot. So everything had to be front lit, but I had to make it look like it was lit from the side and from the back so that everything was playing in the shadows. Especially difficult was shooting in the house; that was a real nightmare. I said to Don Shanks and Donald Pleasence and to the girls, 'Look, I'm going to have lights hidden all over the place, and you're going to have to find them. So find the lights and play those lights for me.' Donald Pleasence was great; he said, 'You mean like Marlon Brando in *Apocalypse Now*?' And I said, 'Exactly!' If you have a look at the moment when he's climbing up the stairs, there are a few shots where his head comes into the light and then it comes back out. That's his Brando shot. But I had to use hard light a lot; I couldn't use soft light because it would have gone everywhere and there would have been no way of controlling it. So that is what was pushing it towards the film noir style without having a lot of heavy backlights. And one of the things that Dominique and I talked about was using more of the set, using the set foreground–background separation the way the old masters did, like Rembrandt and Vermeer and Caravaggio, who would separate foreground and background by light and shade . . . light in the foreground and dark in the background. So we didn't use heavy backlights, which was the traditional film noir thing to do and it was a big plus not having those because we had nowhere to put them."

Another notable aspect of the film's photography is the dynamic sense of immediacy and movement achieved using the Steadicam. One of the benefits of using the Steadicam was it allowed for moments of subjectivity, as Dean Cundey had done so brilliantly in the opening scene of John Carpenter's *Halloween*. These first-person perspectives shot from the point of view of Michael Myers not only increase tension in limiting the photographic plane to that of the protagonist but also make the audience complicit in his stalking of the characters. The Steadicam shots in *Halloween 5* were operated by acclaimed cameraman Ted Churchill, who came with a history of notable Steadicam work on major studio films, such as *The Shining*, *The Right Stuff*, *Ghostbusters*, and *Dirty Dancing*.

"We did use a lot of Steadicam on *Halloween 5*," Draper confirms, "and we had Ted Churchill, who is regarded as one of the greatest Steadicam operators of all time. Garrett Brown invented the Steadicam, and Ted made it popular. And Ted was an old mate of mine, and he came on and did all this Steadicam work on that show. He was there for about 12 days, which was unheard of, especially for a low-budget film. So we were able to have a lot of Steadicam stuff. With the laundry sequence, where you think it's Michael chasing Danielle and she runs down into the laundry room and all the sheets are blowing, that was something we had no idea how we were going to shoot, and I said to Dominique, 'What if I just put up one backlight and we have the sheets in there and have people flapping them and blowing them. I will do it all handheld. And we'll have them just darting around, and we'll see shadows.' He thought that was a great idea, so I was adding to his desire to use a handheld camera. We kept inventing more and more stuff that could add to it, like that sequence where Danielle runs into the furnace room and a camera rushes out and then it rushes back. All that sort of stuff was really dynamic on the wide-angle lens."

Churchill brought immense skill but also a sense of authority, which occasionally rubbed his director the wrong way, and his presence and approach created some tension between Othenin-Girard and Draper. It was a brief but bumpy road before the two were open enough with each to reach a harmonious creative union.

"I love Rob Draper, but we almost parted ways," Othenin-Girard reveals. "I wanted the Steadicam to do a lot of stuff, and this movement and immediacy goes with my personality. Rob understood this, so he said, 'Dominique, I'm going to get you the best Steadicam operator in the world, Ted Churchill.' Then Ted arrives, but he is not young. We have a blimped 35-millimeter camera, and it is so fucking heavy. One time I said, 'Okay, Ted, let's start here outside the house; we go towards the house, we climb the twelve steps to the front door, we go inside, and we attend to . . . ,' and he interrupts saying, 'What's the signification of the shot?' And he starts to talk with Rob for a quarter of an hour on the side debating what kind of signification they have for that shot. I said, 'I don't have this time you guys. Let's just do the shot; then you can talk later. This is the shot that I want.' They were starting to get on my nerves because they were using this discussion of signification to justify the fact that Ted could not carry the camera for so long, but they were not telling me this because they're such professionals. That was one aspect; another was when Jamie is in the clinic, which had night lightning. I told Rob I want this effect. Rob said, 'Okay, Dominique, but you know it takes time to shoot lightning and stuff.' I said, 'Yeah, let's do it. And I want 30 shots that night, not only all of Jamie's scenes on the bed with the shots of her blind writing "he's coming" and some really precise angles of Michael's hand, but I also want the whole corridor, the staircase entering into the operating room, the scalpel ready to cut, and Loomis.' This was huge. The whole night I have about 30 shots that I want, and Rob said, 'You're fucking crazy doing that; you can do 10 shots at night well-lit, not 30.' But I said, 'I need 30. I want the dolly on the feet of the gentleman from the point of view of the gurney, on the face of the girl on the side. I want to go through the staircase . . .' and so on. I write my shot list way before I go to shoot.

So I brought my shot list and told everybody what I'm going to do. I speak to my AD and go through all of it. And when we arrived at the operating room location, we were exhausted, but I said I want the camera to be on top of the door. And Rob is like, 'What?! We need to put up a rig to set the camera on top of the door.' I said, 'I want movement. I want the camera upside down so that the world goes upside down because the girl can't read.' I wanted to be expressive with the camera, but Rob said, 'Another film-school shot.'"

The director continues, "I went to Moustapha and said, 'Moustapha, I can't work with Rob. It's tough. And I have too many problems with the Steadicam operator. Rob is great, but I can't work with him.' I asked Moustapha to talk to him so that he would get a little bit jolted into working with me more instead of me having to beg and fight to get the shots. I said, 'I can't fight. I'm going to be exhausted. I have so many things to deal with. I have new actors who have never acted before.' So Moustapha said, 'Change him. I can get you someone different tomorrow.' Moustapha says this to the line producer, Rick Nathanson, whom he wanted to have as an enemy to me by putting a lot of pressure on me. He would not allow any overtime or any more rigs and so on. But what I was asking for required more than what his budget allowed, so Moustapha gave him a little more money but not much. He was squeezing everybody. But I don't speak to Rob; I just know he is at home with his wife and child, and they are packing. And at 10 p.m., I go to his home because I can't leave it like this. And I see the suitcases are ready, so they are about to leave. So I start to talk to him, and he explains to me his point of view, why he had these talks with Ted Churchill. Because Rob was very, you know, Australian comparing himself to this great Czechoslovakian DP, Miroslav Ondříček, he is always saying, 'You know, I'm like him,' and I would say, 'Yes, Rob, you can be very good; I can see it. But let's not have these kinds of talks. Let's do the movie. And be close to me. Don't go away and make me go search for you. Is that okay? We can cancel the other guy who is supposed to come in the morning at 10 p.m.'"

The director's appeal worked. Draper stayed on the production.

"We had the best of time together. The attitude of Rob has now changed, and my attitude also changed; I became more open to what he had to say. And he offers me these big set pieces for the interior of the house. I would say, 'Rob, I want something impossible, you know that?' And he would say, 'Go ahead!' But now he's laughing, and I'm laughing too. That was the difference after our talk. I said, 'I want to enter nighttime with Loomis going into this space, and I want to see the whole space.' Rob was like, 'At night? Okay, Dominique.' He doesn't complain; he puts light beams outside the windows and allows me the shot. In fulfilling my request, it gave him the possibility to become great. And it is great photography. We worked together to create the best possible shots."

Style and aesthetics agreed upon, there also remained the physical challenge of pulling off the stunts. Michael Myers was played in the film by actor and stuntman Don Shanks, who is not only physically imposing but also somewhat graceful in his movements. That is not to say there weren't a couple of near misses when it came to getting as much carnage on camera as

Michael reaches for his mask of anonymous evil to kill again. Author's Collection

possible, as Othenin-Girard recalls one night that put his own health in jeopardy:

"The special effects team and stunt team almost killed me that night!" the director admits. "I have to say, mea culpa. And I will tell you why—we did the barn and all the exteriors in one night, which was so much work. We shot in the field before the pine tree forest, and we had to have the car go through it. And Billy was running and jumping. And the car turned around to go after Jamie, and then it is crushed and so on. And the car would not be able to drive inside the pine trees. Because there was mud, it would not go fast. So we had to precut every tree before so that the car would do this. And then the car would be on top of the tree and would not run on . . . such a hell! And then I'd say, 'Come on, we can spend another two hours on those trees. Let's do it in the forest.' So then we have Jamie turning around, and the car goes after her. And the team are saying, 'Are you crazy? There's a driver in there. He's going to kill himself!' And I said, 'No, no, no, go ahead!' So I walked to where the car would drive, and I placed the camera there. Don Shanks wanted to do the driving himself as Michael Myers. Don is fantastic; I love him. He would just say, 'Okay, I'll do it.' And he would do it and give us such great shots in the parts of the car going crazy. And then there will be the shot of the crash, and that was a big talk because Don would be sort of harnessed to the seat of the car. It was planned to go 30 miles an hour, and I said, 'Well, that is not fast; you have got to do 100 miles an hour.' And all these stunt guys said, 'No, you're crazy!' I was just joking, but I said, 'Just give me a real crash.'"

The director continues candidly, "And then we're all sitting there. I have my three cameras, and they said, 'Dominique, are we are going to say action?' There is a procedure for stunt action, which is like, 'Camera rolling?' Yeah, yeah, yeah, yeah. And then, 'Action!' And then Don goes and hits the tree. It's fantastic. But I don't say cut, and I've got the stunt coordinator saying, 'Dominique, say cut! Cut, cut cut!' I said, 'Wait!' and he is like, 'Dominique, cut!' and I said, 'Wait, it's so beautiful. Six seconds!' So after he crashed the car then I left the camera running for six seconds and then they would rush to the car. I did that because I knew they would never recreate the feeling of the smoke rising from the hood of the car that I needed to show. Don Shanks was offended that I would not cut immediately. He said, 'What if I had an emergency?' For him, these six seconds felt like 10 minutes. It was this subjective sense of time, and he talked to the newspapers about it saying, 'This crazy director never cuts when it's time to on stunts' and 'This guy doesn't have respect for stunts' and so on. But then we talked again, and then he realized that it was not so long. No, it was not 10 minutes; it was 5 to 10 seconds maximum. But sometimes you need to be hated to get the shots. And thank God, Don was perfect. He did not injure himself. And he did an amazing shot. In fact, he was really well health-wise because later that night we shot him killing Tina."

Another scene that took some filmmaking ingenuity to stage is the claustrophobic laundry chute scene in which Jamie hides from Michael until he hears her and begins stabbing through the steel. So fierce and brutal is the scene that the MPAA [Motion Picture Association of America] took umbrage with the depiction of a little girl being subjected to such terror. Othenin-Girard says, "I had to cut four shots from the laundry chute scene because of censorship, the two major shots. One shot was where we are looking at the girl from Michael's point of view; he tries to get her hand, and she lets go and falls. We are the camera on top of her, and she falls away from us. That was such a scary shot that they carried out censorship. There was no gore, no blood, but it was such an emotional thing imagining that the little girl falls several floors down. So they cut it. Another thing that they cut was the knife stabbing her leg. I had a fake leg made and shot the knife stabbing her and the blood spurting out." The director continues, "That was a very tough scene to do. Rob was not there one day. So I had a guy help me to storyboard the scene, and then I showed them to Rob. I said to him, 'I want this shot, that shot, and the profile. I want . . . ' and so on. And Rob said, 'Okay, Dominique, but you do realize I need to light this.' So we created seven pieces for shooting in a warehouse where everything was done on tables and with skateboards; the girl was on the skateboard. So she was horizontal. The camera was in the tube, and we were pulling her with ropes on a skateboard. It was funny and easy for her. It was a game."

For Draper, the divinity of Orson Welles once again provided a source of inspiration: "When you get to the end of *Touch of Evil*, you feel like you've got to go and take a shower because you just feel dirty and grubby and grimy, and that is exactly what we wanted to try to capture for *Halloween 5*. Especially in the laundry chute sequence, we wanted that to feel claustrophobic so that you feel like you're covered in grease and grime. We wanted the whole film to have that filter as much as we could."

"Danielle never suffered and was never scared," Othenin-Girard affirms. "I was playing Michael Myers when we were shooting on her because the actor, Don Shanks, was not there. I would be running with her around the house, and when we would get tired, I would say, 'Roll the camera!' Her willingness of playing the part plus the real feelings of being so exhausted and being covered with the fake blood, which would be warm on her after running like crazy, all added to the authenticity. So we got the performance. Rob saw how much I involved myself with Danielle, and he said, 'Okay, I need to help Dominique by anticipating. And he knew what angles I wanted, so he would prelight the whole attic really well so that he would be ready for me to shoot. We really formed a team."

Draper recalls receiving some online criticism over the perceived realism of the violent scene, much to his bemusement:

"I've had a couple of arguments online because there was someone who commented about the laundry chute scene and they said we'd stabbed Danielle in the leg because when she got out of the laundry chute, she had blood on her leg. And someone else wrote, 'That's illegal, you can't do that on a film set; if you did that on a film set, you people should have gone to jail for that.' And I was like, 'Hang on; it's a movie! The blood on her leg was fake blood.' But they had heard somewhere that we used a real knife and we actually stabbed her in the leg. We did use a real knife in the shots when he was stabbing through the laundry chute, but when Danielle was in there, we didn't have any shots of the knife. And if there were shots of the knife, it was a fake knife, like the one where she puts her foot on it and throws herself up. That's obviously a fake knife. There is a scene that we shot where the knife comes through, stabs her in the leg, and then pulls out and blood spurts out. That was a fake leg! And they cut that out because it was too graphic. But that's why when she comes out of the laundry chute, she's got blood on her leg because in the story she was stabbed. But I had to explain to people, 'Look, if you slow it down, you can tell that it's all fake. It's a movie!' It's hilarious. 'Did they really kill that guy in that film?' There was another issue with that sense of realism when we shot the scene of the guy getting the three-prong thing in his head. We shot it, and it was so realistic that they had to cut it about four different times before the studio would accept it. It was so brutal that everyone nearly threw up when we shot it, even though it was a rubber head."

With all the pressures of a production to attend to, Othenin-Girard still had to contend with an actor who didn't really want to be there, and it wasn't just any old actor but the inveterate star of the franchise, Donald Pleasence. After much cajoling from his director, the actor came around and delivered a brilliant performance, which required moments of greater physical effort and emotional range than was required in the previous entries, and the effect was seen in the thrilling showdown between Loomis and Michael in the Myers family home in the climax of the film.

"Donald Pleasence did not want to do the movie, but Moustapha told him that contractually he had to. When we met, it was very good. And I said, 'I really need you to have this scar because of the fire and so on. I want something scary.' And he said, 'No, I'm not scary.' I said, 'Yes, because I like antagonists. I want you to be an antagonist in my movie.' And he said, 'But I'm Dr. Loomis. You don't know the story. I know who my character is much better than you, Dominique.' Yeah, yeah, yeah, yeah. 'But, Donald, this is my movie. Let's do it as I please.' So he suffered during the two hours of makeup every day on the hand and on the face and so on. Those makeup guys were great, but it takes time to put latex on the face so that the latex doesn't become green. We did a 35-millimeter test with Rob, and we shot the daylight scenes, the hospital scene, the clinic, and so on. But I said, 'Donald, there is no urgency or rush; if you don't show me urgency and put some pressure on the girl, it's not going to work; I need it.' Then he was great. Because he would take it, he would go and offer me what I wanted, and I would be scared myself. So we worked well. He's such a prodigious actor."

Othenin-Girard continues, "I just love English actors. I worked with John Hurt on my first feature film, *After Darkness*, and he told me how to direct actors. He said, 'Don't ever tell me what you want. Just tell me what you don't want.' I was 23 years old, and I had only three takes possible on *After Darkness* because it was shot on film and really low budget. John worked for a very low price because he liked the project and the screenplay. And so I would often shoot without rolling the camera to see what Julian Sands would do because Julian is the guy who would say, 'I'm best on the first take.' But John would rehearse and would offer me this and then that, and he would sort of create his character. And John said, 'My character comes from inside.' I would invite him to come and see the dailies night after night. And then I would be worried that he doesn't like me because he doesn't want to come and see the dailies. We were screening them in a theater in Geneva. And he said, 'No, Dominique, the dailies are your point of view on what I do. If I look at them, I start to think "how do I look?" instead of how I am inside. For me to create the character, it's about who I am, whereas you have the freedom to shoot it and to move the camera the way you feel. But don't short-circuit my process.' I saw this kind of English approach to acting in Donald Pleasence. He did the same."

"Donald was awesome," Draper acclaims. "He was a really nice guy, and nothing was a problem for him. He was always friendly and chatty and always wanted to hang out by the camera. He definitely didn't have the air of an old movie star or anything like that. Acting was his craft, and he wanted to do the best he could. And he was always willing to work with us to help achieve that on camera. He was up for it. You've obviously seen the film a few times and knowing how we had to light it, you can see the way he plays in the light. I just had to tell him, 'I've got a light here, and I've got a light there, and I've got a light there, so all you've got to do is feel your way from light to light.' It was like Little Red Riding Hood dropping breadcrumbs. If you pick up the breadcrumbs, everything will be great. There were times when people were going, 'I don't know where the lights are!' But they found them eventually."

Othenin-Girard recalls, "One time where I had a clash with Donald was with him talking to the forest, calling for Michael to come home, that long monologue. He could not remember that monologue. He thought it was shit. He thought it was badly written. He hated the monologue. He was drinking quite a bit too. And it was late at night, and we didn't shoot at 10 o'clock when he wished to shoot it. We shot it at 2 o'clock in the morning. We had to get him out of his trailer. And he was waiting, and he was hating it. And he would come and say, 'Michael, come out of the forest. Come out of the forest.' But I said, 'Donald, start slowly and then crescendo, step by step, and then give it to him. So he did it, and I said no. While he was saying these lines, I would speak over him during the take—'Go, Donald, go!'—because he would leave some pauses. I do that from time to time when I would get an actor to do a scene, I would say, 'Do it again, do it again, do it again,' and I would not cut the camera. And Donald was getting exasperated with me. And he put it into the scene. He really gave it to us, and he was great. At the end, we shot him beating Michael up with the two-by-four, and even the crew members were saying, 'You made him crazy! He is going to go ahead and kill Don Shanks! Put some pads on Michael Myers!' We thought he was going to kill Don Shanks and then die of a heart attack. Because Donald didn't want to do the role, he made a deal with Moustapha Akkad that he was allowed to die in this one. So I had the law; I was allowed to kill Loomis because he had enough of the *Halloween* movies. But he came back afterwards in the sixth film. He changed his mind because I guess the paycheck was always strong. So he enjoyed this moment. I know that he was really satisfied to be able to express so much in his acting. And in the end, he liked that we went so far with his character in a new place. But he went reluctantly towards this character that was changed so much from the previous films."

Unusual for the *Halloween* franchise, Othenin-Girard decided that he would instill some humanity in the monster. Among several glimpses into his erstwhile blank canvas of a soul are moments such as when Michael takes off the mask and we see a glimmer of his face. In a brief, tender moment, Jamie, seemingly doomed to meet her imminent demise at the hands of her uncle, appeals to his long-dormant conscience and gestures to him to remove his mask, saying, 'Let me see.' He does, and he cries. It is hard to imagine Moustapha Akkad easily embracing the moment. Did Othenin-Girard finally go too far?

"Moustapha did not want that scene," the director confirms, "although he allowed me to have it. He said, 'It's interesting, but I don't think it's going to work.' He was positive but really fearful about it. Moustapha would come in from LA to Salt Lake City twice a week from time to time smoking his pipe. He would give me his point of view when it was going well. But for the setup—the coffin on top of the bathtub—I took some ideas from my second feature film, in which I have a scene that is very similar, although the roles are reversed. In that film, I had put my evil character inside the coffin because he wanted to feel what it is to be dead. And he put lots of candles around the coffin, and he had set it up on top of the bath, where his girlfriend was taking a bath inside—I'm very lyrical in my sort of way. But at some point, he offends her because he's talking like that, and he has painted his face and so on. And then she gets up—she's naked—and he grabs her. And the coffin almost falls, very dangerous, crazy stuff. And I thought about this for *Halloween 5*, so I set up a beautiful, romantic room with a coffin that Jamie goes to. She knows it is for her and knows that this is the room of memories. She understands that, and she goes into the coffin. I did not put the coffin in a normal position on the floor or on chairs, something stable, because I wanted to have her tilt so that she could get out because of the rage. And then they would destroy the whole space. It gave me that. From that other film, I learned to tilt the coffin in a precarious position. So I had the end, and I had the beginning. And now, I gave her the vulnerability and the courage to ask him, 'Show me, boogeyman.' And then when we briefly see him, it is Don Shanks, who is this big guy with long hair. I probably should have made him more of an average guy, but I didn't care. I showed Don, and it is such a great scene. Less is more, so we could have shown less of him. But his presence is just a little bit on the side of the camera, and it's in the darkness, which is where the boogeyman comes from. So we showed just enough of him.

The director continues with affectionate applause: "I love them so much; they were great in that scene. Don was so gentle with Danielle. She was always around, so she was close with us all. I would be working on another shot that she was not part of, shooting with other people, and I would feel my hand being taken away, and she would bite my little finger and so on. She was just saying, 'I'm here, Dominique! Take care of me.' She was such a sweet little girl. It was fun having young people around. We had a 12-year-old girl train the kittens, and she was the daughter of Doug Seus, who was the animal wrangler for *The Bear* [1988], the French movie by Jean-Jacques Annaud. After shooting, I would get on my motorcycle to visit Doug because I loved him and he absolutely loved me because I allowed his daughter to do the wrangling. I told him to go away with your wife; let your daughter do this film. She knows the kittens so well; she trained them with the whistle. And he said, 'But, Dominique, you have so little time, and you are rushed,' but I said, 'She will be fine. She'll do it.' And they were so pleased that I trusted her and made her the head wrangler for these kittens. And they behaved so well with her; I mean, it was all a game."

Michael's methods of stalking and voyeuristically gazing at his victims have always carried something of a psychosexual impulse and methodology, going all the way back to the opening scene of the first film. In a perverse way, this is something that further humanizes him. Othenin-Girard explores those tendencies further in this film, and the manner in which Michael reacts to the cavorting teens here results in some of his most violent actions yet. Take the barn love scene in which Sam (Tamara Glynn) and Spitz (Matthew Walker) practice safe sex, which is notable for the explicit point made by Spitz that he is using a condom. This is particularly rare in horror cinema of the 1980s, in which teen characters are usually seen engaged in promiscuous and audaciously unprotected sex . . . or at least, if they are being cautious, it is never mentioned. In the scene, Michael watches voyeuristically, moving slowly toward his chosen farm implement, which will function somewhat phallically in his killing of Sam. Michael moves leisurely enough that he gives the couple enough time to almost reach a climax, but they are denied such pleasure as Michael penetrates Sam in his own deadly perverse manner, impaling her with a three-pronged pitchfork.

Othenin-Girard considers it crucial to the horror film that there be an element of punished sexuality, which was rather pertinent in the era of the AIDS crisis and the perceived flagrant sexuality of the 1980s. The issue of the devastating disease wouldn't be limited to just intellectual themes depicted within the fictional frames of a film, but the reality of the issue came crashing home when it came to shooting the intimate barn scene. As if to acknowledge the social panic that existed in America around the AIDS panic, not only does Spitz conscientiously wrap his member before coitus ensues, but the filming of the scene was also fraught with anxiety, as the director recalls: "It is the pleasure of sex that needs to be punished. When the person experiences their first enjoyment of sex, you kill them. That is part of a horror film, but that was a difficult scene to do. It was between Tamara Glynn and Michael Walker. But we were in the time of AIDS, and he was gay. Tamara learned about this a week before, and she didn't want to do it. She said, 'I'm afraid because we didn't know if AIDS was transmitted by skin or whatever.' She was scared frozen, so all the shots of her being unbuttoned were with my fingers. You can see that he was so uncomfortable because he felt guilty of being gay. We knew there was no problem with it, but people were scared because of the AIDS propaganda that was around all the time; it was everywhere back then. But the whole situation was making him sweat so much; when he tried to carry her, he was very awkward. There was no sensuality, no eroticism. It was very, very difficult. We encountered stuff like this where we had to function fast. It's difficult to imagine the impact it had at that time. It was terror on everyone all the time."

Amplifying the psychosexual element, there is something particularly perverse in how Michael watches Rachel, which is aided by the subjective use of the Steadicam as we watch from Michael's lascivious gaze. And then there's the moment with Tina, where she thinks Michael is Mikey, her boyfriend, when Othenin-Girard allows for a hint of sexual tension as underscored when Michael performs a very subtle head movement toward his flirty companion. It is a playful, psychological element of the film that may not appeal to all *Halloween* fans, who may prefer John Carpenter's idea of Michael as motiveless evil. But then again, Othenin-Girard always intended on stretching the rules to the breaking point, even if that meant giving Michael some kind of emotional impulse for the rage that he harbors. Some sequels have Michael functioning as a robot, a soulless phantom, or as some say more positively, "a force of nature," but Othenin-Girard renders Michael as something much more than a mindless, senseless murder machine. He offers his villain as a physical embodiment of great emotional rage. The director points out KNB effects wizard Greg Nicotero for having crafted a mask that had more of a recognizably human countenance than what had been used before, which was something that aided him in bringing some personality to Michael.

"Greg understood all of this," Othenin-Girard affirms, "because the mask had features; it was not a plain plastic sort of thing. It had character. And I wanted to give Michael Myers the character of a suffering soul. I did not want him to be just a mechanical robot, a killing machine. That was not interesting for me. So the scene with Tina in the car was my idea. We had a lot of fun breaking the rules. We even broke the rules in the houses we chose, as our house was not like the house of Carpenter. For a start, I had to make the film in Salt Lake City because there was some finance coming from the city, so we had to shoot it there. That meant I didn't have the California flat house that we were used to seeing in the Halloween films. And that was good for me because I wanted to have romantic things. So I asked Moustapha if I may bring some romantic elements to it, and he said yes. At that point, he trusted me. He wanted a *Halloween 5* that was good. That year, all the sequels were going really low quality and were doing badly in the market. *Friday the 13th Part VIII* had failed, and others were not doing well. So Moustapha allowed me to go ahead and make the film the way I wanted to make it. The only point where we really didn't agree was the first character that sort of saved Michael, the hermit."

That disagreement would change the course of the *Halloween* narrative irrevocably, to the point that the formal franchise would die with the sixth film, which carried the burden of having to explain themes set up in this film due to those disagreements. Enter the Man in Black and the Cult of Thorn. In the original opening of the film, which followed Michael's being blasted by multiple firearms, he is saved by an eccentric, young occultist hermit (Theron Read), who is named "Dr. Death" in the initial script. Michael awakens after having a telekinetic episode with Jamie, and he immediately dispatches Dr. Death despite the good doctor's saving his life. This scene was ultimately replaced by the opening that was reshot, featuring the older mountain man hermit. One shot that was kept from the original opening was that of Michael's wrist displaying a runic tattoo, which is later revealed (in *Halloween: The Curse of Michael Myers*) to be the Mark of Thorn.

"I had a fantastic actor, Theron Read, who weighed around 40 pounds and was seven feet high. He was like a skinny sort of wire. And it was weird. The art department did such a fantastic job. Brent Swift created a shack with a lot of voodoo stuff that we all took down, hoping that Ramsey Thomas was not going to shoot the scene with the shots of the old guy [Harper Roisman]. Moustapha said that if Michael kills an old man, then everyone will feel sorry for him. And this was probably because Moustapha was an old man! So he changed that opening. I was very unhappy to have my great first character be replaced with very poor front light. Rob lights from behind; that was our trick, backlight. We wanted to kill this character in backlight. And this poor guy, Ramsey Thomas, had a crew of four. And he did all the shots on the old man inside the cabin, and he front lit it. 'Nooooo!' It was like Rob and I had died."

The rune is left ambiguous in *Halloween 5*, as is the mysterious Man in Black who arrives in town resplendent in silver steel-toed boots, overcoat, and stylish bolero hat. His presence is unexplained (again, until the following film), save for the fact that he functions as something of a guardian angel to Michael. Othenin-Girard explains the rather arbitrary inclusion of the character:

"In the middle of the shoot, Moustapha said to me, 'Dominique, I need another character.' We were literally four weeks into a six-week shoot, and he said, 'I don't know who but someone saves Michael from the police station at the end of the film.' I just went, 'Okay, Moustapha, with this new character, I don't want to show his face because I don't have time to cast him. I want him in silhouette.' And that happened with the Man in Black. I said, 'As it is Zorro, give me a guy in silhouette with Zorro boots, a hat, shoulders square, and cigarette.' This is how I describe his image to the costume designers. So these four guys were now ready to put him in and shoot him at the last moment. We were shooting an exterior street with Tina and Michael Myers in the car, and we had the street lit. And we were ready to insert the character; it took 15 minutes to add the character to the shots, to write him in as much as we could without knowing who the character was, frankly. I was communicating with Michael Jacobs and said, 'What do you think?' And he said, 'We're going to make him part of a sect or something like that, so I want him to have a tattoo because that links him to it. We could say it's blood or so. Let's do that, and we'll sort it out later in the next film.' So we quickly invented the tattoo that is a rune; it's a force, it's a link, and we reshot a lot of the close-ups to facilitate this storyline."

With the film in the can, it came time to cut the picture. Working with editor Jerry Brady, Othenin-Girard found himself collaborating with someone who had more traditional ideas about piecing the film together, which suited the director just fine, as he was under too much temporal pressure to have an editor's trying to leave any stylistic impressions. Brady just wanted to tell the story economically:

"Jerry was an old-timer movie editor," the director affirms. "He was all meat and potato, no frivolous things. He would get the story to progress all the time. And it was good for me to have a guy who's not a creative editor trying a lot of stuff. We had no time for this. We were shooting in 35-millimeter, so this was 24 frames per second. And in the editing room, it was just the two of us, no assistants. I was with the Moviola, and he was on the flat bench. It was crazy; we had six weeks to edit the movie. In the editing room next to ours was Oliver Stone, who was doing *Born on the Fourth of July*, and his son would prefer to hang out in our waiting room because it was always more fun. There was more blood and stuff, so he liked being with us. Oliver would always come to our editing room and apologize for his son intruding. I would say, 'He's okay; he's helping us.' And Oliver's editor, Pietro [Scalia], would also come to the editing room, and we'd have a lot of fun talking.

"And then Moustapha would say, 'Okay, now you've got to have credits. What do you want, Dominique?' And I never thought of the credits before, so I said, 'Fuck, I want blades.' 'What do you mean blades?' 'I want the name to appear, and then it is slashed off with a slice and then the next name, and so on.' So Moustapha said, 'Okay, okay, find the money and talk to these guys.' And he brings three guys into the editing room who are going to shoot these blades because I have no time, as we are full-time editing. I explained to them what I wanted. And they came back three days later with slow-motion footage of the inside of the pumpkin full of seeds, and the blade comes in slower. And Moustapha asked me if that is what I want. 'No.' And he said, 'What do you mean? You asked for the pumpkin, you asked for the blade, and they gave you this.' I said, 'Moustapha, the credit must get me so scared and anguished; it's got to sum up the whole movie and tell the audience 'You're going to get it for your money.' I want it to be scary, but this thing with the slow pumpkins is just child's play.' So Moustapha said, 'Well, tell them to throw it out and do it again.' So Moustapha was great. I was unhappy but didn't think I could tell them to redo it. So I went to help them shoot what I had in mind. I said, 'I want the reflection of the light inside the blade to shine with very quick slashing and then the name.' And we did it, but it was during editing, you know; it's like, everything is thought out."

Bringing some *Halloween* history to the proceedings as well as adding some unnerving tones to Othenin-Girard's unorthodox imagery was composer Alan Howarth, once again providing the theme music but this time, adding some twists at the encouragement of his director, who was at once a radical originalist and honorable traditionalist:

"Dominique's personality dictated a lot of what I did on *Halloween 5*. He wanted to go back to the original *Halloween*, so it was very piano oriented and very simple. It stands on its own with the characters and the activity. Imagine you're a director and you have got to mount a new *Halloween* movie. The thing is, you can't go too far, but you want to do something that is your style, something nobody else could bring to it. Dominique's sense of humor and the way he wanted me to translate that musically meant we got to laugh for the first time in a *Halloween* movie; it was Dominique who brought some absurd sensibilities to it with the goofy cops and the girls going out to the party. However, the creepiness remains, and that was most important. It's all there in the scenes around the house, in the basement. Michael's working wherever he's lurking. There are some great scares in *Halloween 5*, especially where they have Jamie in the laundry chute and Michael is stabbing through the metal, and that was a great scene; I like what I did with it the way the hits are done. Also, the opening of *Halloween 5* was an interesting thing with the slashing of the pumpkin credits. That was one where the technology and the tools of the day really helped what I came up with; that was the first time I was able to take the *Halloween* theme as a whole track and put it on one key of the emulator sampler and be able to play it back on that key while playing other music. There were some real avant-garde samples used in that opening; I thought it was really successful."

Once again, the shrewd producers of the *Halloween* franchise accommodated their closest media ally, *Fangoria*, which duly gave their much-coveted front cover to the latest *Halloween* film in exchange for decent publicity materials. The magazine's editor, Tony Timpone, recalls the symbiotic relationship between his publication and the film's producers:

"Back then, I was dealing with Paul Freeman the most in terms of promoting the movies and whoever the unit publicist was at the time. They were very hands on, but they never restricted us in any way. They were great to deal with because they realized that we were a great ally in promoting the film. So once again, they flew our writer to the set in Utah, and they gave us exclusive access to anyone we wanted, including Donald Pleasence, the director Dominique Othenin-Girard, and any of the actors, you name it. They were great; they were always very, very cooperative. And back then, *Fangoria* was the only game in town. There weren't any other horror magazines, and there were no horror websites. We weren't lumped in with a dozen other journalists to cover the same few scenes being shot. We were the big guys on campus. We were the only ones there. They really rolled out the red carpet for *Fangoria*. So that was a really good time. We were in a great position to get what we wanted because we didn't have any other competition sharing the limelight with us. It was a case of 'Okay, you want the *Fangoria* cover and a big spread in the magazine? Give me some good gory photos!' And they were totally onboard."

Despite riding on the coattails of the successful fourth entry and with the support of a respected genre magazine, *Halloween 5* was said to have struggled to draw a significant audience to the theaters upon its theatrical release. It's hard to imagine a *Halloween* film not doing good business in the 1980s, but the horror boom was in serious financial decline by the end of the decade. The two other major horror franchises of the era—*A Nightmare on Elm Street* and *Friday the 13th*—both experienced a decline in commercial value as they tallied their lowest box office numbers in 1989 with *A Nightmare on Elm Street 5: The Dream Child* and *Friday the 13th Part VIII: Jason Takes Manhattan*. According to the reported figures, *Halloween 5* ranks alongside them as being the least successful of its franchise, although its director, Dominique Othenin-Girard, disputes this and has a different opinion about the film's financial success, having learned a little about Hollywood accounting:

"I learned one thing about the business side of things, and it has to do with Moustapha and my agent. Everybody thinks the film had no success that year, but it enjoyed a much better success than the box office figures that were published suggested. This is because Moustapha wrote to *Variety* asking them to stop printing the numbers, and that is because my agent said, 'There is no way Dominique is going to make this film without back-end profits.' And Moustapha replied, 'There's no way Dominique will have an accounting company looking at my figures.' So what do they do? Moustapha came up with this: 'Let's take the *Variety* box office figures and as it passes over $12 million in income, Dominique will get $20,000 for every $500,000 made. But at $12 million, Moustapha asked *Variety* to stop printing the figures and said, 'If you print numbers on *Halloween 5* again, I will sue you.' So I never got anything. But a year and a half later, *The Hollywood Reporter* showed the figure to be $57 million worldwide gross. There were two figures inside this data: one was like $30 million, and then worldwide total, it was $57 million. But I couldn't go back to Moustapha or Malek on my money side. That was the trick Moustapha played on me, and it is really ugly. And it made the film out to look like it was unsuccessful, which is not true. It worked much better than all the other sequels; this was the year where the sequels to the other major horror films were really a catastrophe. You learn from your mistakes. But I'm an artist; I delegate these things. I don't look at these things going into every film, and that's probably why today I'm not rich."

"For all the film's faults," Tony Timpone says, "I think that Dominique Othenin-Girard at least had some kind of mad vision for *Halloween*. He brought great visual sense to it. And it was really well shot by Rob Draper; it looked really good. The problem with it is you can see that they were sowing the seeds of a silly mythology, but that's what they wanted to do. To keep pushing the franchise forward, they had to come up with some different tangents, some different ideas. The problem is that didn't necessarily work for Michael Myers because as John Carpenter always said, Michael is a force of nature and when you do try to explain him, it takes the terror out of the character. He's a shark in the water, something you don't know how to relate to or how to survive it, for the most part, but when they started to humanize him and find a method behind his madness, it kind of deflated the whole thing."

For Draper, despite his reluctance to work in the horror genre, the film proved that becoming known for one's work in that genre wasn't such a bad deal after all, as some significant jobs were on the horror horizon. Following *Halloween 5*, the cinematographer would continue to work in the horror field, first on the big-screen adaptation of the small-screen anthology series *Tales from the Darkside*, and then brought his eye for television terror to an HBO show that was being produced by a significant quintet of Hollywood power players. *Tales from the Crypt* was made by David Geffen's production company and executive produced by none other than Richard Donner (*Superman: The Movie, The Goonies, Lethal Weapon*), Walter Hill (*The Warriors, 48 Hrs., Southern Comfort*), David Giler (*Myra Breckinridge, The Parallax View, Alien*), Robert Zemeckis (*Used Cars, Back to the Future, Who Framed Roger Rabbit*), and Joel Silver (*Predator, Die Hard, Road House*). Draper recalls his canvassing efforts to get on the show, which ultimately paid off:

"When I saw that those guys were attached to it, I thought, 'Oh, my god, I gotta get onto that show!' So I drove them crazy for about nine months, calling and calling. And eventually, they said, 'Look, we're going to shoot new wraparounds, and Dick Donner doesn't like the way it is all done like a comic book with a lot of color. So if you can tell us that you can do it with a different visual style, we will get you to come in and do 20 of the wraparounds.' I was like, 'Aces! Off we go.' So I flew out to LA, and Kevin Yeager was directing them because he also made the Cryptkeeper [host of *Tales from the Crypt*]. Kevin and I hit it off, and we shot the wraparounds. After the second day of dailies, Dick Donner called me into his office and said he absolutely loved it. So now I had my foot in the door. Then Kevin told me he was doing an episode [of *Tales from the Crypt*] called "Lower Berth" about a two-headed man set in a 1920's sideshow, and that was right up my alley. So I begged him to let me shoot that, and he had no problem. I shot it, and then it won their first CableACE Award for cinematography. The thing about that show was they wanted feature-quality photography because they were all feature guys. So not only did you have a lot of freedom, but you also had total freedom to do whatever you could do and however you wanted to do it because they brought you in as a DP [director of photography] that they respected and there were no guidelines for that other than it had to look fantastic. That is why the cinematography on *Tales from the Crypt* stands up."

Draper continues, "It was definitely a big thing for those guys that it had to have a real feature-film look to it. And they spent money on it too. They had good budgets, and I think we had seven or eight days to shoot each half-hour episode, which was fantastic. For example, when I do *Creepshow* these days, we've had to do a one-hour episode in six days. And we've got two stories to shoot, two half-hour stories each to shoot in three days, so I've got to go like a bat out of hell. It was on *Tales from the Crypt* I met Manny Coto, which led to me shooting his film *Dr. Giggles*. One thing just kept leading to another. The unfortunate thing was that back then, there was such a long time between shooting the film and the film coming out, which meant that by the time the film came out, you were already on to something else. At one point after *Tales from the Crypt*, I was asked to do *Free Willy*, but I was doing something else. Also, I thought, 'Who wants to see a film about a whale?' Oh my gosh, that was a mistake."

In the 35 years since its release, *Halloween 5: The Revenge of Michael Myers* has remained a divisive entry in the series, splitting fan opinions. There are those who love Othenin-Girard's unique style and European flavor, but no matter what side of the camp one falls on, there is always a special kind of derision reserved for the bumbling comedy cops and other awkward moments of humor throughout the film. However, Draper takes a more sanguine view of the film's legacy and considers the benefits of fan culture and its power to revive interest in works that weren't widely appreciated upon release and can instigate a turnaround of critical appreciation. Such has occurred with *Halloween III: Season of the Witch*, so there is always hope.

"I do feel *Halloween 5* is being appreciated more these days," Draper says. "I think what tends to happen is younger people don't necessarily want to go back and watch the older films, such as the original *Halloween*, so they might be inclined to seek out a later film in the franchise, such as *Halloween 5*. Eventually *Halloween 5* will be someone's favorite one because it will be the first one that they see, or the only one they see. I'm proud of it. It was really my first big feature film. I had done a few other very low-budget, small-scale films, but as my agent said, 'That's your first Hollywood film.' So yeah, I'm still quite proud of that. I never thought the day would come when I would say that, but then I think in terms of the craft and the difficulty of shooting it and the things I had to do to get it to look the way it did. I look at some of the things now, and I can't work out how I did it. When I look at it I go, 'Hang on, where were the lights in that?' The sad part about it was I didn't get to do the final color grade on *Halloween 5* because I had already gone on to another film, and that was a real shame. Some people have said they don't like *Halloween 5* because it looks too different, and that is perhaps one of the problems with having too much creative freedom. But even though Dominique brough his very distinctive style to it, we still had to work within certain parameters that Moustapha wanted us to adhere to; he still wanted it to look and feel like a *Halloween* movie. After a few days of dailies, they were a little bit concerned that the film was going to have a very different look to the other *Halloween* films. And I think, in a way, it does, but I think we did a pretty good job on the film. My son is a director now, and he loves *Halloween 5*. It might be because I'm his dad; if he doesn't love it, I'll kill him. But I would never have any qualms about saying to someone, 'Look, this is an example of my work.'"

For Othenin-Girard, the viewers he aimed to please the most assured him that the film could stand proud among the other entries of the franchise, as the director recalls: "Moustapha and the producers were very, very happy with the film. That was really evident when they said, 'Okay, now we've got the great movie we were looking for!' They took advantage of me until the end; they sent me to Toronto to supervise the printing of the prints. It was something like 1,400 prints, and we were watching one in every hundred to make sure it was to our specifications. So I spent four or five days in Toronto, free of charge, which was, of course, part of my director's agreement. And mea culpa,

Wayne—I never saw *Halloween II* and *Halloween III*. I saw the first *Halloween* several times. And I saw *Halloween 4* to know where I was going with *Halloween 5*. To this day, I haven't seen them. I like John Carpenter; I thought his idea was great: spend a few hundred thousand dollars to make a simple story where the stakes are very clear. With *Halloween 5*, I felt like I got the opportunity to respect that and to use it as my template and then to do something different."

Othenin-Girard was further surprised to learn that his film was inspiring the future generation of *Halloween* filmmakers when Moustapha Akkad's son (and now chief of everything *Halloween*) Malek showed him Rob Zombie's reboot:

"I like Malek a lot; I have a very good relationship with him. He was nine years old when I was shooting *Halloween 5*; he used to come on to the set all wide-eyed. And now he is making them. He wanted me to do another *Halloween* film a few years ago, so he showed me one of the Rob Zombie films. Wayne, I was shocked by what I saw. Malek told me, 'Rob was inspired by your movie,' and I said, 'No, Malek, he copied my movie! You have the two girls walking in the Steadicam shot; you have Michael Myers killing the guy by crashing the window of a police car and then strangling him. One event after the other is like what we did!' I was totally shocked. I said, 'Malek, pay me some copyrights! Your father already fucked me over, and now you're copying my movie, shot for shot!'"

To quote Oscar Wilde, "Imitation is the sincerest form of flattery."

Chapter Four

A New Dimension

"Michael's work is not finished in Haddonfield." —Tommy Doyle

When *Halloween: The Curse of Michael Myers* was released in the fall of 1995, the horror genre wasn't yet riding the wave of postmodernism that emerged following the massive success of Wes Craven's *Scream* the following year. Bob Weinstein's Dimension Films was still churning out straight-to-video sequels and original films to little fanfare, beyond the genre lovers and those dedicated to the franchise brands that the company was exploiting with name recognition. Dimension Films was founded as a horror specialist subsidiary of Miramax, the legendary independent distribution company and later Disney partner, founded by Bob and Harvey Weinstein. The horror genre was nothing new to the Weinsteins; they had been attempting to break into the low-budget slasher market as far back as 1981 when they made the controversial cult classic *The Burning*. Bob had written it, with Peter Lawrence, based on a story by Harvey, Tony Maylam, and another future studio mogul, Brad Grey. But this kind of product wouldn't be Miramax's stock in trade for long, as they would soon be distributing world cinema, arthouse, and sophisticated independent fare, such as Steven Soderbergh's *Sex, Lies, and Videotape* (1989), Tom DiCillo's *Johnny Suede* (1991), and Neil Jordan's *The Crying Game*, before they would get into business with Disney and begin their seeming dominance of the film industry for several years after they released Quentin Tarantino's *Pulp Fiction* in 1994. That moment was perhaps the commercial and cultural zenith of the independent boom, instigating a whole subgenre of hip, cynical, intellectually absurdist films that could cross over into the mainstream, eligible for and often winning prestigious prizes at both the Cannes Film Festival and the Academy Awards. Miramax became respectable, that is until Harvey Weinstein's bad behavior helped usher in the #MeToo movement, which took him and many other lecherous Hollywood power players down and their reputations with them.

It was throughout Miramax's rise in the industry that Bob Weinstein had the good idea to open his own subsidiary specializing in horror. Dimension Films took a particular interest in producing straight-to-video sequels to preexisting horror titles that genre fans would be familiar with. Among their first releases would be *Hellraiser III: Hell on Earth* (Anthony Hickox [1992]), followed by *Children of the Corn II: The Final Sacrifice* (David Price [1992]), and soon in their sights would be the *Halloween* franchise, which would imminently become the property of Dimension for three films. And the second of those releases, *Halloween H20: 20 Years Later*, would reinvigorate the reputation and commercial value of the brand, but that film was released in the post-*Scream* climate of slick, self-referential, ironic horror films that were very much in vogue in the mid- to late 1990s. In 1995, *Halloween: The Curse of Michael Myers* wasn't anything so hip as to be looking inward at itself and philosophically wondering, "What is a horror film?" and, therefore, playing with the conventions of such. It was too busy being an actual horror film to care about such intellectual masturbation.

As such, the sixth installment of the franchise aligns perfectly with the tone of *Halloween 4: The Return of Michael Myers* and *Halloween 5: The Revenge of Michael Myers*, which is to say that it treats its subject matter seriously. And perhaps this was part of its downfall and failure to find a suitable audience in the era of ironic postmodernism. Here was a film that not only played straight another night of terror with Michael Myers stalking his remaining family members but also dealt with some heavy themes involving the breakdown of the family unit, teen pregnancy, social expectation, and in some people's view, incest. So it was not exactly what the *Beavis and Butthead*–weaned Gen-X audiences were looking for in their Friday-night slasher flicks, but those are the very elements that make *Halloween: The Curse of Michael Myers* redeemable in this writer's eyes. The fact that it doesn't naval gaze upon its own place within the genre, is willing to inject some kind of social subtext into a franchise not normally known for such, and gets straight down to the business of being a slasher film in the tradition of the *Halloween* franchise is testament to screenwriter Daniel Farrands and his approach to the material. Indeed, this film came from a place of sincerity, the jackpot wish fulfilment of a 19-year-old fan who found himself sitting opposite *Halloween* godfather Moustapha Akkad in his office on Sunset Boulevard and pitching his contribution to the franchise that he loved so dearly. How Farrands got there is the kind of story that would warm the heart of anybody whose youth was spent in front of the TV gorging on horror movies and dreaming of someday making one of their own. And Farrands didn't just dream it; he willed it into existence.

"*Halloween 5* was the one that galvanized in my head what I needed to do. You know how it is said that you must envision your future and that you manifest things. Well, I don't necessarily mean to sound new age because those words are kind of overused, but in a weird way, I did manifest that. I'll never forget it. And I have witnesses! When I saw *Halloween 5* at the Studio City Theatre, I walked out, and I noticed there were not many people there. People weren't lining up around the block or anything, and I'll never forget walking out into the lobby of the theater and saying, 'I'm going to write *Halloween 6*!' It wasn't just 'maybe I'm going to write it,' and it wasn't 'if I could write it.' It was 'oh, yeah, this is what's going to happen.' Now, the journey from that statement to doing it is strange, circuitous, and weirdly the timing was just right. They do say timing is everything. I made my declarative statement to the universe at that moment and then just went about doing that, but then I thought, 'How am I actually going to do this?'"

Evil rises. Author's Collection

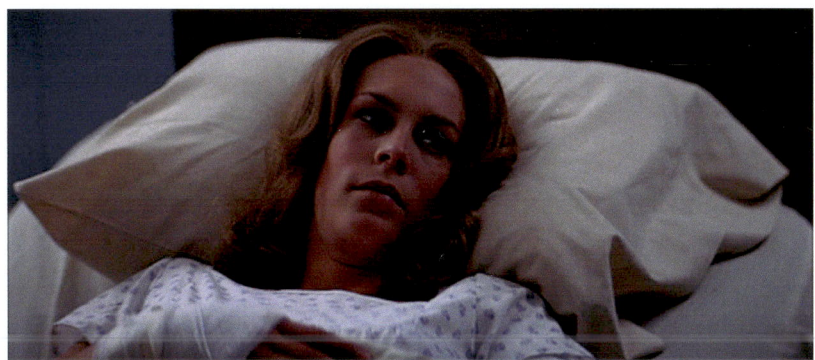

Laurie Strode (Jamie Lee Curtis) tries to recover from her night of terror. Author's Collection

Trick-or-treaters prepare for the Big Giveaway in *Halloween III: Season of the Witch* **(1982).** Universal Pictures/Photofest ©Universal Pictures

Dr. Dan Challis (Tom Atkins) and Ellie Grimbridge (Stacey Nelkin) check out the deadly Silver Shamrock masks in *Halloween III: Season of the Witch* **(1982).** Universal Pictures/Photofest ©Universal Pictures

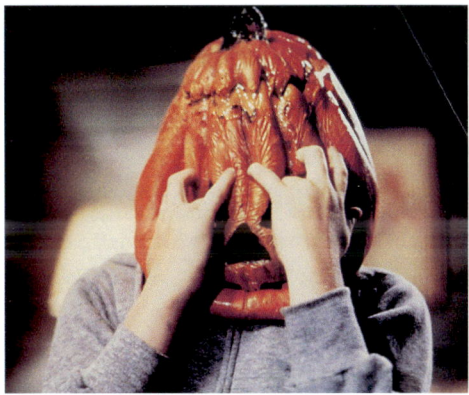

Little Buddy Kupfur's head is melted by the Silver Shamrock Big Giveaway. Pictorial Press Ltd/Alamy Stock Photo

Danielle Harris and Ellie Cornell star in *Halloween 4: The Return of Michael Myers* **(1988).** Anchor Bay Entertainment/Photofest ©Anchor Bay Entertainment

The man in the mirror: Michael Myers in *Halloween 4: The Return of Michael Myers* **(1988).** Pictorial Press Ltd/Alamy Stock Photo

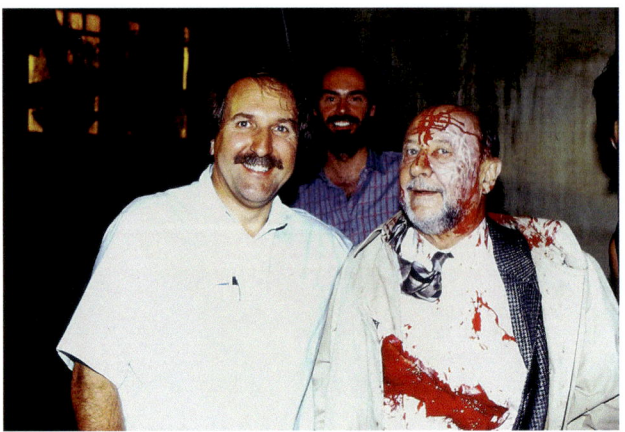

On set with cinematographer Rob Draper (left), director Dominique Othenin-Girard (center), and actor Donald Pleasence (right). Courtesy Rob Draper

Michael Myers (George P. Wilbur) terrorizes in *Halloween: The Curse of Michael Myers* (1995). Miramax Films/Photofest ©Miramax Films

Veteran actor Mitchell Ryan as Dr. Wynn. Author's collection

Adam Arkin (left) and Jamie Lee Curtis star in *Halloween H20: 20 Years Later* (1998). Dimension/Photofest ©Dimension Films

From left: Bianca Kajlich, Brad Loree (as Michael Myers), and Busta Rhymes in *Halloween: Resurrection* (2002). Miramax Films/Photofest ©Miramax Films

Sheri Moon Zombie and Daeg Faerch appear in Rob Zombie's remake of *Halloween* (2007). Dimension/Photofest ©Dimension Films

Daeg Faerch (young Michael) and Sheri Moon Zombie (Deborah Myers) on the set of *Halloween* (2007). Courtesy Phil Parmet

Dr. Loomis comforts his troubled young patient. Author's Collection

Michael Myers is almost ready for his close-up. Courtesy Phil Parmet

Calling action on Tyler Mane as Michael Myers on Rob Zombie's *Halloween* (2007). Courtesy Phil Parmet

Sheri Moon Zombie films a scene as Michael's mother, Deborah Myers. Courtesy Phil Parmet

A surreal vision of young Michael and his mother. Author's Collection

David Gordon Green monitors the action on the set of *Halloween Ends* (2022). Universal Pictures/Photofest ©Universal Pictures

Halloween: The Curse of Michael Myers (1995) poster art. Miramax Films/Photofest ©Miramax Films

It all began when Farrands was a young film aficionado whose immersion into cinema occurred with a viewing of *Jesus Christ Superstar*, an unlikely starting point for the man who would resurrect Michael Myers years later, but nonetheless, a powerful experience for the enthralled lad.

"It was the music, the visual dynamic, and everything going on onscreen," Farrands enthuses. "I was about three years old, and it just blew my mind and showed me the power that a film can have. The spectacle of cinema grabbed me at an early age. It was the way the camera moved and the flashing lights. It was a very famous film at the time, and the music had already been famous. Also, being raised in a very Catholic household, but I'm not a very religious person anymore, so I fell away from all of that. But I think film is, in a weird way, like a religious experience for a lot of people, and it was like that for me as well. The idea that it is communal and where all our emotions can be tied into something all at once, we experience something collectively. That was very profound to me at a very young age. The '70s were an interesting time for film, television, and pop culture, so being a young person and around all that really opened my eyes. It was a very formative time for me. I was born on the East Coast in Providence, Rhode Island. And when I was seven years old, my parents had the high-minded idea to hightail it out of there and come to California, and we came to Los Angeles. This was around 1976. There was something of an allure for me because I knew that's where they make the movies. And the idea that there was a Universal Studios . . . I was just enamored with the place from the time I can remember. My parents weren't necessarily artistic, and I don't think there were any artistic aspirations in my family, although my father was sort of a musician. There were certainly no aspirations to be in the film business. I didn't have an uncle working in the industry or anything; I'm not a nepo baby. It was just my passion and drive for storytelling and make-believe. And I think most of my generation, which is Generation X, saw this movie that came out in 1977 called *Star Wars*, and that really captured my imagination, everything from the spectacle to the visuals to the special effects and the music. I don't know how to explain it, but for my generation, *Star Wars* just moved and inspired us."

The screenwriter continues, "Weirdly enough, given my Catholic roots, horror was not necessarily encouraged or supported in anyway in my household, but like a lot of kids, I found horror movies by osmosis. There were always these stories and movies that we weren't allowed to see, the stuff you talked about with your friends in the playground or in school, things like *When a Stranger Calls* and *Halloween*, and I vividly remember *The Exorcist* coming on TV one time and just running out of the room in stark terror. I was always kind of afraid of things; I think religion in some ways instills fear by its very nature, and that's what it's intended to do. And I don't mean that as a slight against anyone who has a belief, so I think there was a little bit of that. But I was a very curious child, and I always wanted to find out what's behind the curtain. So when I got over the shock and fear, it became a thing where I wanted to explore how and what it was, to understand the nature of fear. So I didn't see *Halloween* when it was released because I was a bit too small at the time, but I do remember my mom taking us to see *Omen II*, and that was okay with her because it shows a battle with the devil. Of all the horror movies, that was the one I was allowed to see.

"*Halloween* didn't come into my world until 1981. And it was the week that it was going to air for the very first time on network television, and it was a Friday-night *Movie of the Week*. So now, we thought we could watch it because it was on television. And I remember we all sat around to watch it, but one by one, everyone began disappearing because it had gotten too scary, until it was only me left on a couch in a dark living room with a bunch of pillows piled up around me and I'm peeking through the pillows. As you know, the movie becomes darker and darker, and the point everybody else checked out was when Laurie Strode walks across the road and goes into the house . . . that's when I was left alone! My memory of it is that I was so terrified, but there was an enthusiasm for it that I hadn't experienced before. And at that point, we were one of the families around that owned a VCR, and we happened to put a tape in and recorded it. So now, I had it on tape, and that started my mimicry from there. I had to experience this movie again and again and again until it was more or less committed to memory."

The result of Farrands's passion and labor is *Halloween: The Curse of Michael Myers,* perhaps the most divisive film of the *Halloween* franchise, or at least the formal franchise. The film is concerned with Michael Myers's pursuit of the infant son that his niece Jamie Lloyd (J. C. Brandy) gives birth to early in the film. It has been six years since Myers terrorized the town of Haddonfield, where the seasonal celebration has been banned because of the trauma it has caused the tight-knit community, but old wounds are reopened when Jamie, who has been kidnapped by the Cult of Thorn, gives birth and Michael's pursuit of the child leads him back home . . . again. In the alternative cut of the film, known as the *Producer's Cut*, the child is revealed to be Michael's after a ceremony is staged where Michael inseminates his niece. Regardless of who or how and which cut, Jamie has given birth and escapes the clutches of the cult. Michael gives chase, catching up with Jamie and killing her. But her child lives, having been left hidden by Jamie in a bus terminal before somewhat self-sacrificially leading Michael to her at a farm as a diversion to save her son. The boy is saved by none other than Tommy Doyle (Paul Rudd), the reclusive survivor of the 1978 killings and the one who is obsessively pursuing the meaning behind Michael's madness and the runic symbols associated with him. Naming the infant Steven, Tommy brings him home to care for him with the help of his neighbor Kara Strode (Marianne Hagan), who is the first cousin of Laurie Strode. She is living in the Myers house because her real estate agent uncle couldn't sell it due to its association with the evil that resided there. Her father, John (Bradford English), bought the house because no one else would; however, the property is a constant target of neighborhood pranksters who pick on the house, although those pesky, taunting kids are nothing compared to the terror that will reign at the house on Halloween night, when Michael returns home in pursuit of his last living relative, baby Steven.

The film expands upon the introduction in *Halloween 5* of the mysterious Man in Black, who in that film, observed proceedings and broke Michael free from his cell in the climactic police station massacre. It is revealed here that the trench-coated one is in fact the leader of a Druid cult who has been controlling Michael all along through his experiments in the black arts. It is further revealed the Man in Black is also Dr. Terence Wynn (Mitchell Ryan), friend and colleague of Dr. Loomis (Donald Pleasence) and the chief administrator of Smith's Grove

Sanitarium. Screenwriter Daniel Farrands recalls the efforts he made in uncovering, not unlike Tommy Doyle perhaps, the meaning of the mythology surrounding Michael Myers that Dominique Othenin-Girard and his collaborators cooked up in *Halloween 5*.

Dr. Wynn (Mitchell Ryan) and Dr. Loomis (Donald Pleasence) in deep discussion in *Halloween: The Curse of Michael Myers* (1995). Dimension Films/Photofest ©Dimension Films

"In those days the Internet wasn't what it is today; it was a smaller Internet, of course. You couldn't just IMDb someone or find them on social media. So we had this thing called the *Hollywood Creative Directory*. It was a little paperback, like a little book that you could pick up at any newsstand in Los Angeles, and maybe other cities, but definitely here. So I picked it up, and I looked for the production company behind the *Halloween* movies. And there was a name and a phone number for Ramsey Thomas, who had produced *Halloween 5*, so I wrote this letter in which I introduced myself as a writer and explained my passion for this. So I got a call from Ramsey, and he said, 'You know what, we're going to be making *Halloween 6* right away; send me something. I thought, 'Oh my god!' I had a script that was not a *Halloween* script. I've read stories over the years that said I wrote a *Halloween* script and they bought it, but that's absolutely not what happened. I'd written an original horror script a couple years before; it's the one thing I had, and I sent it to Ramsey sort of hoping, but maybe not fully expecting, that I would hear anything. But he called me maybe even a couple of weeks down the road, and he's like, 'Okay, I've read this, and I think it's good. I want to start bringing in writers to come up with a pitch and have a meeting with Moustapha Akkad.' To me, it was like being summoned to the principal's office. I had to prepare.

"And that's when I started to put together this very exhaustive sort of bible of the Halloween franchise in which I detailed every character. I went to this New Age place called the Bodhi Tree Bookstore, which is sadly out of business, on Melrose, to ask them about this weird symbol on Michael's wrist that has something to do with the guy with the black hat, the coat, and the boots who shows up at the end of *Halloween 5*. I wanted to know what that was. So I drew a picture of it to show them, and they were like, 'Oh, that's a rune.' 'What the hell is a rune?' And they said, 'Come with me!' and they brought me to a book that is called *Rune Magic* that was written by a guy named Donald Tyson. I still have the book. I looked up the symbol, and it is the mark of the devil, essentially. So I'm like, 'Wow, so they must know where they're going with this! I'm going to work that into my bible. So I started to make a family tree and note who was related to whom. I just went through it all as a fan."

Farrands recalls the crucial moment that would change his life, the moment he went from Halloween fan to filmmaker: "I'll never forget that meeting. Moustapha's office at the time was on Sunset Boulevard. I walked in and sat down, and he sees this 19-year-old kid sitting there. He was looking at me from behind this big desk, with his little smile and his pipe, and the impression I got was that he's thinking, 'Who the hell is this kid?' I don't think he was expecting a teenager. And the meeting lasted maybe five minutes; it wasn't much. And I showed him my bible and how I incorporated that Thorn symbol into the logo, which ended up in some versions of the film. To this day, I honestly don't know what he was thinking. And this is before his son, Malek, who is my age, really became Mr. Halloween. He has inherited the whole thing from his dad. Malek was off at college, as was everybody else our age, while I was just trying to make movies. So that meeting was a surreal experience. I remember seeing the posters for *Halloween* all the way up to *Halloween 5* on the wall behind Moustapha. Ramsey was there too, and he was nice to me, if a little gruff. He was somebody who was kind of a journeyman; he was doing this for a long time and was more of a nuts-and-bolts kind of guy. I was a little intimidated by him, but he was very nice and told me what to say and what not to say. I just kind of had my momentary audience with The Man. His name is the first thing you see in all the *Halloween* movies: 'Moustapha Akkad presents . . . ' To me it was a huge moment; it was like meeting George Lucas."

Principal photography began in the fall of 1994, which afforded the filmmakers an authentic seasonal vibe for filming, as Farrands recalls: "We were lucky that we literally started shooting on October 30th. No kidding. So all the leaves and the fall atmosphere and the Halloween vibe that you see in that movie is for real. It's not like we had to try that much. It was all there; those really were orange leaves; it wasn't like when they were making the earlier movies where they had a bag of leaves and would have to spread them around somebody's lawn and then pick them up because they didn't have money to buy more of them. We had leaves that were falling off trees and piled up on lawns. So we had the benefit of filming at that time of year."

Cast in the lead role of Kara Strode was Marianne Hagan, who had appeared in various episodic television shows, including *Who's the Boss?* and *SeaQuest DSV* before landing her first lead role in a major feature film with *Halloween: The Curse of Michael Myers*. Things began happening for Hagan while she was attending the Circle in the Square Theatre School in New York City; a brief appearance in the Dudley Moore comedy *Crazy People* led to her getting an agent, a Screen Actors Guild card, and calls to come out to Hollywood. But the native New Yorker harbored dreams of treading the boards of her city's theaters and wasn't best pleased with the idea of heading west to pursue her career. 'My agent said I should go to LA, and I was like, 'LA?! Eurgh! Why?' and they said, 'I'm going to set up some meetings for you out there. I think it would be good for you.' So I went. And things went really well really quickly, as I was getting jobs, not your dream job kind of jobs but guest spots on little sitcoms here and there and other small parts on TV shows, like *SeaQuest DSV*, which nobody remembers. But it was produced by Steven Spielberg, and it starred Roy Scheider. So I got a two-part thing on that, and then my manager called and said, 'I have an audition for you for the new *Halloween* movie.' And I was like, '*Halloween*? As in Jamie Lee Curtis *Halloween*?' I didn't know much about that franchise other than I had seen the first film while I was in middle school and I saw *Halloween II* on TV while I was in high school, but I hadn't seen parts three, four, and five. My agent told me that Harvey Weinstein and Miramax just started a new arm of the company called Dimension and it is headed by Bob Weinstein and all the movies are going to be focused on sci-fi and horror. The first thing they did was they bought the *Halloween* franchise, and I said, 'Okay, this sounds classy,' because Miramax was known for quality back then. This was before the Harvey Weinstein scandal broke out. So I went in for the first audition. And it was Moustapha Akkad and the casting director, and I think Daniel Farrands was there too. And then I walked out, didn't really think about it, and I got a call back and went in again and thought it went well; then I got a call saying, 'They love you,' and that they wanted me to go back in for a chemistry read with their first choice for Tommy Doyle, which was Paul Rudd.'

Rudd was on the cusp of celebrity with his appearance in Amy Heckerling's *Clueless*, a major Paramount comedy that would introduce him to the world upon release in July 1995. That film would enjoy massive success at the box office, become a 1990's cult classic, and make Paul Rudd a star. But while making *The Curse of Michael Myers*, Rudd was just another struggling actor trying to make it out in Los Angeles, as Hagan recalls:

"Paul and I met at the audition, and because we were such serious actors, we were going over our stuff and not really talking

From left: Marianne Hagan, Devin Gardner, and Paul Rudd in *Halloween: The Curse of Michael Myers* (1995). Miramax Films/Photofest ©Miramax Films

to anyone. I remember specifically I was standing off to the side because Paul had a scene that was just him, and I watched him do it. And I thought to myself, 'This guy is going to be a star! No question.' And then I did my stuff, and we did our scenes together; then a few days later, we found out we were going to Salt Lake City, where they shot the principal photography, and off we went! Paul and I had an absolute blast. We would go to the Blockbuster in Salt Lake City and get a bunch of movies, but we would decide on the theme, which could be something like 'Paul Newman movies.' So we'd get *Hud, Cool Hand Luke, The Sting*, and we would sit and watch them and comment about how amazing he is. And we just laughed and laughed. And that's when I said to him, 'You need to do comedy!' At this time, he had a final callback for *Clueless*, and he had to get a day off in Salt Lake City to fly back to LA. And so I coached him on it. In the film, he plays this pretentious stepbrother from back East, and in one of his lines, he has to say the name Nietzsche. I told him I only have one note: you need to pronounce Nietzsche as 'Nietzsch-ah,' because all the pretentious people and those in academia say 'Nietzsch-ah.' So he said he would do it, and I told him it is guaranteed to get a laugh. He came back, and he said it got a laugh. And I said I knew it would. And then he found out the next day that he got the role. So we celebrated and had a lot of fun. With Paul and I being so young and naive, we said, 'We are going to make the best horror movie ever!' We were talking *Rosemary's Baby*, bringing back the original *Halloween*, we're not going to go for the crazy blood and guts and all that kind of stuff. That was really our goal. We knew it had to be good because Daniel Farrands, who has an encyclopedic knowledge of the *Halloween* movies, made us very aware that the fans were very antsy because there hadn't been a sequel in six years."

Halloween: The Curse of Michael Myers stands out for being rich in some relevant themes that some of the other sequels steered clear of in their pursuit of more immediate thrills. With Hagan's character in particular, Farrands introduced some worthy contemplations upon family dynamics when the perceived social order of middle-class life is disrupted by deviating, and deviant, behavior. In this case, it is the Strode's daughter Kara having a child in her youth out of wedlock and having to return home to her father's shame after a failed relationship with the child's father. The film presents an interesting discord between the daughter and her father, who has taken her life's course as a slight on him, the family, and their way of life.

"I wanted that lead girl to be very sympathetic to the audience," Farrands says, "and to not just be fighting against what Michael Myers represents, like external threats, which is very similar to the original. Laurie was this very shy, repressed girl, but with Kara, I wanted to show that she already had obstacles in her life. And I think the family dynamic was something I related to on a personal level, that kind of dysfunction. So I wanted this family to feel like they were already troubled, haunted, to be kind of stalked by something that had nothing to do with a slasher killer coming into their world. And I think that their emotional dysfunction was a setup for her ultimate discovery of her inner strength."

Marianne Hagan applauds what Farrands achieved in writing the character and the attendant themes: "I read the script and loved it, especially the part of Kara because she was a thinker, and she doesn't take her clothes off. If she did, I wouldn't have done it because I never would have done nudity in anything I've ever done. My parents are very Roman Catholic, and they would have just died if I had shown my naked body onscreen. I may be wrong about this because I'm not a horror movie fan, but my idea of horror movies was blood and guts and women with their shirts off and this puritanical thing of if you see a woman showing her breasts, then she is going to be killed within 30 seconds. But what I liked about *Halloween 6* is that there was none of that with Kara. She was a student who moved back home. And yes, she had a child out of wedlock, but that doesn't make her a slut. She is going to the local community college, majoring in psychology. She was very thoughtful. In the original script, she had a lot more to do, but the way it ended, for a lot of different reasons, because of the weather and switching schedules around, a lot of my scenes were cut. Kara was in the library all the time; she was on the computer looking up Thorn, trying to figure it all out so that when she does interface with Tommy, they trade information. But because the scenes were cut, it just becomes me holding a baby and saying, 'Tommy, you're so great! You're so smart! How did you figure it all out?' So that's what I loved about Kara."

Indeed, the themes of family discord in the film add a layer of subtext sorely missing from many horror films, and franchise sequels in particular. Perhaps those difficult themes are close to the bone for viewers who just want some gore with their popcorn, but in a film that functions on the rote stalk-and-slash routine, it is most welcome that there are characters who are not just fodder for the villain and who depict relatable situations. Hagan recalls, "When I did the scene at the breakfast table where my father, played by Brad English, God rest his soul, smacks me across the face, I had this conversation with the director Joe Chappelle, and I remember saying, 'Just because this is a horror doesn't mean that this scene can't be something serious; I think we should treat it like *Ordinary People*. It should be psychological; we shouldn't indicate that it's a horror film and the shit is going to hit the fan later.' Now, clearly, it is nothing like *Ordinary People*, but I felt that it should really be about the family dynamic. We have the mother giving me the money, as mothers often do; the father being pissed at her for giving her all their money; they've got a bastard in the house; and then my brother Paul is trying to lighten everything up. Daniel Farrands and I talked about this for so long. He was on the set in the beginning and was an endless font of information."

"This is long before the #MeToo movement," Farrands says, "but I wanted to have this young woman who was resourceful, smart and who wasn't a sexualized person. If anything, her sexuality had caused a problem in her life, or her early experience with someone else resulted in her getting pregnant and having to leave home, so she had to come back on her hands and knees. I thought that a lot of American teenagers can probably relate to this. I also think I was rebelling against the carefree nature of the teen characters in *Halloween 5*. And it was nothing against kids having a good time, but I just wanted to make her a little bit older, not a high school girl, maybe early junior college. So Kara is around 22 or 23 years old; she is young enough that she's still vulnerable and doesn't really know where she is going to land in life. She is going to try to get an education, and she must live at home with Mom and Dad while she does that. But she's got this little kid that she had when she was 16, after which she went off with her boyfriend, but it didn't work out. All of that caused a huge rift between her and her parents. I had that story in my head. I felt like it gave her more dimension."

For Farrands, the *Halloween* films are intellectually richer than their closest horror rivals, and that is down to the implicit psychosexuality of Michael Myers. It is a theme that is hard to ignore, as very often the filmmakers throughout the franchise have often chosen to present scenes shot from Michael's first-person perspective, the film's frame his subjective gaze as he surveys his prey. There is a voyeuristic quality to these shots that implies a certain lascivious motivation, even all the way back to his first victim, his sister. The entire opening scene of John Carpenter's *Halloween* is viewed through young Michael's eyes, spying on his sister Judith and her boyfriend as they fool around before going upstairs to have sex. Once the boyfriend leaves, Michael is free to creep up to Judith's bedroom, where he finds her nude and stabs her to death. And while notions of incestual desire are to be speculated on at the viewer's or critic's

Marianne Hagan plays Kara Strode. Author's Collection

privilege, the fact that Michael's niece is forced into giving birth to his son in the *Producer's Cut* has led to some misinterpreting Farrands's intention in introducing the idea.

"Everything was sex driven in the original movie!" Farrands says. "I feel that there is a participatory vibe to these films, and people have written their college thesis on these themes. So it goes much deeper than I could ever imagine going, discussing the knife as a phallic symbol, how it's all psychosexuality, and analyzing what is going on in this creeper's head. Those ideas are always interesting to me. There are layers to Michael Myers that you don't see in the likes of Jason Voorhees from *Friday the 13th*, who is more like a monster living in the woods and stalking teenagers at their summer camp, or Freddy, who is this creature who lives in your dreams. And both of those are obviously so scary, but Michael just seemed like somebody who could be out there, like this is something that could happen. But there is also that weird tendency to take the psychosexual aspects of it too far. It's interesting to me how those who've seen the *Producer's Cut* call it 'The Incest Version.' And it's just weird to me because I remember so vividly when we went down that road of the baby being Michael's child, I was so emphatic in saying that this is not about Michael Myers being incestuous with his own niece; that's not what this is about. And they were like, 'No, no, no, no, no, we understand what it is.'"

Farrands continues, "I think there are people who only look at these films on a superficial level. They miss the themes and the symbolism; they don't read past an image on the screen. I think the way that the impregnation sequence was put together, it literally looks like Michael is going to have sex with his niece. That was supposed to be symbolic. Essentially, she was being impregnated with the same evil that had infected Michael. It wasn't a literal rape; it was certainly a violation, but it wasn't a physical rape. I always likened it to the impregnation scene in *Rosemary's Baby* where she's in a drug-induced stupor and there's the weird faces and everything is kind of morphing around her in this bizarre dreamlike state, and then she sees this demonic face. And then suddenly she is like, 'What is it?' I just didn't want to be too on the nose, or to be so pornographic;

that would be just so gross. So for the record, that was never the intention; it was never a thought in my mind. But it's interesting how there's like a faction of toxic fandom that wants to say, 'That's an incest movie!'"

The *Producer's Cut* that has been referenced thus far refers to an initial edit of the film that was made before the studio decided that it didn't deliver enough generic thrills and spills to appease its potential audience after test-screening results dictated a change in direction. Reshoots were ordered to amplify the violence and increase the carnage, while further changes were made that altered the narrative of Farrands's original script.

"I ran afoul of people who thought they knew better," Farrands admits. "There is a lot of politics in this business, and I put myself in the middle of all that. I was so young, and this meant so much to me that I didn't care if I was burning a bridge along the way. It just felt to me like there were people involved in this movie that saw it as a piece of merchandise or product that just needed to be dealt with, handled, graded, put out, and moved on. And I'm not talking about the Akkads; it's certainly not them because *Halloween* is their lifeblood, it's their legacy, it's their IP [intellectual property] that they protect. However, on the studio level, even on the more nuts-and-bolts level of releasing the movie, there was a cadre of people who, to me, were looking at it as just another movie and who didn't have a lot of respect for the original and not a lot of respect for what we were trying to accomplish. So that was frustrating, and as a result of that, so many things in the script that I felt were necessary to tell the story properly and to give it the appropriate context were just excised before we even got them to the camera. So it was like the scenes weren't even on the editing room floor; they were on the production room floor. Just pages of script being pulled out. And for me, it was like, 'Oh my god! Why bother? Why did you bother having a script if you are just going to tear out pages, crumble them into a ball, and toss them in the trash?' And I get it. Some of it is production. I've directed enough myself to know some of it is due to time, and some of these things are made on a very limited budget. But I also feel like you have to balance that with a vision of what you're going for and having a director that would really fight for that."

"Dan was basically kicked off the set," Hagan reveals. "They didn't like the writer being there. John Guare, the writer of the Louis Malle film *Atlantic City*, famously said, 'The writer on a film set is like the hooker who got fucked and paid but won't leave.' And it's kind of true. But they asked Daniel to leave, and we were devastated. The actors were devastated because there was nobody else who we could go to for information and guidance. The director, God bless his soul, Joe Chappelle, it was his first big movie and there was so much pressure on him. He was dealing with the Weinsteins, the producers, and he had so many other things on his plate that he wasn't really there for anything like, 'Oh, Joe, I have a question about what my motivation is in this scene.' It's pathetic now that I think about it."

"I really liked the director as a human being," Farrands says. "He is a nice guy. He had studied a lot; he came from a film school in Chicago and made a student film that had gotten a lot of attention for him. I thought we were going to be in good hands. But I felt like Joe just wasn't at the point in his career where he felt he could do whatever he wanted to, unlike me, who was kind of a renegade in that I just wanted to make the best *Halloween* movie that we could make, being the über-fan, and knew what would make a *Halloween* movie work. But Joe had a lot of pressures around him that I did not like too much. That was the dynamic that went on in the beginning, and I just knew it wasn't going to end well; for me it felt like I was on a sinking ship."

Hagan recalls her shock at being summoned to Los Angeles for reshoots on a film she had presumed to be finished: "We wrapped the movie in Salt Lake City. And we went to a cast and crew screening in the spring, and we thought that was it, it was done. And what we saw wasn't quite what the script was; it lost something, but it was not overly gory or bloody. Then over that summer of '95, Bob Weinstein held some test screenings in Harlem, which consisted of 14-year-old boys, and they hated the movie. The notes that came back had comments like, 'More blood and gore!' and 'The ending sucks!' So after thinking that we were done, we got a call saying that we had to go to Los Angeles because they are going to do a week of reshoots. And I was like, 'What?! We're done! We just saw it.' But they said they have to add more blood and gore; every kill needs to go from a 1 to a 10. So we were like eurgh. I was in New York at the time because I was in the process of moving back here because I wanted to do theater and artsy stuff, and *Clueless* had just come out with Paul. *Clueless* was shot after *Halloween 6*, but it came out before it. So we show up on the set in Los Angeles, and they are trying to match what we shot in Salt Lake City. The costume designer thought the movie was finished, and she sold off all the costumes. So for continuity's sake, the new costume designers had to watch the movie and stop it to take notes. I'm wearing this white dress, because there was supposed to be this underground cult in the town, which gets completely blurred out, and they had to completely remake that dress. I think it worked. But they had to redo everybody's clothes, and it all had to match. And that was no small feat. I had cut my hair, so they had to put extensions in my hair because it was very long in the scenes that we shot in Salt Lake City. Paul had grown his hair longer. And he didn't want to cut it, but he had to in order to match the previous footage. So there were some unhappy people on that set."

The result of the reshoots is what fans were given upon release in September 1995. After acting upon the reports of the test screening and increasing the violence, those viewers for such material remained elusive, as the film underperformed at the box office. Farrands recalls the response that greeted the film: "When the film first came out, it was just dragged through the mud, both critically and in terms of the fan base. I mean, there were always fans who loved it because it was a *Halloween* movie, but I think there was a huge portion of them that were like, 'What happened with this movie?!' It was disappointing. I was trying to do an A24 movie before there was an A24, in terms of the style. And I don't know if the style necessarily found its way through with all the miscommunication that was going on, and that was sad. It was a 'too many cooks in the kitchen' kind of thing. And we were dealing with a studio that was still, at that time, relatively new, and there were a lot of big egos there."

Tony Timpone, then-editor of *Fangoria*, was, as ever, keeping a professional eye on the *Halloween* franchise, but in the midst of the sixth film's release, he immediately felt the negative impact from the magazine's constituency, as he recalls: "*Halloween: The Curse of Michael Myers* was so awful. At least *Halloween 5* was coherent in most ways, and it was really well shot by Rob Draper. But the fans were pretty disgusted with it. Things went south when the Weinsteins took over and started making *Halloween* films. This production was very troubled because the Weinsteins became very controlling and drove the filmmakers up the wall, so there were a lot of clashes. And we suffered as a result of that because they were very uncooperative with us. We weren't given access to the set, and they didn't really supply us with any good photos of Michael because they didn't want to 'give away any of the surprises.' We did ultimately do a cover for *Halloween 6*, but I'm not sure how we did it because it was particularly hard to get any good material from the studio for it. It was also tough because by the time they got to the sixth film, there really weren't any new angles to explore, so there wasn't much new that we could say about the movie or the series at that point. But we covered it as much as we could and ran articles on it. And we even got into some hot water with the Weinsteins when we ran a review of it after one of my interns got to attend a test screening of the film and trashed it. The cut of the movie that they saw was made up of the material that exists as the so-called *Producer's Cut*, so it was before they reshot and recut it, which was a whole other debacle. The fans were clamoring to see the alternate cut because they wanted to see something that was close to Daniel Farrands's vision of the film. I never saw the *Producer's Cut* because the theatrical version was so bad, I just didn't want to revisit it at all."

And it is no wonder why the general response to the film has been so schismatic over the years, as there has never truly been a definitive version of the film released. The two versions that do exist are very different, though neither truly represents what Farrands initially envisioned for the film. Both versions, the theatrically released *Halloween: The Curse of Michael Myers*, and *Halloween 6: The Producer's Cut*, function around the same basic storyline, though the two cuts are wildly divergent in tone and narrative direction. After two decades of existing only as a much-discussed bootleg work print, with its grubby picture and sound quality adding to its illicit allure, the *Producer's Cut* was finally granted an official release by boutique physical media company Shout! Factory under its specialist label Scream, so *Halloween* fans could finally see the alternative version of the film in the clarity of high definition, and it is a markedly different experience, for both better and worse. Unfortunately, Billy Dickson's cinematography has been given something of a cold blue tinting, which desaturates the lush autumnal brown and orange color of the theatrical version, toned down, one presumes, for a chilling effect, but all that this digital grading does is give the film the surface look of a contemporary streaming service production. But the main differences aren't just aesthetic; they are narrative, and they are many. The *Producer's Cut* places much heavier emphasis on the Cult of Thorn and the significance of the runic symbol that was ambiguously introduced in *Halloween 5: The Revenge of Michael Myers*. This cut of the film certainly makes for a more subtle psychological horror film, placing more emphasis on mood and tone than on excessive gore.

Farrands recalls the effort involved in bringing the *Producer's Cut* to the marketplace in a legitimate form: "The issues of getting that officially released was the bane of my existence for 20 years, just dealing with everything and trying to figure out how we could definitively release it. And finally, it happened with the support and persuasion of a lot of people at the studio level. However, it took a long time. And it's crazy to me that it still isn't available in certain parts of the world. It wasn't long after the theatrical mess came out that the work print of the *Producer's Cut* somehow landed and fans started getting their hands on it when it began showing up at conventions all over the place. Suddenly, it was a whole new movie, and I was fascinated by it."

Hagan recalls, "Dan Farrands really wanted to bring *Halloween 6* back to the original *Halloween*, where John Carpenter used the Hitchcockian devices of suspense and the use of music to enhance that suspense, and the implied violence. I don't consider either of the two cuts that are available to be the definitive version of the film. I think Dan would agree."

And he does: "My opinion of the *Producer's Cut* is that it represents a little more of what my script intended it to be. Even though we had some intense scenes in *Halloween 6*, we never went in with the intention of being that extreme or full-on with the violence. When they did the reshoots, there was certainly a little bit more bloodletting, but it still wasn't as extreme as some of the stuff that we've seen in the more recent films. All the effects in those are great and are really terrifying; they pack a punch. But I think some of the later films went a bit too far with the gore, especially Rob Zombie's films. I think that level of violence just felt too extreme. I felt that they could have been moodier and scarier. It's just not curious enough for me. I remember when Michael would pop out of a closet and all you would see was the shadow; those scares were more tastefully achieved. Like in John Carpenter's first movie, when he hangs Bob on that wall, you can feel that knife going through him, but it's not done in this explicit way."

Hagan says, "As much as I think that the theatrical version doesn't make a lot of sense and some of the kill scenes are just so gross, the *Producer's Cut* wasn't the script either, for all the reasons I said, such as cutting stuff out and stitching together what they had. If you read Daniel's script, there's a beginning, there's a middle, and there's an end. It all makes sense; there's a real trajectory to the story. And that's not in the *Producer's Cut*. So neither one is truly representative of Daniel's script. There are certain things I like about the *Producer's Cut*, and I also like certain things about the theatrical cut, such as the way it moves faster as we get toward the end. I particularly like that I get to beat up Michael Myers with a lead pipe, which was really a Styrofoam pipe spray-painted metallic; that's my favorite scene, hammering evil to death."

For composer Alan Howarth, the business side of the situation reminded him of what had gone on before, when the first *Halloween* film became such a success that outside corporate interests became involved, thus diluting the creative control at the artistry level on the ensuing films.

"This film was done with a bigger studio than *Halloween 4* and *5*," Howarth says. "The Weinsteins bought the rights to do it. And that meant that we had to deal with the Hollywood business part of it, and the lawyers and the accountants always mess it up. In some ways, the same thing happened with *Halloween II*. That was a Universal film, so there were additional commercial interests involved. The theatrical cut is the definitive version of *Halloween 6*; it is the one that was released and has been out there for the last 30 years. The famous lost *Producer's Cut* was intended to be the definitive, or close enough to it, but it wasn't what the market wanted nor what the investors wanted."

One of the positive elements of the *Producer's Cut* is Howarth's reprisal of John Carpenter's original theme music in place of the very mid-1990's grunge and alternative rock songs that soundtracked the theatrical cut, allowing for a more unsettling atmosphere to permeate. However, the acquiescence to studio demands for another cut of the film meant Howarth was to take an alternate approach with his score, as he recalls having to change tack to accommodate the Weinsteins' vision for a more hardcore *Halloween*:

"The *Producer's Cut* was done in a way that was consistent with *Halloween*, as was my score for it. But then the Weinsteins got involved, as this was a Miramax film, and they wanted to amp it up to have more violence. So the score for that cut had to be more hard-edged. So I went in and did a second version of the score to the new cuts with the new visuals; I brought in drums and guitars and just went all out with a rock version. And that is a really good one, it holds up on its own. Each *Halloween* score has a different flavor. As a composer, you just want to improve and keep doing better. I was able to do some interesting stuff on *Halloween 6* with the rock version of the theme and with the Thorn theme that I had going. It was original to me; it wasn't just the *Halloween* theme anymore. I got to make some new stuff, and it worked well. Opening the films up to these backstories, like the Druid people and all that, meant I could bring more flavors and textures to the music. *Halloween* always took place in the house, upstairs or downstairs, in the basement, or outside in the backyard. And now we went to other places and other scenes;

we went to the hospital and other locations. So it was a larger canvas, like the opening scene when Michael is trying to get the baby and stuff like that. After *Halloween 6*, it was a whole new regime; it was new directors, new editors, new composers, etcetera, so I haven't really participated in anything after that film."

For Farrands, the film remains an experience of mixed feelings. It has been a surreal journey, from sitting in his living room devouring the *Halloween* movies to then writing one of them. The business side of it has been brutal: to see his work butchered almost beyond recognizability from what he thought would be the ultimate *Halloween* movie for the fans by a fan, to one that certainly has its qualities but also its share of flaws. Regardless of how the film turned out, the franchise remains for him a touchstone in cinema and in his life.

"*Halloween* has become much bigger than just one film now," the screenwriter says, "much bigger than one character. It has made its way into the zeitgeist, into cultural iconography. And it's not just American culture but culture around the world. Michael Myers has become emblematic of the Halloween holiday itself. I don't think there's a neighborhood in America on Halloween night where there isn't a five-year-old trick-or-treater with a Michael Myers mask on. It has just become bigger than life. And I think, in terms of its importance to culture, it is just as big as and probably as recognizable as *Star Wars*; it has that longevity. I mean, we are at the 13th movie now. For me, it's still like a mixed bag, as in I was thrilled to be there. It was the opportunity of a lifetime, especially for me because of my adoration and love for the franchise, and just having been considered, much less anointed, with that responsibility, that was a great honor. I had to take a step back to take it all in, every moment of every second of every day that I was a part of it. I couldn't escape that monumental feeling of achievement. I'm looking around, and there's cameras and lights and actors and makeup and trailers. And then there's George Wilbur standing in the corner, and he has the mask. And then there was an epic moment for me when Donald Pleasence walked on to the set; it felt like it was a dream, and I was going to wake up any moment. But then I'd remember that this is real."

Farrands continues, "I don't know about the writers of *Halloween 4* or *Halloween 5* and how much working on a *Halloween* movie meant to them, but it meant everything to me; it came from the fiber of my being. It was a life-changing moment; it opened doors for me that I don't know would have ever opened had that not been on my résumé. Writing a *Halloween* movie gave me exposure to a lot of people. When I got the movie, I didn't have an agent at all. I had nobody in my camp, so to speak. And so it just helped me move to the next level. And some things I don't love, but to have a career after all these years and be still doing it is just so amazing to me. And I never thought about it in those terms; I didn't have a long-range plan. I just wanted to write *Halloween 6*. It was like I got my wish first time out, so now what? It is flattering to me that people still want to talk to me about this film that was made almost 30 years ago. It's kind of surreal and gratifying. Because of the documentaries I have made on *Elm Street* and *Friday the 13th*, I have been asked by so many fans about when I'm going to do a documentary on the *Halloween* franchise. I always say that I'm probably not and the reasons for that are there's been so many documentaries out there already on the home-video releases, especially on the Scream Factory releases; they have literally got a making-of documentary on every film, and they are incredibly in depth. So I don't know if there's much more I can add. Another reason is that having been associated with the series and having had my own experience working on the franchise, I don't know how objective I could really be at this point. I don't know about the kind of perception people would have about that, the optics of the writer of one of the movies making a documentary about the series. It would feel a little tainted or weird. A bit incestuous I guess is really a better word, and no pun intended.

"So many people's careers started in this franchise. I got to know Debra Hill a little bit in the years prior to when she passed, and she was really encouraging to me. I used to write letters to her too, and when she heard I got it, she was very supportive. At that point, she and John Carpenter had sort of pulled away from the whole series, but she was always in the background kind of watching. It was Debra who suggested that Dominique should be the director for *Halloween 5*. That was an interesting choice, and the film was very different. When I got the job on *Halloween 6*, she said, 'You know what, I'm so happy, so proud of you, and I didn't have a hand in any of it. Honestly, it was Moustapha who decided. But I'm glad it was you because I know how much you care. And I hope that it's going to be the beginning for you and that we'll see *Halloween 7*.' Just hearing from people whose names were on the screen in those early *Halloween* movies and just having them acknowledge you in some way, as small as possible, genuinely meant something to me. Even Jamie Lee Curtis called me on the phone a couple of years ago. It's a weird thing. Even though we all worked on and contributed to different movies in the franchise, the fact is we all kind of acknowledge each other, and it's like, 'You did this one. And I did that one.' There's a weird family element to it, a strong dysfunctional family. And that's fantastic. When we made *Halloween 6*, everyone involved was like, 'They're making a sixth one? A *Halloween six*?!' People were aghast, like, 'Who's going to want to see another one of those?' And the one who was scratching his head the most was John Carpenter, although I think he's grateful for the royalty check."

There would be many royalty checks to come for Carpenter and significantly so too, as following the unfortunate reception of *The Curse of Michael Myers*, the franchise would take a massive change in direction, one that involved bringing back the second biggest star of the brand (behind Michael Myers, of course), Jamie Lee Curtis. Not that this was the initial intention of Dimension. They, the Weinsteins, took control of the property, but as Marianne Hagan recalls, they had fumbled the sixth film so badly that it required a commercial makeover with major star power and an entire retcon of the Thorn story arc and Jamie Lloyd narrative strand, meaning Hagan and Rudd would not be returning for the seventh film.

"When Paul and I signed on to *Halloween 6*, we were also forced to sign a letter of intent for *Halloween 7*, and we thought, 'Why are they making us do this? We don't know where we are going to be two or three years from now. And who says we're going to even want to do it?' We were such brats about it, rolling our eyes and all that. We were told that Jamie Lee Curtis wanted nothing to do with *Halloween* ever again. She did the first two, but she hated it; she felt it turned her into a B-movie actress and she had to work so hard to undo that idea of her being this scream queen. So it never even occurred to us that she would ever want to come back. It was even in her publicity contracts that you cannot ask about *Halloween* movies; that was how much she wanted to distance herself from it. But after *Halloween 6*, Bob Weinstein figured out everything that went wrong with it. And so he brought in this writer, Kevin Williamson, who wrote a script specifically for Jamie, and they brought in a great director, Steve Miner, so she jumped onboard. We were so surprised because we had been told that she wanted nothing to do with the franchise ever again, and then I read an interview with her in which the journalist said that he heard that she would never do another *Halloween* movie and she said, 'Well, I have two kids going to college now, and that helped my decision.' Basically, they were going to pay her a shitload of money to do it."

And so, with the industrial might of the Weinsteins, now major power players in the film business, and with a Hollywood heavyweight in Jamie Lee Curtis returning as Laurie Strode, *Halloween H20* was born, and the franchise became part of the pop-cultural conversation once again.

"Oh, we've got a psychotic serial killer in the family who loves to butcher people on Halloween, and I just thought it in bad taste to celebrate." —John Tate

Few followers of the *Halloween* franchise could have anticipated that it would continue after what felt like its natural demise following the production difficulties and dismal release of *Halloween: The Curse of Michael Myers* in 1995, and sure enough three years went by before the next film would arrive. But what nobody expected was that Jamie Lee Curtis would be onboard. It was new and novel, a sequel that would have the legitimacy of not just a returning main character and Michael Myers's archnemesis but also a major star. For fans, it felt like *Halloween* was breaking out of the confines of the horror genre and into the mainstream. The story would not acknowledge the threads of the Thorn Trilogy; rather, it would take place 20 years later and far from the suburban streets of Haddonfield, Illinois, in the sunny Summer Glen community of Northern California, where Laurie Strode is living in anonymity under the assumed name of Keri Tate and employed as the headmistress of what she calls "a very posh secluded private school." She has a son, John, with whom she is obsessively strict. We learn that John's father is something of a deadbeat dad, an "abusive, chain-smoking methadone addict," who sends his son birthday cards months too late and accompanied by a few dollars to make up for his absence. Laurie herself is a functioning alcoholic and relies on the stock of prescription medication that fills her bathroom cabinet as well as drinking to get her through the nightmares of her brother's acts and the anxiety of his impending and inevitable arrival.

As expected, Michael tracks down Laurie and finds her at the Hillcrest Academy, where brother and sister will face each other in an epic night of terror that pleased fans like few *Halloween* sequels before it. *Halloween H20* not only benefits from the return of Jamie Lee Curtis, and a renewed sense of authenticity provided by her presence, but also from the film's being aesthetically slick and well produced, achieved by having much more mainstream sensibilities than the previous three films of the franchise. If anything, the film feels more aesthetically similar to Wes Craven's then-recent *Scream* films than it does to the last three *Halloween* films, and this is true for a variety of reasons. Like Craven's box office hits, there are occasional nods to slashers past, such as the cameo of Curtis's mother, Janet Leigh, which at one point, is accompanied by a brief musical cue of Bernard Herrmann's *Psycho* score in acknowledgment of her iconic appearance in Hitchcock's 1960 classic.

Such self-aware in-jokes bring an element of comic subtlety to the film that the previous and generally austere prior sequels largely eschewed. With the exception of the bumbling cops and vivacious teen girls of *Halloween 5*, the franchise had, up to this

Halloween H20: 20 Years Later (1998) poster art. Dimension Films/Photofest ©Dimension Films

point, been largely serious in tone. But this was the era of postmodernism and pop-culture referencing thanks in large part to the phenomenon of Quentin Tarantino and the hyper self-awareness of his massively popular works as well as the postclassical nature of *Scream*. And while the humor of *H20* is passable, as the

Mother and daughter scream queens, Janet Leigh (left) and Jamie Lee Curtis chat between takes on *Halloween H20: 20 Years Later*. Dimension Films/Photofest ©Dimension Films

suspense takes precedent, it was the follow-up, *Halloween: Resurrection*, that amplified the comedy. Indeed, capitalizing on the success of *Scream* and its sequel, the power players at Dimension Films ended up incorporating several elements of what made those films so appealing to contemporary audiences into the construction of *Halloween H20*. For starters, the film was written by the man behind those films, Kevin Williamson, and they also pulled music from those films and integrated it with composer John Ottman's original score, a controversial decision discussed in-depth pages ahead.

To direct the seventh entry, Dimension Films brought in Steve Miner, a filmmaker whose name might not have been fashionable or known to the general moviegoing population of the late 1990s, but within the horror community, he was known as someone who could craft a decent horror sequel, as he had done so before with the enjoyable *Friday the 13th Part II* and the excellent *Friday the 13th Part III*. As a journeyman studio director, he was proficient in producing slick mass entertainment, such as the comedies *Soul Man* (1986) and *My Father the Hero* (1994), and importantly, he had previously directed Jamie Lee Curtis in the romantic fantasy *Forever Young* (1992), which had been a big box office hit for Warner Brothers. He was evidently the right man for the job, as *Halloween H20* is a terrifically efficient horror film that gets back to the basics of the *Halloween* franchise, which presents its thrills and spills with a brisk pace and deftly cut editing. The film is also a slick, handsomely photographed affair by the brilliant cinematographer Daryn Okada, whose career has seen him emerge from the independent horror underworld of the 1980s, working on the likes of *Phantasm*, *Microwave Massacre*, and *Lady in White*, to lensing contemporary major studio fare, such as *Mean Girls*, *Just like Heaven*, and *American Reunion*.

Okada grew up in East Los Angeles without any connections in the film business but with an intense interest in movies and cinematography. With school guidance counselors unable to help steer him in the right direction, the teenager spent his early days of high school teaching himself the principles of still photography and exposure. A voracious viewer of film, he quickly developed his tastes and a distinction between what made good movies and bad movies, as usually this was down to his understanding of the quality of the photography and the lighting. This was during the New Hollywood era, when films began to take on new styles while breaking away from the classical, invisible aesthetic of the Golden Age studio picture. With idiosyncratic artistic indulgences, such as Dennis Hopper's *Easy Rider* and John Schlesinger's *Midnight Cowboy* (both 1969) becoming huge successes and cultural touchstones, emboldening a new generation of artists and filmmakers to bring an alternative approach to the screen, Okada found inspiration in this movement, which piqued his interest in pursuing the profession.

"The cinematographers of the New Hollywood were changing things up," Okada affirms, "and that's what I couldn't understand at first, which was you had those guys who made it look like this was really cool and then you had this other group which were stuck in the style of the past, making everything look like they did 20 or 30 years ago; it wasn't a technical thing, and it wasn't a lens thing or a camera thing. It was just what you decided as being the cinematographer behind it. So that instantly got my interest. It wasn't the size of a budget; it was how you used it all. I started reading about those guys—Vilmos Zsigmond, László Kovács, Conrad Hall, Gordon Willis. Even as a teenager, I knew those names. I was reading about them and finding out about who was doing what, and that really interested me more than anything else, such as following sports or stuff like that. I wasn't going to get anywhere in school, and so when California brought in the proficiency test that you could take to get your diploma and leave school early, I did that. I was in the first group in the first year that they brought that in. I just wanted time to be out in the world."

One of the things that Okada stumbled into outside of academia was an initiative that aerospace company Rockwell in Downey, California, offered. Okada signed up for a five-month program at the company, which was at the time making a space shuttle and had an entire department that required what they called "photo documentary." The department needed to shoot pieces of the space shuttle as it would undergo stress tests, to see at what point something would break. What made it tricky for any cameraman was that it had to be done at high-speed photography; those behind the lens had to know exactly when something would happen because the cameras would ramp up to speed. Okada got to hang around and work with the photographer, and it would be here that he received some training with equipment and gained knowledge of photographic technology that would serve him well, as he recalls:

"The fun part was going out to the middle of this field at the Rockwell Downey plant and actually setting up different cameras for different pieces. It was 16-millimeter, 35-millimeter, and at different resolutions because on a fast camera, it would be a rotating prism as a shutter and we would try to capture what we thought the engineers needed to see, which also involved explosives. So there was a lot of prep for that moment, but that kind of thinking really got me into wanting to work on movies. It was like a hands-on film school, and after that, I had it in my head how it works. So that was my first moment with film cameras and that kind of stuff, and since I had all this free time, I was able to teach myself to be a projectionist."

While attending East Los Angeles College in the late 1970s, the institution received a National Endowment for the Arts grant to mount a program of films, and Okada duly embraced this opportunity to get involved. With a thousand-seat auditorium that housed three carbon arc projectors that nobody knew how to use, the eager student took advantage and taught himself how to project the prints and got hired to screen a series of films programmed by UCLA film students. And with this, Okada was exposed to world cinema, experiencing his first Kurosawa films from the projection booth while running the reels. "It was literally like *Cinema Paradiso*," Okada says. "These were beautiful prints, and to be able to handle them and to present them is where I get a lot of respect for projection. You are part of presenting whatever that show is for those people down there that have paid to come see it. That was a whole area that I had no idea about, so it was a whole other side of my film education, which was 'earn as you learn, try it and do it.' I was getting my hands on the gear."

Further practical education was to come for Okada, as independent horror was beginning to get attention and gain traction in Los Angeles. The East Coast had Sam Raimi and his groundbreaking low-budget gore fest *The Evil Dead*, so it was time for the West Coast equivalent to emerge. Enter Don Coscarelli, the mastermind behind the eerie 1979 chiller *Phantasm* and its subsequent franchise. Okada recalls landing work on the film and the independent spirit with which it was made:

"I got to meet Don Coscarelli, who had previously done a movie that he had sold to Universal, and which made money in Japan, and we went and did this other little movie called *Phantasm*. That movie was made by us just figuring out how to do it; it was just a small group of us. One of the attractions of working on that film was that Don and his producer, Paul Pepperman, had money to use a Panaflex with four lenses, shooting it on Kodak film—brand-new film, not short ends—and they were going to process it at Technicolor. Everyone else was grabbing things where they could. But we had all of that going for us, and that was the difference there. Don did the operating, Paul pulled focus, and all of us did everything else trying to light it and mounting cameras. By the time we got to make *Phantasm II*, it was different. What we did on *Phantasm* wouldn't have been allowed on a studio film. When you meet people and get into the groove of working together, there is a core group that forms and which is always there and able to figure out what's going on and how to do things. Don and I became good friends, and we remain so to this day. And it all goes back to *Phantasm*. He has always been so gracious. Don makes the kinds of movies he wants to make; he likes the genre, and he doesn't need to make it epic or make it some crazy thing where it's a big movie made by committee."

When *Phantasm* began making money, people took note of those who could turn a low-budget production into a valuable product; all of a sudden, those making nonunion films wanted the people who made *Phantasm*. One of those that Okada would go on to work with was his *H20* director, Steve Miner, when he took the job of shooting *Elvis*, the 1990 ABC miniseries that detailed the singer's days as a burgeoning musician in mid-1950's Memphis, Tennessee.

"*Elvis* was this half-hour, single camera–style show," Okada recalls. "Nick McLean, who was the cinematographer of *The Goonies* and was the cameraman on *Close Encounters of the Third Kind*, shot the pilot, and I did the rest of the series. I saw that pilot and thought, 'Wow, this looks good!' It was shot on 35-millimeter film, but the rest of the series was done using 16-millimeter, which was great but also a challenge in trying to preserve the look of the pilot. The series got picked up by ABC, and Steve was the director and producer of it. So that's how we began working together. We shared a similar taste for how to solve things, and it was like how Steve and Nick worked. In those days, it was hard to get two cameras. It was always a special thing when you could, and we made it an important element of the show. With Steve, it is about getting the most work done that you can in an efficient amount of time. His thinking was that it keeps everything fresh, and I totally agree with that, if you can keep the pace. And of course, there is a look to it, but there's a point where you hope you have figured out enough stuff where you don't have to waste time fiddling with little things. Steve would let you do anything as long as you weren't going to be spending a million hours on stuff. We were doing things that they weren't doing on television. It was Elvis the early years, so it was everything before the '60s right up to the early '60s. And we were on location in Memphis. It was us and a crew that was mainly from Memphis, and we had to figure out a way of hiding things that weren't of the period that story was set in. So I resorted to shooting all our exteriors using long lenses. That way we could just dress some small portion of the set, maybe using some period cars in the shot. Steve was really into that, and that's how we got away with the legitimacy of it all and made it work."

After *Elvis*, Okada would continue his collaboration with Miner, this time on the depression-set Disney film *Wild Hearts Can't Be Broken* (1991), which was made for a little less than $3 million in 28 days in South Carolina. Following that came another Disney picture, the 1994 comedy *My Father the Hero*, starring Gérard Depardieu, a remake of the 1991 French film also starring Depardieu, *Mon père ce héros*. Then when Miner was preparing to direct *Lake Placid*, again with Okada lensing the film, the production hit a bump in the road and was briefly derailed. But that film's misfortune was to benefit the *Halloween* franchise.

Okada remembers, "We were scouting locations for *Lake Placid* for producer David Kelley, and it came with various complications. Stan Winston was a friend of Steve's, and Stan jumped into it. But he thought that *Jurassic Park* would be the last big thing that he would physically make, but the crocodile in *Lake Placid* was going to be this 30-foot animatronic. And then when we looked at how the weather and how everything else in Vancouver was going to be at that time of year, we thought, 'This is the wrong time to start this movie.' But Steve, who is like a cat who always lands on his feet, gets a call from Jamie Lee Curtis about doing *Halloween H20*, and he says to me, 'Hey, do you want to go do another movie before we do *Lake Placid*?' So we started talking about *H20*." Not being a fan of the Thorn Trilogy, Okada sought influence from those whose style defined

Chris Durand (as Michael Myers) and director Steve Miner on the set of *Halloween H20: 20 Years Later* (1998). Dimension Films/Photofest ©Dimension Films

the franchise early on. "I hated the *Halloween* movies after *Season of the Witch*," he admits, "I thought those ones were just really exploiting the whole thing. So our way of thinking going into *H20* was to use as much of John Carpenter's and Dean Cundey's aesthetic and what they did thematically and tonally, picking up from *Halloween II* and using that kind of range. I had gotten to know Dean over the years before that, and I got to know about the difficulties of the style they used. But I also got to see what using anamorphic brought to the film and why it created such a distinctive atmosphere. So we were going to shoot in that format, and there were a lot of issues as to the exteriors and what we wanted them to look like; there were times when we wanted it to be half overcast for certain things."

Okada details some of the key visual elements that were considered in bringing this latest *Halloween* to the contemporary horror-movie landscape, which had recently undergone a mainstream transformation with the success of the *Scream* movies. *Halloween H20* was going to be slick and stylish without being showy and intrusive:

"We thought a lot about John Carpenter's early use of Steadicam and the look that gave the first film, so we were very careful about how we used it; it wasn't just putting some Steadicam here and there. Certain shots would be dolly shots, but with others, we knew what we wanted to say with the Steadicam. You couldn't overdo it because it would have aged it in a way, and I didn't want to copy Dean. It was more about resurrecting the visual soul of it. We also didn't want to go for a flashy, MTV style of filming, which some of the previous *Halloween* sequels had opted for, and by 'we' I mean Steve, myself, and Jamie. We chose to be really faithful to the original film, and we didn't know if it was going to work or not. But we knew what had been done with the previous films, and we knew that our senses were telling us to stick to the original as a visual reference, advancing on that in subtle ways. Miramax didn't really care about the style; they knew they were getting a movie one way or the other. They were too busy looking into other elements of the production. I was surprised when they started making other sequels and saw that those filmmakers decided to make it as flashy as they did, taking the machine-gun approach, trying to hit a target that might be in there somewhere. It's not a very deliberate approach, but we were very deliberate when it came to *H20*."

Indeed, *Halloween H20* looks beautiful and accomplished in the manner of a commercial enterprise; this is horror filmmaking for the masses, as Okada complements his beautiful stars with appropriately lighting while the photography is resplendent in its juxtaposition of tones, contrasting the lush daytime exteriors with the appropriately moody field of shadows for Michael to lurk and stalk through when he goes to school. The aesthetic that Okada gleaned from the masters of the 1978 film and utilized here makes for a rich visual experience. "Steve and I looked at it like it was music," the cinematographer reveals. "We wanted that song to have the same melody that gets played in different ways, and those are your tools at your disposal in filmmaking. We used everything that we knew cinematically to tell the story. We didn't know if it would play or not, but we felt it was the right way to do this movie. The biggest disappointment on *H20* was that Panavision ran out of anamorphic lenses. And I had a great relationship with them, and they were trying to get a set. But unfortunately, one of the Scott brothers took everything in town. I was able to get a couple anamorphic lenses to do the tests to see how I could make it feel right, framing it and what focal lengths were important. I didn't want to make it like a cropped Super 35 kind of thing, even though that was eventually how it was going to be, but one of the things about anamorphic is the way things fall off. There were some lenses that I adjusted that weren't anamorphic that had a slightly different feel, but where everybody said I was totally crazy was that in anamorphic, you are using so much negative vertical space and compressing it to expand it back when you project it. Even though the lenses may not be technically perfect, there is a richness to looking at that much film material, and I found there is no other way I can get that except in a slower-speed film stock. So for a film that has a lot of dark stuff, we did not use the fastest, most light-sensitive film stocks that were available. I shot all those night scenes at ASA 200 because I didn't want that high-speed grainy look; I wanted it to have that same feel as *Halloween*, so that meant I also had to be very precise in what the shots were going to be because we weren't going to be lighting it up. There were no digital video ways of judging it. You train your eye to see what it is going to see; you see what you shot and move on day by day."

With the visual aesthetic finely honed, the accompanying music would be of utmost importance. For the first time since *Halloween II*, Alan Howarth would not be tasked with providing the score. Instead, Steve Miner had an ear for the work of John Ottman, a multihyphenate composer-editor-director-producer who has, on some projects, worn various combinations of those hats. Ottman made a significant contribution to the success of Bryan Singer's 1995 crime mystery, *The Usual Suspects*, serving as both editor and composer of that fine film, and followed that with Ben Stiller's *The Cable Guy* (1996) and John Badham's *Incognito* (1997), showing remarkable range and distinctive musical signature across multiple genres. Ottman considers the rarity of his multitasking abilities:

"There's not too many of us who do editing and composing, and sometime producing as well, because why would anybody put themselves through that agony. On *The Usual Suspects*, I told Bryan that I just wanted to write the score. But we had just won at the Sundance Film Festival for the previous feature that we did called *Public Access*, on which I had done both the music and the editing, and he said to me, 'You're never going to be the composer for me unless you are the editor.' That's how the blackmail basically began. And then I also ended up at some time producing the film because he wasn't around a lot; so that's my plight."

Ottman is that other rarity of being an autodidact in an industry largely comprising classically trained film composers, which could be some way of understanding the uniqueness and originality of his compositions. Without the strict parameters set by music conservatories and the limits of the theory that they teach, Ottman was able to experiment to find his own musical voice while under the influence of some old masters.

"I am self-taught," he confirms. "If there's a cocktail party with a piano in the room, I'd be really fucked because I cannot play very well. Jerry Goldsmith and John Williams were my teachers just from listening to them, also the original *Star Trek* series because that had a fantastic score written by film composers of the day, luminaries of the time. Of course, they were very motif driven, and they couldn't afford to score every episode. So the music editors were the unsung heroes there because they reused the thematic material and gave the show such thread and consistency. I really absorbed all of that; in fact, a lot of my sensibilities come from that show. And when *Star Trek: The Motion Picture* came out, I, of course, went bananas for the score, which is one of the best scores ever written, and then I went back and listened to every Jerry Goldsmith score that I could hear. So I learned my sensibilities from those guys; they were my teachers."

Ottman continues, "I could write tunes with a pencil way back when I was in high school. And I played the clarinet, and then I went into filmmaking and sort of forgot it all. And then when MIDI technology came along in the '80s, I bought some secondhand equipment and just taught myself how to use it. I went to Tower Records, and they used to have experts working there based on the section. So I went to the classical music section and asked the person there if they could get me every piece of classical music that sounds like film music. And the guy gave me Gustav Holst's *The Planets* and *Sinfonia antartica* and all these other symphonies. I learned them by listening to them. And I would go watch them if they were being performed in my town, and I learned by watching the orchestra. I learned all of this in a very strange way, so I fell into professionally composing. I was always a film score fan. But I was always making movies in my parents' garage since before grade school so by the time I went to USC film school, I was sort of a veteran of making little movies. And then I ended up cutting a film that Bryan was a PA [production assistant] on, someone's thesis project film, and that was how Bryan had a bird's-eye view of what I did. I disassembled the movie and did my stuff, and that's why he hit me up when he had this short 20-minute *Diner*-type movie that he did, which I ended up codirecting with him for reasons that are hilarious but which I won't go into. So I was always a filmmaker. And then I fell into the music thing, and I loved it; it's like giving birth to something. I love editing because of the power and the control over the project, but it's such a long haul; it's a year or two of your life, or you can compose and be in and out in a couple of months."

Steve Miner envisioned his *Halloween* sequel breaking tradition by bringing in a thematic Bernard Herrmann–style soundtrack, which would, indeed, be unusual for the franchise, as John Carpenter and Alan Howarth's music had always excelled in its minimalist electronic modes. Ottman would endeavor not to deviate too far with either approach, accepting Miner's request while honoring what came before. Ottman would incorporate the essential elements of Carpenter's original score and infuse it with the grandeur of an orchestral revision, as he recalls:

"Steve had heard my work, and thought I would be the guy to do something along those lines. When we met and he told me what he wanted, I was like, 'Hell yeah! I'm totally onboard with that concept; that would be fun.' When he referenced Bernard Herrmann's stuff, it meant that I had a license to use a big orchestra, even though we had no budget. But the concept was to make it feel like it was a big orchestra. So I used this tiny little orchestra in a small studio here in the Valley [San Fernando Valley]. I didn't have a long time to work on the score, maybe about eight weeks, which can be enough time; I've done scores in two or three weeks sometimes. But there was no budget. It was like a package deal where I was responsible for delivering the whole thing. They give you money, and you take what you want from it. But in a lot of those cases, the composer will do a synthesized score because they can just take all the money. But I never did that; I always spent a lot of it or most of it on recording with a real group. So we had an illegal date behind closed doors with union musicians in a little studio in the Valley. They call it a 'dark date' because you are using musicians who shouldn't be doing it because they are part of the union; we also had some nonunion guys in there as well. I was excited about doing it with this approach because then I could take the John Carpenter material and make it big and orchestral in a way it had never been heard before, especially the staccato piano rhythm. The Carpenter score is so simple. You don't even need to look up the written score; you can just listen to it and play it on your keyboard. That simplicity is what makes it work so well and goes right to the core of dread. Those big ominous chords behind the main melody give it the sound of oppressive horror that gets right to you, and it is super memorable immediately. So turning Carpenter's main theme into a big orchestral Bernard Herrmann–esque kind of thing was fun for me; I loved doing that and coming up with a secondary theme within that for Laurie Strode. Steve was a pretty laid-back director, which I love! He wasn't breathing down my neck or coming into my studio and standing there while I'm trying to play something, which is my worst nightmare; it's like when someone stands over you when you're trying to type. He was very receptive to my ideas, and he liked how I could push the film further and make it work; he trusted me and let me do my thing. And I loved that."

Unfortunately, things didn't quite go to plan. Dimension Films bosses Bob and Harvey Weinstein, who had meddled so detrimentally with *Halloween: The Curse of Michael Myers*, were unaware of the kind of score that Steve Miner wanted Ottman to write and were not best pleased with the idea of incorporating music that would evoke an older style of composition. And so, on the demands of the Weinsteins, the music editors would reduce Ottman's score and stitch together elements from Marco Beltrami's music from previous Dimension properties, *Scream*, *Scream 2*, and *Mimic*, to score portions of the film. Ottman recalls the debacle that ensued:

"The Weinsteins assumed that I would do what a lot of composers do, which is to rip off the temp score, because the film was testing very well with the audience using Marco Beltrami's music from *Mimic* and *Scream* for the temp score. So from a producer's point of view, it was a case of 'if it ain't broke, don't fix it,' because the audience liked the movie; so they didn't want to change anything. It was all unknown to me that this was happening, and it was all unknown to them that I was writing this Bernard Herrmann score. So when they heard it, they were like, 'What the fuck is this?' There was a very nice note from one of the Weinstein brothers that said, 'The score is extremely thoughtful, too thoughtful for this movie.' But unfortunately, a lot of those ideas were thrown by the wayside, and then they threw in this frenetic, crazy *Scream* music and stuff. I strongly believe that if you can make people care for the characters, then you can make them believe in the world the story is set in. If you immediately walk in and hear screeching violins, then the audience is going to pull back from the film and look at it as more of a joke. So my concept was to pull people in, but that approach was ultimately thrown out. So we needed to make it all clanks and bangs and to make it obvious. So from there, we had to go put the score through a Cuisinart and chop it up. As it remains now, it's my score, then 30 seconds of *Mimic*, then back to my score, then *Mimic* again, and then four minutes of my score. In my view, it is a train wreck of ideas and styles. Steve was so checked out during all this process that it really became his editor's task. I guess to anyone unaware of all this, it worked, but to me it's frustrating because there's certain cues where I had done the John Carpenter motifs and I thought that at least those should have been preserved. My score would have elevated the film and made it bigger, but not elevate it in such a way that it wouldn't have made it scary anymore. But that was the idea, was something richer. Listening back to it now without the emotional attachment that I had to it at the time, I can hear a lot of it is standard orchestration stuff, but it all came from the characters or from the psychology that was under the surface of a scene, whatever the pain of the characters was. It was too deep for the movie. There are little musical cues from the first film that I recorded and wanted to put into the score. They were kinds of things that I thought would really turn on the audience . . . but I got deep-sixed. There was no soundtrack release because the Weinstein brothers felt that it would expose the drama that went on behind the movie and what happened, and some people thought that they didn't want to be seen as being guilty for having dumped a full, thoughtful score. So it meant I had to release my own album, but I couldn't call it *Halloween H20*."

As with the previous sequel, Dimension Films was not keen on playing ball with the media regarding publicity and preview material, a stance further cemented given various production issues with the film. Tony Timpone recalls the lack of assistance *Fangoria* received when trying to hype the sequel to their readers: "When it got to *H20*, I couldn't even do a cover because they wouldn't supply any photos. And there was only the one image of Michael Myers that they released, and it was the one that you see in the trailer with Laurie looking through the door and she sees Michael; that was the only shot of Michael. The Weinsteins made it a real challenge for us to cover *Halloween 6* and *H20* because of the way they controlled things. It was all made worse because they were having a lot of trouble with the look of Michael in the movie; they had to do a lot of reshoots with the mask, as they weren't happy. So that might be why they didn't give us the photos we wanted, but I was getting excuses like, 'Oh, we want to preserve the mystery of Michael Myers.' They said they wanted to keep him hidden, which never made any sense because everybody who has seen the previous films knows what Michael Myers looks like. So that was another kind of argument I was getting, that they wanted to keep the mystique of the character, even though he had been overexposed countless times already."

Despite the issues that the film faced, it was released to a very warm reception in August 1998 and quickly became the most financially successful film of the franchise until David Gordon Green's 2018 sequel. With Jamie Lee Curtis's presence giving the film some canonical authority, as well as grounding it in the diegetic worlds of the first two films, it was giving fan service before fan service truly became something of a unique selling point in today's franchise-heavy marketplace, the kind seen with the aforementioned Green film and its two sequels. *Halloween H20* also had the added appeal of up-and-coming stars Josh Hartnett, who was poised for teen idol status, and Michelle Williams of the fresh-faced ensemble on the popular television drama *Dawson's Creek*. This film would be both Hartnett's and Williams's feature debut, and pairing them with Curtis gave the film a greater commercial advantage and afforded it a much wider demographic to appeal to beyond the horror fan base that other entries in the franchise only considered appeasing.

For Ottman, the wounds of his brush with Michael Myers (or perhaps more precisely, the Weinsteins) were too raw to appreciate the film upon release, and it has taken time for him to consider it all. While still hurt by what occurred, he remains sanguine in his acknowledgment of what was achieved under difficult circumstances and the collaborations it led to:

"I still don't have enough separation from it; I'm unable to disassociate myself from everything that happened. It was very traumatic at the time to be there at the dub stage and basically bartering and arguing about what cues they're going to dump and which ones they're going to put back in. When the film came out, I didn't go to see it, and I didn't attend the premiere because I was so upset at the time. Since then, I've seen it on TV. And I still think it's a hodgepodge score, and it bothers me because I always see what the film could have been. There's just no flow to the music in the movie because it just gets interrupted by the other stuff that was not originally part of the plan. The Bernard Herrmann *Psycho* theme reference is a residual of the score that I was writing. It felt so natural when that came in because of this whole pastiche that I had done. But now it sticks out as a joke, and it is a great in-joke for people who know *Psycho*. Thank God that got preserved. I've seen videos where fans have reconstructed my score from the tracks on my album, and they have put the whole thing together on top of the movie or on scenes from it. I saw one scene where they were running through a forest, and I thought, 'Okay, maybe that piece was a little too thoughtful.' Maybe I should have just done some crazy shit there, but not to the extent that they did in the final version. I'm glad people like it and dig up the original score and give it some life. It would be cool to be able to go back and do a real mix with my original score; that could be fun. I'm proud of many parts of it, particularly the main theme and some cues, but if I were to tier my favorite scores, I wouldn't put it near the top."

The composer continues, "This was early in my career, and I was horrified about the situation. But as a filmmaker and knowing the producer mindset, I understand why they did what they did. Whether it was the right choice or not, we'll never know because they never released the film with my full score to see how that would have done, but I understand their way of thinking because they had test screenings that were going through the roof and they had that temp score on there for those screenings.

And if I were the producer, I would be terrified to go a whole other route and release the movie without testing it. If there had been time, I would have pressed them and said, 'Why don't you dub the film with my score and then test it and see how it compares to the other one.' It probably would have tested the same, or maybe more, who knows? But there was no time. So they had to go with what they were working with, and I understand that. Despite everything that happened, I'm pretty glad that a good chunk of my score was preserved in the final cut. And I got to work with Steve again on *Lake Placid*. He felt terrible about what happened on *Halloween H20*. But he loved what I had done, so he just let me go for it on *Lake Placid*. That was a fun score to do, and it all remained intact. There were some issues with postproduction on *Lake Placid* when the temp score wasn't really working, which was great because I could just come in and dump it and do my thing."

For Daryn Okada, knowing how badly the previous three films were received by some, he wasn't quite prepared for the huge embrace that would await Michael Myers when in the company of his little sister, Laurie Strode. "I went into it unsure if it would be written off because it was a sequel, being the seventh movie in a franchise, and people were just trying to make money off it. But Jamie was totally onboard with everything. She had worked with Steve before, and it was a fantastic time; it was like we were making the first *Halloween* movie. And our goal was not to make it bigger or more spectacular but to try and get into the character more and stay in that world and have it that nothing much changed in those 20 years. Steve and I flew down from shooting *Lake Placid* to attend the premiere, and then we went right back. But then it opened and we heard that the audiences liked it, the critics seemed to appreciate it, and it became successful. That was a great feeling."

"I was a fan of *H20*," Timpone admits, "but the problem I had with the film is that aesthetically it feels more like a *Scream* movie and less like a *Halloween* movie, even though Jamie Lee Curtis is terrific in it. But whatever kind of excitement they had built up with *H20*, especially with bringing back the character of Laurie Strode, casting Jamie Lee, and connecting it back to the first two movies, they killed all that excitement and goodwill with *Halloween: Resurrection*. That film was just another routine movie like *Part 6*, a straight formula horror movie."

"Trick or treat, motherfucker!" —Freddie Harris

Halloween: Resurrection picks up three years later from *Halloween H20*. That film arrived with a sense of prestige, or at least a sense of importance, within the context of horror cinema and the *Halloween* franchise due to the return of Jamie Lee Curtis and the attendant legitimacy that carried. *Halloween: Resurrection*, however, feels much more formulaic, like one of the other franchise sequels that Dimension Films was in the habit of releasing, but entertainingly so and albeit with a higher budget and production values. Its goals aren't anything as lofty as continuing or concluding a legacy in any definitive manner (despite Laurie Strode's death here, Jamie Lee Curtis would return eventually); rather, it aims simply to please. The film unspools with immediacy and without any precredit sequence to shock us into the first act. The credits roll on; before we know it, we see Laurie Strode dispatched in what feels like a contractually obliged kill-off, or perhaps kiss-off, but a well-mounted one at that.

The film opens in a sanitarium where Laurie Strode is presently locked up after it is revealed the man in the mask that she decapitated at the end of the previous film was not Michael Myers but was, in fact, a paramedic whose larynx Michael crushed and then switched clothes with. As always, Laurie is anticipating her brother's arrival to once again sever their familial connection for good. This time he succeeds. Cut to a year later, and we once again get the *Scream* vibes as a bunch of hip, self-aware college students are chosen from a competition to appear in a supposedly innovative Internet reality show called Dangertainment being directed by fame-seeking Freddie Harris (Busta Rhymes) and Nora Winston (Tyra Banks). The contest that the college students must endure is to spend Halloween night in the old Myers house. Webcams will be set up throughout the house to document their efforts and reactions to various obstacles and scary props. They will also be equipped with the 2002 equivalent of GoPro cameras so that viewers of the show will experience the trials and terror of the contestants subjectively. What the stars and viewers of Dangertainment don't realize is that Michael Myers (Brad Loree) is coming home again, and he doesn't take kindly to strangers in his house. By the end of the night, when Freddie is asked by a news reporter what he can tell her about Michael Myers, the entrepreneurial director will have a revelation that also functions as an ironic self-reflexive response to audiences of the *Halloween* franchise itself: "Michael Myers is not a sound bite, a spin-off, a tie-in, some sort of celebrity scandal. Michael Myers is a killer shark in baggy-ass overalls that gets his kicks off of killing everything and everyone that he comes across. That's all." Indeed! So much for one's deep thematic analysis.

Just when you thought there was no way to bring Michael Myers back to life, having been supposedly decapitated by his axe-wielding sister at the end of *Halloween H20*, what else could resurrect the career of a 1970's and 1980's icon? Well, reality television, of course!

The horror subgenre of the found footage and its various offshoots of surveillance footage/faux documentary/first-person perspective had appeared sporadically across cinema history of the past 50 years, with the likes of Ruggero Deodato's controversial 1980 film *Cannibal Holocaust* being the most infamous and notable example. It would be almost two decades later when the style was popularized and brought to cultural consciousness with the phenomenal success of Daniel Myrick and Eduardo Sanchez's *The Blair Witch Project* in 1999, a film that captured the attention of audiences with its claims to reality and grainy handheld 16-millimeter production values. When technology permitted in the 2000s, the craze truly took off. Low-budget productions could now use their limitations as an aesthetic device and make huge profits, as did *Paranormal Activity* (Oren Peli [2007]), *Rec* (Jaume Balagueró and Paco Plaza [2007]), the anthological *V/H/S* (multiple directors [2012]), and others in becoming

Halloween: Resurrection **(2002) poster art.** Miramax Films/Photofest ©Miramax Films

franchise mainstays. Soon, it was the stuff of mainstream cinema, as blockbuster producer J. J. Abrams partnered with Paramount to release *Cloverfield* in 2008. Even legends of the horror genre, such as George Romero, got in on the act with *Diary of the Dead* that same year. And it has persisted ever since, becoming a fixture of the straight-to-video world and oversaturating the independent horror industry, with only the occasional title, such as *Project X*, produced by Todd Phillips and released by Warner Brothers in 2012, being novelty enough as a found footage comedy to make it to the big screen.

Rarely discussed within this generic context, however, is *Halloween: Resurrection*. Partly because the film breaks the illusion of being found/surveillance/webcam footage by cutting back to its traditional fiction film narrative, but the picture does function much along the lines of the subgenre's form and also from the *Big Brother*–style surveillance camera aesthetic. Created by Dutch media tycoon John de Mol Jr., *Big Brother* was the modestly produced show launched in 1999 that swiftly became a television sensation in the same year that *The Blair Witch Project* turned cheap into commercial within the film world; the influential show featured contestants directly addressing the audience in a confessional manner while the main voyeuristic aesthetic of the show was presenting the action in a seemingly authentic real-time observatory situation, as *Halloween: Resurrection* adopts for Freddie and Nora's webcam show.

Brad Loree, the man behind the Michael Myers mask, acknowledges the film's foresight and anticipation of surveillance entertainment as a low-risk/big-reward potential for production companies, such as the film's fictional Dangertainment. "*Halloween: Resurrection* was ahead of its time in a lot of ways, with the way Deckard and Sarah are text messaging, the Facetime kind of stuff, and the parody of online reality shows. They made a reference to *Survivor*, which was the big reality TV show at the time."

Cinematographer David Geddes was instrumental in creating the dual aesthetic on which the film functions entertainingly. Geddes had worked prolifically in television through the mid-1980s and early 1990s photographing the popular youth-oriented dramas *21 Jump Street* and *Beverly Hills, 90210* before going deeply into the direct-to-video and made-for-television market. *Halloween: Resurrection* was to be his first major theatrical feature film, and it all came from a phone call from an agent who knew director Rick Rosenthal, who was returning to the franchise after delivering the solid first sequel, *Halloween II*. Geddes and Rosenthal were a good match personally and professionally, finding common ground on what the style of the film should be and developing their approach as the project progressed. Geddes reveals how the film's novel aesthetic emerged from his work on the hit TV show *Dark Angel*:

"Rick and I worked out the photographic style together. Some of it I brought with me from doing the TV show *Dark Angel*; I had just finished season one or two of that. I had been experimenting with looks for that show, such as the use of pacific blue lighting, which transferred nicely over to *Halloween: Resurrection*; that was used as a dystopia look for *Dark Angel*, but it worked in the context of *Halloween* too. The use of digital video cameras for the reality show look was interesting because that technology was new to all of us. I had never worked with it before, and it was complicated to get it to be technically acceptable. The wireless setups were nothing like we have now, where we have itty-bitty cameras that you can paste to your forehead and that's all you need. But back then, we had power packs and transmitters and things that had to be hidden in the wardrobe. It was at times clunky, but it did help the film look different and give it a sense of reality. In fact, looking back at it, I realize that the clunkiness of it added to the reality of it. It was gritty and grainy. All that footage was done on the fly; they turned the cameras on and basically recorded 24/7. It must have been a nightmare for the editors to cherry-pick all of the pieces that ended up in the film, and that is like true documentary filmmaking, where everything was somebody's POV [point of view]. A lot of it we step back from to tell the story, and we continue for a long time with that handheld feeling so that it wouldn't be a big jump with that particular look."

While this unpredictable and loosely filmed footage was a major element of the film, and a technical challenge at that, there was also the more traditionally disciplined and refined film photography to deal with. With the bar set very high throughout the *Halloween* films, thanks to the stunning camerawork and lighting styles of Dean Cundey, Peter Lyons Collister, Rob Draper, Billy Dickson, and Daryn Okada, Geddes would be joining a list of considerable talent in bringing his own unique aesthetic to the *Halloween* franchise. Geddes reveals an insight into his approach:

"The biggest thing with horror is that darkness is your friend; there is always that infamous scare of things coming out of the dark. You don't want to give the audience too much information; you want to let them use their imagination to figure out things like whether it's a person or a monster or a creature, whatever it is. You are treading that fine edge; you don't want it murky, black-gray nothingness; there needs to be detail but not detail to the point that the mystery can be easily recognized. I did go back and look at some of the previous films, but the producers didn't handcuff us at all; they let us go forward and put it together as we felt. We didn't have a lot of time, and it wasn't a particularly big-budget project. But we did work with color schemes and went back to figure out the level of darkness and how much we wanted to show and how much we didn't want to show. It was all challenging, but the hardest thing in terms of the cinematography is to not light or to light and then eliminate light; it's a lot of work. With a day exterior, you say, 'Okay, let's shadow this and shadow that.' But a lot of the time, the treatment that you want to give the scary stuff means you've got flags going up because you've got to get rid of that light and so on. It was up to us as to how we wanted to shoot Michael Myers, but of course, he's got that white mask, which is difficult to deal with in the dark. But a lot of that was the actual actor, Brad Loree; Rick worked with him a lot to get the physical motion of the character right because you're not seeing any facial expressions because of the mask. It was really good the way he worked with him to get the body movements just enough that you know not only is he scary but that he is strong. A lot of the time, we gave Brad even more detail because we needed to see more of him; we had wide shots and needed to sell that sense of him being out there."

Of all the actors in the franchise, Loree is the one who had the advantage of being lit in such a way that he is visibly expressive through his eyes as well as his physical gestures. The weight of such was not lost on the actor, who studied those who set the template, as he reveals:

"I watched all the Michael Myers, and in particular, I looked at Uncle Dick—who is Dick Warlock, but I call him Uncle Dick—and I looked at Nick Castle. I looked at the way he walks across the street toward Laurie Strode and the kids that she is looking after; it's that long walk, and I watched it over and over and over. Rick Rosenthal described it as it's like your upper body is sitting on a pedestal made of your hips and legs and your legs are just transporting your upper body—you don't swing your arms. It's so methodical that it's almost robotic. That was good direction to have because when I first went in to meet the executives about doing it, I quickly realized that all they were looking for is someone who understands English. And everybody was there. You'd swear it was so important, but the truth is they might as well have been looking for a guy to transport the mask around. I was the only person they looked at; it was like, 'Yeah, you'll do!' The producer and cowriter of the original *Halloween*, Debra Hill, apparently wore the mask in one shot of that film, among others. When they fired Tom Morga off *Halloween 4*, they hired George Wilbur to be Michael Myers. Well, there's a difference in height, but they don't give a fuck as long as the guy can walk from here to there to stab somebody; that's all they care about. I can tell you I put a lot more thought into the character than they did."

Loree's path to film stunt work began with his interest in karate as a six-year-old kid growing up in a small town outside of Vancouver. It was there that Loree became fascinated with Bruce Lee and martial arts, inspiring him to enroll in the local karate school, where he was instructed by a gentleman named Tony Morelli. He continued his green belt studies all through junior and then senior high school until young love persuaded him onto the rugby fields. While his sporting interests were briefly dictated by his hormones, he soon returned to his passion for martial arts when Morelli returned to town a hero of the discipline.

"I had gotten into rugby because the girl I was in love with was a rugby girl," Loree admits, "but then shortly after I got out of school, I went to the big stadium here in town to see that my former green belt karate instructor was now a full-time professional full-contact kickboxer and he won the world title, which just blew my mind. So I went back to the school, and I told myself that I would find a way to become that guy's sparring partner. And sure, Wayne, I did. He recruited me because I had grown up. And because he was world champion, he started doing commercials here in Vancouver and eventually did stand-in work in the film industry. And then stunt guys said, 'If we have a world champion in our midst, it would be a real feather in our caps,' and they took Tony aside and said, 'You should be a stunt guy.' And they dragged him into the stunt world, and he dragged me along with him because I was his protégé and one of his best friends. I looked up to Tony so much that it never entered my mind that I could ever be on the same playing field as him; if he was a stunt guy, then I was going to be an extra. But it was Ken Kirzinger who took me for a beer after working for Tony one time, and he said, 'Brad, if you get a pager, a headshot, and a résumé, I'll take you around and introduce you to everybody.' And sure enough, us and another guy were inseparable, and that's how I got into stunts full on. I always wanted to be an actor, Wayne, but I didn't have the confidence; my experience was in the stunt world, and that's how I ended up in film."

Loree found work that would ultimately lead to *Halloween*; he was the stunt coordinator and stunt double on a low-budget kids show for Fox called *Los Luchadores*, which was about Mexican wrestlers by day who become crime fighters by night. When the eighth *Halloween* movie was hiring in town, the show's first AD [assistant director] had just finished work on its first season and went to interview for the film, though he had no intention of taking it, as it was merely a professional courtesy and networking opportunity. However, he did recommend Loree to them when the *Halloween* people revealed that they had not yet found their stunt coordinator nor their Michael Myers.

"I was busy working on *Los Luchadores* and making good money," Loree says, "and then one day, when I was driving, I got a call out of the blue from this production manager who said, 'Hey, can you come in to meet the executives?' Because I was driving, I was only half paying attention. And so I thought that they were looking for a stunt double for Mike Myers, as in

Austin Powers, and I thought, 'Boy, his career sure has gone downhill!'"

However, Loree was not a horror-film enthusiast and wasn't too keen to apply, but with the encouragement of those who did know the relevance of *Halloween*, he realized the opportunity was too good not to consider, as he admits, "I was not a horror guy, Wayne. When I was 19 or 20, I dated a girl who loved horror, and when we broke up, I thought, 'Great! I never have to watch horror films again!' Well, suddenly, everyone's talking about this *Halloween* movie. And I had no interest in it, but my cousin told me she really enjoyed the film. And so I rented and watched it and thought, 'Wow! This film is not bloody, it's not gory, it's not overly violent, but it's suspenseful!' and I love suspense. So I went to the interview and met everybody, including the director, then at one point, the producer said, 'Now, Brad, you don't have the job yet; you're the first person we looked at. But if we do decide to go with you, we want you to know that we're going to have to fly you to Los Angeles to cast your head for the mask.' And I said, 'Whoa, whoa, whoa . . . I gotta go to LA just to double some dummy actor?!' And they said, 'No, no—you're not going to double the guy; you are the guy!' And the actor in me said, 'Oh, Brad, you have got to do this!' And so I took the *Halloween* job, and my buddy Dean [Choe] took the *Los Luchadores* job for the second season. As an actor, it's kind of embarrassing because you're wearing a mask and you don't speak the whole time, but as a stunt guy, it's my one day in the spotlight."

After being hired to play the star attraction of the new *Halloween* movie, Loree went to have his head cast for the mask. Being a fan of the bloodless classic original film, the actor anxiously asked producer Malek Akkad just how bloody and gory this sequel was going to be to get a measure of how the filmmakers would be approaching the material. Loree reveals, "Malek told me that what they were trying to do was to go back to the original and that kind of suspense, and so I was really nervous about doing a good job. Even though I didn't have lines to memorize, I wanted to move right and do a really good job. I was so nervous, even in the mask. When I was a kid, there were camera pictures before church on a Sunday morning. And if you had a cowlick, then you got a smack in the head. So it was like I had this existential thing when I had a camera pointed at me. And Rick [Rosenthal, director] did have to remind me a couple of times to move slowly, take my time, that it's not a race. That was important to remember. I really liked Rick. He is a very economical director, and I got along with him very well, except when we had one little issue over the scene where I'm stabbing the guy with the tripod. I'm sure I was listening to everything that he said, but I wasn't doing what he wanted; I don't know if I have ADHD, Wayne, but when I get tired and lazy, my focus goes off. I was not proactively asking a lot of questions because I felt that I was just there as an employee; I wasn't there as part of the collaborative, creative team, so he got a little short with me at some point there. But shooting horror is almost like shooting TV. You only have so much time to get your day's work done; they're on a real tight schedule. We shot for five weeks and had another week of reshoots, so all told, I worked on it for six weeks."

Halloween: Resurrection essentially functions as a "take a bunch of people to a house and chop them up" scenario and is structured within the claustrophobic confines of the long-abandoned Myers family home, which has been set up with

Michael (played by Brad Loree) is ready for a showdown in the fiery basement. Author's Collection

a variety of props and paraphernalia to scare the Dangertainment contestants, so with the majority of the film taking place in a single setting with the illusion of limited space, there were several reasons to have the location built in an environment that could be entirely controlled as required. Cinematographer Geddes reveals the movie magic behind the production:

"It looks like we had limited space within the confines of that house, but we shot that house in a huge construction warehouse. It was a building that was used to construct ships, car ferries, and that type of thing; it was quite huge. The reason we did that is because we shot that show in Vancouver in May/June, and of course, being this far north at that time of year, there is very little night. When you get to the longest day, June 21st, there is only about four to five hours of light, which doesn't give you much time to do what you need. You will have three months of work if you only have half a dozen hours of work every night, so it was necessary for us to build it all on a stage. We also had to build the neighborhood, so we had to construct the houses behind it and the houses beside it and the road in front of the house. We had a huge blue screen, something like 60 feet tall, so we could put in a deep background. It was a big, big setup, but doing it this way gave us a lot of freedom. And the greatest thing was we didn't have to work all night; we could just shoot it during the day because we were onstage. That allowed us so much freedom, such as with the part in the film where Laurie Strode drops off the building down into the trees. That was done for real; it was supposed to be the roof of the clinic, but it was a different building that we dropped her off. But Jamie Lee actually fell into a blue-screen bag. All that other stuff you see there in the shot, such as the trees that she disappears into as she falls, that is all CGI [computer-generated imagery]. That was another reason to build the sets on a stage; it gave us a lot of freedom to develop the look of the film."

Geddes continues, "The daytime exteriors at the start of the film when Busta Rhymes is standing there in the middle of the street looking at the house was shot on location in an actual suburban street, but then everything he is looking at and the house that everybody goes into was shot onstage. That was complicated because it required a huge lighting setup to sell the fact that it was daylight on that set; especially as the exterior location shots were done on a very bright, sunny Vancouver day, and we had to match that. The producers panicked a bit because it was only a few pages in the script to introduce that house in a daytime exterior, but it was probably the most expensive part of it because of the tons of lighting gear and power used to light up that street that we built in that big warehouse. That was a great challenge to do; I think we had enough power to go back to the future, 1.1 gigawatts! It worked because it had to. But once that was out of the way, it was all-night shooting, which was great because being onstage you can rig the lights however you like and put stuff wherever you want. When you are shooting practically and on location, you come up against it because you might need to put a light in the neighbor's backyard, and then you have to go wake them up to ask permission. But we owned it all, so we had total control over what we could do physically; it was just a matter of doing whatever needed to be done. It was also a lot better in terms of safety because we had people climbing out of windows and on the roof. But we could put all the required safety gear in there, and they were easy to reach with different types of cranes. I love the challenge of working on a film like this. A director or stunt coordinator will come to me, and we'll get into discussion about how things should be done, when we ask each other, 'How do we do this?'"

"I had some of those questions!" Loree admits. "The stunt where Busta Rhymes kicks me through the window, they wanted me to start my backwards run from about six feet, and I'm telling you, Wayne, I had no room to spare on either side of my shoulders because it was a bedroom window, which was kind of narrow. A couple of times during rehearsal, I caught myself on either side, so I was nervous about whether I was going to get through there. But on the actual take, I made it through there, and that was the one where I was nervous about how it would go. There was also the moment where I roll off the roof, and I'm hanging. We were very careful, of course; I'm in a harness. But I must have had 12 feet of rope, and anything can go wrong with 12 feet of rope if you were to get tangled in it. My dad was there to watch it, and when I described everything to him, he almost had a heart attack! If you look closely at the moment that Jamie and I go over the side of the roof with the rope rig on my legs, when I'm reaching back, the idea is he is hanging on with his right hand, and he is reaching out to her with his left hand. After she drops, you can see that because of the angle and my inflexibility because the way my arm was twisted, I could only hang on with two fingers, and I haven't had anybody come back to me having noticed that. But if you look at it, you can see that it looks like he is hanging on with only two fingers. Hanging on was very difficult, even though I was cabled in, but whatever the angle my arm was at, I just couldn't hang on with my full hand. The scene where I'm in the garage on fire and I sit up, that was tough too; there were a couple of times when I had to squirm away from the fire because I tell you, it was hot!"

Geddes continues, revealing further logistical complications: "A lot of the more difficult stuff was in the basement when we had it collapsing and some of the tunnel work because we couldn't just build a big tunnel to work in comfortably; it had to be a creepy, slimy little tunnel, so that gets complicated to light. The hospital scenes with Jamie Lee Curtis were a real location. It was an old hospital, and interestingly, that building was a psychiatric ward with bars on the windows, the weird hallways, and the big locking doors; that was all practical. So we didn't have to do much with that. We put some new paint in and aged

Evil ensnared. Author's Collection

down a lot of the set. It's a government-owned building; it's not very expensive to use, so it is a popular place to shoot. It really does have a great look. I shot there going back to *21 Jump Street*. The biggest tunnel there is under the building, like a dirt hallway underground that we used to shoot for the beginning and the end when he is walking in and out."

Once the principal photography was in the can, it was time to layer on that most crucial element of a *Halloween* experience, the music. After the debacle of the score on *Halloween H20*, composer John Ottman was never going to return, so producers had to look elsewhere. Miramax music executive Randy Spendlove had been impressed by the speed and skill of erstwhile television composer Danny Lux after he had been enlisted to help save the score of a recent production; spotting someone who could produce results with great economy, Spendlove approached Lux about providing the score for *Halloween: Resurrection*. This would be Lux's major feature debut after two decades working in television music, with credits that include hit shows, such as *Ally McBeal*, *Dawson's Creek*, *Party of Five*, and *NYPD Blue*.

Like Ottman before him, Lux is an autodidact, having learned music himself rather than academically, nor did he have any ambitions on going into film and television scoring. As a drummer with intentions on going down the band route, music theory was something he felt he didn't need in order to write and perform his own work, and what he did learn of the craft was through his accidental apprenticeship with legendary television music man Mike Post. Lux became a protégé of the prolific composer of memorable theme tunes from *The A-Team*, *Magnum P.I.*, *Hardcastle and McCormick*, *NYPD Blue*, and *Murder One*, among many others. Lux lucked into this crucial collaboration when he was only a couple of weeks out of high school back in 1987. One day, an employee of Mike Post was looking for a music store in Burbank, California, but mistakenly walked into the print shop owned by Lux's father. That misstep would change young Lux's life, as he recalls:

"My dad wasn't super supportive of the music thing back then, but he asked this guy, whose name was Charlie, what he was looking for. And Charlie says, 'I'm looking for this music store,' which was actually just across the street, and my dad perked up and said, 'Oh, my son is into music.' And Charlie gave my dad a phone number and said, 'Have him call us! Maybe we'll have something for him.' So I did, and about two weeks later, I got hired to help put together three keyboard setups and an electronic drum setup because they were still doing every score with about 30 musicians. So right out of high school, I started doing that. I kind of fell into it, and I was just hanging out watching these sessions go down and troubleshooting during the sessions. And then that led to Mike hiring me to be his gofer, his studio guy. And that guy Charlie, who walked into the wrong place, and which led to me getting this job, quit after about a year, and then Mike gave me another opportunity. I was already pretty adept as an engineer because I had been doing it all through my teen years as well as producing, so he would have me work on a few things. And he was impressed enough that I became his engineer at the age of 19, and by 21, I was writing on some of his shows. But my ending up as a composer for film and television was a total fluke because I don't come from a music theory background; I'm totally self-taught. The only thing I really studied for a long time was drums, and that doesn't really translate to this stuff. I came up through Mike Post and learned the craft working for him. The music that he writes for TV is kind of a different genre than some of the more sophisticated harmonic stuff in film. I've studied some of it on my own, and I've a fair amount of knowledge now. But it's all self-taught and self-learned; I didn't come out of a university system or anything. But I worked with Mike for nine years, and when I left, my career just exploded. Right out of the gate I had multiple TV series and have ever since."

With consistent work within the television industry, Lux only felt the pull of the film world after he switched representatives in 2001. His new agency had merged with another company that was focused on getting their clients work in film, and being that he hadn't done much film work to this point, he felt it was time to take advantage of what they had to offer. The first opportunity to come up was the Wayans brothers' spoof sequel *Scary Movie 2*, which was being produced by Miramax's horror division Dimension Films. What should have been Lux's first major score for a film ended up being an unfortunate experience, one that yielded the positive result of getting hired for *Halloween: Resurrection*.

"*Scary Movie 2* had its score thrown out, and they were panicking," Lux recalls. "So they had me and another composer come in for a couple of days; it was a weird experience. It was like, 'Watch the movie, pick some scenes, and start rewriting the score!' Ahhh, okay! So I rewrote a few cues, and this other guy probably did too, and then in a couple of days, we were told, 'Go ahead and stop because we just hired Marco Beltrami and his team. They are going to rescore the whole movie in four days with 11 or 12 people writing on it.' Ultimately, I think I have two cues in the movie. Randy Spendlove, who was head of film music at Miramax at the time, was impressed enough to say, 'You only worked on it for two days, and you did a great job!' and through his relationship with one of the agents, I got mentioned for a new *Halloween* film that was coming up at the time. But right before then, there was a series on HBO called *Project Greenlight* that Matt Damon and Ben Affleck were executive producers on. It was like a contest where the author of the winning script was made to direct the movie. So Miramax made me the composer of that movie, which was called *Stolen Summer*. It was a fun experience. I only had nine days to do it, but it came out good. Because of those two experiences with Miramax, I was offered *Halloween* when that came up. I was like, 'Wow!' because I love the franchise; I thought it would be such a blast just to do one of them. I remember being invited down to a screening of the movie, and there were about 30 or 40 people present in this small screening room. Robert Rodriguez was there watching it, and a few other people that I recognized. I wasn't totally sure that I had the movie at that point, but talking to them afterwards, it sounded like the job was mine. So it was like, 'Oh, okay, great!'"

Knowing about what had happened to John Ottman and his score on *Halloween H20*, Lux was careful to approach his compositions with limited ambitions to Hitchcockian themes and melodies. Lux shares Ottman's love of Bernard Herrmann, John Williams, and Jerry Goldsmith, but he knew it was important to deliver what was expected, which was to keep it simple and keep it fun.

"*H20* is a cool movie," Lux says, "but I heard the story about John Ottman getting most of his music thrown out because the Weinsteins said, 'This doesn't sound like music for a *Halloween* movie!' And then they ended up tracking a bunch of the music from Marco Beltrami's *Scream* score. So when I got onboard this one and talked with Rick Rosenthal and the producer Paul Freeman, everyone was hyperaware of what had happened on the previous movie's music, and so the basic overall instruction was to make a fun slasher movie score; don't get all Hitchcock on us. The previous score for *H20* was trying to pull from Herrmann, but my approach to this score was fairly ambient at times because if I remember right, they tend to have much of the scenes in the house scored with this really low-ambient rumble. It's there throughout the whole thing, and so I was hyperaware they were keeping that and it was needed to keep it part of the soundscape of the movie. So a lot of the score is creepy and ambient. And then there's a lot of action, and there's certainly a bunch of jump scares in the movie, which gives it that dynamic with the quieter stuff."

Lux continues: "We talked about reusing some themes from the original film, but ultimately, I only reused the main theme. John Carpenter has made a lot of scores, but I don't think any of them are anywhere near as good as the *Halloween* one. There is something about it, especially when you consider the time that it happened; you can't help but realize how much of an interesting score it is, a very smart score. Every time I go back and watch the original now, I wish I had paid more respect to some of the other themes, which are pretty cool, but nonetheless, that's not how it went down. Basically, every time Michael appeared onscreen, the main theme is reprised a little bit, and it is fun to redo that theme in general. My approach was just to give the classic theme a new production. And the process was fairly easy, although the biggest bummer for me was I got hired and it's a horror movie, so the first question I had was, 'Am I going to get a real orchestra?' because especially back in 2002, the samples for orchestral stuff are not what they are today; they were really in their infancy back then. With a real orchestra, you can do some crazy-sounding effects, but unfortunately, they told me from the onset to 'write it like you're not going to have one.' And I'm like, 'Man, that really boxes me in,' compared to them saying I can have one. In the end, they gave me a little bit of money to bring in 28 players, not a giant orchestra, but we recorded with them and put that on top of what I had done. We kept everything that I had done because it was enough that the score was done if we didn't have anything else, but it was there if I was allowed to bring in other players to enhance and double pieces. So I think we added about 15 strings, some brass and woodwinds, and just went to town on it a bit more. I had at least three orchestrators that I brought in at the very end, and I said, 'Let's just go nuts!' So we enhanced things with some scary woodwind stuff and some scary string stuff; so that's the kind of thing we added with the real instruments. It was kind of a bummer that they didn't give me that from the get-go, but the biggest bummer was that there was around 63 minutes of score for that movie, and I remember I was writing the last six-minute cue when I got a phone call saying, 'Hey, stop! We're not going to release it this Halloween.' I was literally about half a day away from finishing the thing, and they had tabled it for five or six months away. Then they called me back in after they had reshot a bunch of stuff and recut a lot of it, so I had to throw out about 80% of what I had done because it didn't fit anymore. So I had to go and do it a second time."

After sampling the unpredictably and ever-evolving nature of feature film scoring, Lux returned to the world of television scoring and to great success, including composing music for long-running hit shows, such as *Boston Legal*, *My Name Is Earl*, *The Good Wife*, and *Grey's Anatomy*. "I spend most of my time focusing on TV," the composer confirms, "because that's where I came up and I kind of like the high turnover rate in TV. After being on *Halloween: Resurrection* for nine months, I knew going forward that I didn't want to spend nine months on a single project again. I like people to make quick decisions and then move on to the next one. Nor have I received more offers to do the score for similar movies. Strangely enough, I've just done

one other horror movie. And they are fun to do, but TV shows have a strict schedule where no matter what I'm working on, I only have a couple days to do it and then I'm on to the next thing. And I like that."

Halloween: Resurrection would be the last film in what one might refer to as the formal franchise before Rob Zombie's two films would remake and reinterpret the origins of the characters and their milieu and before David Gordon Green would direct his own trilogy to function as a belated sequel to only John Carpenter's original film. For several of those involved in the creation of the eighth *Halloween* film, it would be their first and last involvement with the franchise; for some, it was a brief detour before life and work took them elsewhere; for others, the legacy looms large.

"I only saw *Halloween: Resurrection* in a theater one time," Lux admits, "and it was an early screening. And it actually sounded kind of weird, and I don't know if it was the theater or what. But the way it was mixed made it sound so wet; I thought they might have screwed it up, and I was kind of disappointed. When I hear it now, it's usually on a TV broadcast, and I don't hear that same issue. So it could have been a technical issue with the theater that we were in. But it was a lot of fun to go watch it in a theater with all the fans because they have such a good time watching these movies. And then when John Carpenter's theme came up, man, they just howled and screamed. *Resurrection* is not the most amazing *Halloween* movie that there is. It was super fun to do; I just love being part of the *Halloween* franchise. I enjoyed the experience of working with Rick Rosenthal; he came with the history of having done the second movie, and he was an easygoing guy to work with. He may not have had the best movie to make, but I thought he did a great job with what he had to work with. And having a chance to work in the horror genre is about as much fun as you can have as a composer. I still like to listen back to some of the cues occasionally, and I still think, 'Hey, that sounds pretty cool!' I don't get to write stuff like that; it's a lot different to writing something for *Grey's Anatomy*, which I've been doing for 19 years now. I do get a kick out of knowing I did a score for one of those films and that I'm a part of that franchise."

"*Halloween: Resurrection* was a fun experience," Geddes admits. "It was a lot of fun to shoot, and I'm certainly pleased with the end product. We shot several endings, but I was happy with the ending that made the final cut. I think they wanted something more in-depth. The original one we shot was fairly simplistic, so they just developed the story better with the ending they eventually went with, which was a stronger ending. Strangely enough, I don't get constant contact about *Halloween*, but I do get a lot of phone calls and emails for my Carpenter connection with *The Thing* [1982], on which I was second assistant. Even working with special effects people on new shows, they are all over me asking about *The Thing*. Up to that point, *Halloween: Resurrection* was my first major crack at the horror genre, so it was a fun challenge to figure all of that out. I like doing big shows and the small shows, but getting in there and doing huge shows is very rewarding. Of course, you can get bogged down a bit because it takes so long and you get distanced a little bit from the storytelling, from the emotion of it."

For Loree, as for anybody else who assumes the infamous visage of Michael Myers, stepping into that mask meant becoming the logo of a legendary franchise and symbol of something greater than a single film; he has now become part of horror-film history. With 20 years having passed since the film's release, Loree contemplates his place within the franchise and the responsibility that assuming such an iconic role can place upon those who accept it:

"I have had a lot of feedback about the job that I did on the film, and Dick Warlock has even stated publicly in the media that he thought I was the best Michael Myers. I appreciate that over the moon and back, Wayne, but Nick Castle and Dick Warlock will always be Michael Myers to me. Now that the film is 20 years old, there's all these guys in their early to mid-30s that say *Halloween: Resurrection* was the first *Halloween* movie that they saw, so I am Michael Myers to this new generation of *Halloween* fans. I went to my first convention in about 2004 because every five years, they hold these anniversary conventions for the franchise in Pasadena, where they shot the first one. Well, I had people coming up to me tearing strips off me left, right, and center for having gotten beaten up by Busta Rhymes! I'm like, 'Well, yeah, it was in the script!' They're chewing me out like it was my fault. 'Dude, I'm just the stunt guy reading the script!' Years later, they came to town to do the *Freddy vs. Jason* film, and the producer of that had seen me being interviewed on the set of *Halloween: Resurrection*. And one of the questions I was asked was, 'Why is Michael Myers the way he is?' and this producer was super impressed with how much thinking and acting I put into it. So that producer had me come in and be interviewed to play Jason, but the director was like, 'Sorry, man, but you're not tall enough.' Then I thought, 'Well, I hope my buddy Ken Kirzinger gets the job!' And sure enough, they interviewed a million guys; they looked at the whole cattle call. And they came back to Kenny, and he got that job. So we go and do the same conventions having both played these iconic characters."

Loree continues, "I remember the last day, we were in this big, giant studio, and Rick had pieced together this 15-minute teaser for the stuff with Jamie. And so we're all watching it, and I'm standing there holding hands with my girlfriend. And when Michael was walking down the tunnel, she squeezed my hand because she was getting scared, and I was getting a little nervous too because Michael Myers has always freaked me out. But then I'm like, 'Wait a minute . . . that's me!' We had a good laugh at that. I thought the acting in the film was great. I was so impressed with all those kids; I got so close to all of them. I'm happy with my performance. And I wish that I got to do it more than once, but it just happened to be the one *Halloween* film that they photographed here in Vancouver. *Halloween: Resurrection* had such a great script, and I just wanted to do the best that I could. The more I watch *Halloween: Resurrection* today, the more I appreciate it."

Chapter Five

All in the Family

> "That is not appropriate babysitter behavior!" —Tommy Doyle

Since the 1980s and the rise of the franchise sequel, brand-name recognition has become crucial to the marketing of horror products. The revolutionary New Hollywood movement, which arguably spanned the mid-1960s to the early 1980s, had produced auteur filmmakers who made some of the most provocative, daring, and artistically unique horror movies that Hollywood had ever released. Some came from within the studio system, such as *The Exorcist* (William Friedkin [1973]), *Jaws* (Steven Spielberg [1975]), and *The Omen* (Richard Donner [1976]). In 1977, Warner Brothers made the bold choice of bringing in John Boorman to revisit a now-teenage Regan MacNeil in *Exorcist II: The Heretic*. Boorman, however, was not a studio journeyman and thus, was never going to turn in a cookie-cutter sequel to William Friedkin's 1973 masterpiece. But Boorman's distinctive style was so different and his vision so bizarre and so wildly removed from the original film that viewers hated the sequel, and yet they returned to it in droves. In a way, this response would set a template for horror sequels to come. They would never equal or rival the original film, and they would expect critical notices of diminishing returns. But their recognizable name, and in some cases, their villain, was enough to draw audiences in to fuel further entries in the series. The huge success of

Jaws inspired Universal to make a swift return to the great white sharks of Amity Island for *Jaws 2* in 1978, the same year 20th Century Fox updated us on 12-year-old Damien Thorn's plans for demonic world domination in *Damien: Omen II*.

Even the horror films that arose outside of the studio system in the independent milieu, such as *The Texas Chainsaw Massacre* (Tobe Hooper [1974]), *Halloween* (John Carpenter [1978]), and *Friday the 13th* (Sean S. Cunningham [1980]), would make such an impact on the box office, and on cinema culture, that they would get into bed with the studios for the production and distribution of their initial run of sequels, giving rise to the mainstream studio sequel and the horror boom of the 1980s. Each studio had their own respective horror properties, and though several franchises saw fortunes diminish by the end of the decade, reaching a particularly low return on investment in 1989, they had made enough of an impact on pop culture that the studios would capitalize on the image of their iconic villains and their brand recognition at the turn of the millennium with an industry of reboots and remakes.

After the period of postmodern ironic horror films of the 1990s ran its course (the characters of which, of course, would have entirely and knowingly anticipated), the post-*Scream* era found the horror landscape barren and bereft of original ideas. Dimension Films was still doing the Lord's work churning out straight-to-video sequels to franchises from the 1980s: *Hellraiser* (*Inferno* [2000], *Hellseeker* [2002], *Deader* [2005], and *Hellworld* [2005]) and *Children of the Corn* (*Revelation* [2001]). New Line Cinema brought a long-gestating crossover bout between Freddy Krueger and Jason Voorhees to the big screen with *Freddy vs. Jason* (2003), while Platinum Dunes, the brainchild of Michael Bay, Brad Fuller, and Andrew Form, would carve out its own niche of remaking revered classic texts with *The Texas Chainsaw Massacre* (2003), *The Amityville Horror* (2005), *The Hitcher* (2007), *Friday the 13th* (2009), and *A Nightmare on Elm Street* (2010). The routine Dimension sequels knew their place. They were undemanding of their audiences and were there to merely service both casual viewers and fans with usually low-budget fare that ticked some generic boxes; conversely, the Platinum Dunes

***Halloween* (2007) poster art.** Dimension Films/Photofest ©Dimension Films

productions were higher in budget and production value and thus, received theatrical releases. However, the studio had the audacity and temerity to tamper with what are, in the eyes of their fans, sacrosanct works and were not at all well received.

Of course, *Halloween* would not escape its fate of being remade in this era of nostalgia for all things 1970s and 1980s, but it would take a brave soul to take on the duty of telling the story of an anointed horror icon such as Michael Myers in this era of Hollywood filmmaking, where the subtlety and nuance that John Carpenter brought to his 1978 film would be something of a relic of a bygone era of cinema. Carpenter's slow, methodical, studied form of filmmaking would not apply to a *Halloween* film made in 2007. Since his film was released, American Cinema had gone through several aesthetic shifts and industrial movements: the post–New Hollywood return to traditional, classical (read, invisible) filmmaking modes after the success of *Star Wars* and the death of *Heaven's Gate*; the rise of MTV and its influence of the music video on feature-film editing and cinematography; and the independent boom of the 1990s, which afforded opportunities for bold new visionaries to emerge and in some cases, mingle with the mainstream. Such cases as the latter didn't always work out well. Acclaimed independent filmmakers, such as Tom DiCillo and Hal Hartley, who found prominence in the early 1990s with their low-budget arthouse classics, would struggle to break into the mainstream despite collaborations with Paramount Pictures (DiCillo with *The Real Blonde* [1997]) and United Artists/MGM (Hartley with *No Such Thing* [2001]). Another indie icon, John Carpenter, felt like quitting the business after working with Warner Brothers on *Memoirs of an Invisible Man* in 1992. It's an age-old tale, an auteur filmmaker in conflict with the commercial concerns of their corporate financiers.

It turned out that Rob Zombie was the hero we needed to step up and bring Michael Myers crashing into the horror landscape of the 2000s, and he, too, was already well versed in such studio bureaucracies and corporate combat. His brilliantly manic and excessively violent debut film *House of 1000 Corpses* was made for Universal, but the film fell victim to the company's fears over its violent themes and content. The film was shelved and passed to another studio before it was shelved again, only to be rescued by Lions Gate Entertainment, a production and distribution company with some independent credibility and a willingness to take risks with left-field material. Already a cult figure in alternative music circles, thanks to his band White Zombie and their well-defined shock-rock image, and now with two films with certified horror credibility to them (including *Corpses* sequel *The Devil's Rejects* in 2005), Zombie seemed the ideal candidate to resurrect *Halloween* after its unceremonious death with *Resurrection* five years prior. As expected, Zombie's *Halloween* was never going to be a slavish rethread of what John Carpenter did. Yes, he would acknowledge the original film with the reverence of a devout fan but with a unique filmmaking style that was so well developed that, even after only two films, this would be Rob Zombie's *Halloween*, for better or worse.

The film immediately sets up a social context in complete contrast to the middle-class suburban ideal of Haddonfield that audiences have been familiar with to this point. The opening of Carpenter's *Halloween* gives no insight into the early life of Michael Myers. If anything, the domestic situation looks, on the surface, to be a perfectly petit bourgeois representation of 1960's suburbia. Zombie, however, renders Michael's upbringing in a decidedly lower-class setting (some may refer to it disparagingly as "white thrash"), depicting a fractured familial milieu with a loving, if preoccupied, matriarch in Deborah Myers (Sheri Moon Zombie), who is making ends meet as an exotic dancer in a sleazy strip club while her children are targeted for abuse and vitriol by her repulsive alcoholic boyfriend Ronnie White (portrayed with relish by the great William Forsythe). White bullies and disparages young Michael for his tender tendencies toward his baby sister Angel (later Laurie), referring to Michael as being gay for showing such affection, while White leers and sexually comments on his girlfriend's teenage daughter and Michael's sister, Judith. This shocking opening scene not only dares to give some insight into the reasoning behind Michael's psychological state, which Carpenter never intended to explore, but also, for the first time, we are offered some alternative sociological context. Up to now, the characters of the *Halloween* films populated an idyllic Midwestern world of white picket fence suburbia, manicured lawns, and small towns; indeed, the American Dream duly enjoyed and perturbed only by the return of a masked maniac every Halloween night. Directly opposing the damaged domestic environment of the Myers household is the Strode abode, into which orphaned Angel was adopted and raised as Laurie. Unlike the sheer decrepitude and moral bankruptcy of the Myers home, the Strodes offer a world of warmth and affection. Rather than the abuse and belligerence of Ronnie White, Laurie's adopted parents are socially, intellectually, and emotionally engaged, a middle-class alternative to a life of misery that could have been.

Zombie goes even further in explaining Michael's fractured state of mind when he reveals that the bullying extends beyond the home and into the school halls, which will be the catalyst for Michael's first murder. It is also revealed that school administrators have been worried about their student upon finding dead animals in his bag as well as photographs of such. This is far removed from the blank canvas of pure evil that Carpenter offered us in 1978, but Zombie should be applauded for offering his own take on the material. Director David Gordon Green would return to Carpenter's idea for his Blumhouse trilogy, but Zombie's film offers a richer intellectual experience as well as a visceral one, as he not only brings in sociological and psychological elements but also incorporates his trademark proclivity for extreme violence and gore. Depicting the familial milieu the way Zombie does affords the audience some fleeting moments of sympathy for Michael, even if we know that he will never reciprocate any such emotion for any of his victims. While his love for his mother is never in question, it is interesting that the person he has the most affinity for is his baby sister, Laurie. Given her age and innocence, she is the one human being who never harasses, denigrates, or belittles him because she never had a chance to. Only in her fight for survival when Michael returns home 15 years later does she antagonize him. When he confronts her with a photograph showing him and her in happier times of youth, she rejects it in not recognizing her nor her brother. Only then does Michael pursue her with murderous intent.

Of course, any self-respecting remake of *Halloween* will have certain touchstones to acknowledge, notably John Carpenter's iconic theme tune, but it is used sparingly for greater effect, such as the opening credits in which Michael flees the school and exacts revenge upon his school tormentor. In a neat and not overt nod to the original, the characters are seen watching the same films on television that their 1978 versions did: Howard Hawks's *The Thing from Another World* (1951) and *Forbidden Planet* (1956). Elsewhere, there is the obligatory reprise of Blue Öyster Cult's "(Don't Fear) the Reaper," and in a subtle allusion to the time and place of the original film's setting, the Myers house has a framed picture of President John F. Kennedy hanging on the wall. In a moment that could be said was the death of a certain kind of American innocence, JFK was assassinated on November 22, 1963, the same year that Michael lost his own innocence when he murdered his sister, Judith, on October 31. Just as the safe suburban world of Haddonfield—itself a vision of American domestic stability—had been shook to its core after the events of Halloween night 1963, the country, too, was rocked by the killing of its 35th president. And after a period of national mourning, the country entered a volatile time of civil and social unrest, a theme that would be reflected somewhat in David Gordon Green's *Halloween Kills* (2021). This image of an iconic American may just be a simple prop to imply the film's temporal setting, or indeed it could be a more meaningful placement, the face of a man that projects ideas of hope in complete and utter contrast to the blank face of Michael Myers, which promotes notions of carnage, killing, and despair.

Former *Fangoria* editor Tony Timpone notes that Zombie's film was the first *Halloween* in a long time to invite any kind of analysis beyond the immediate context of stalk-and-slash generic registers. "Until the Rob Zombie films came along, there really wasn't much analysis to be had," Timpone says. "Parts five and six tried to come up with this mythology to explain him, but every time they deviated from the formula so much, the fans got in an uproar; they didn't appreciate these new approaches which were trying to propel the series in new directions. I think the relationship that fandom has with our horror icons is an interesting one. They don't want them to be human, but Rob Zombie made Michael human. Fans find it scarier that way when they are not human, when they are just monsters or some kind of unstoppable evil, because you can't reason with it. They wanted Michael just the way they remembered him from 1978 and for it to be left at that. Horror fans are very opinionated, maybe too opinionated in some ways. But they want what they want and they like what they like, and there's not much middle ground. God bless them for that."

One of the film's greatest elements is cinematographer Phil Parmet's stylishly gritty camerawork infused with the immediacy of his mostly handheld lensing, which is often contrasted with moments of unique static framing that creates an unusual and distinctly original visual tone for the film. Timpone applauds the aesthetic that Zombie and his cinematographer rendered with aplomb. "I think the first two thirds of his first *Halloween* is a really, really good movie; it's only in the last third of the film when it falls into the pattern of recreating the final moments of Carpenter's film I felt that he stumbled. But I admired the freshness of it. I really appreciated the look and style of it. It's interesting that he brings in someone like cinematographer Phil Parmet, who comes from the New York indie underground scene, and documentaries, who brings a different kind of style to it. It's very well shot but not in a very glossy kind of Hollywood style. He brought this real gritty kind of immediacy."

Indeed, Phil Parmet was not only the perfect choice to be the director of photography on the film given his prior work on Rob Zombie's 2005 sequel to *House of 1000 Corpses*, *The Devil's Rejects*, but he brought with him a history of work in the New York independent scene as well as in cinema verité. Parmet had been behind the camera on Barbara Kopple's Oscar-winning labor relations documentary *Harlan County USA* (1976) as well as Robert Richter and Stanley Warnow's documentary of the antinuclear arms demonstration and concert in New York City, *In Our Hands* (1983). His feature film credits include notable independent productions, such as Alexandre Rockwell's *In the Soup* (1992), as well as Rockwell's segment in the 1995 portmanteau picture *Four Rooms*, and several films directed by Steve Buscemi, including *Animal Factory* (2000) and *Lonesome Jim* (2005). Parmet had been a keen photographer since his early days and all through high school, earning a little money on the side as an aerial photographer. It was while at college that he dabbled in cinematography, shooting his friends' short films and meeting people along the way who could help him earn a living doing what he loved. One of those he met was the pioneering cameraman Garrett Brown, the inventor of the Steadicam, who had seen a short film that Parmet had shot and duly inquired about hiring him for commercials that Brown was working on at the time.

"That was really the start of it for me," Parmet affirms. "I said, 'Oh, it's a great way to make money.' And it kind of grew from there. I did a film that won a national endowment grant, and a lot of people saw it in New York, which led to me getting work. I shot some documentaries, including one for Barbara Kopple that later won an Academy Award, *Harlan County USA*. But I was always interested in trying to do theatrical films, and I got an opportunity when some friends of mine had raised some money in Japan. So I did a little action movie with them and just figured out that I can actually make a living doing something I really love to do, rather than something I hated to do, which was most other things. If you can find a job or you can find something that you love to do and it turns out you can make money from it, well there's nothing better than that. I worked in New York in the '70s and '80s. There was a great independent film scene going on there, and that is where I met a lot of actors."

Parmet continues, "I did this film for Alexandre Rockwell called *In the Soup*, which won at Sundance, and I hooked up with a lot of young New York actors, like Steve Buscemi and Stanley Tucci, people that I worked with and made friends with and shot films for later on. I did three films for Steve Buscemi that he directed, which are not known very well. Steve is one of the great people I had an opportunity to meet in my lifetime. I think that is another great thing about cinematography; it's a world where you can kind of investigate places and people that you are interested in. I've known Steve since the '70s when he was still a fireman. My girlfriend at the time was a painter who lived in the same building as him. I was going to try to do a play, *Life of Galileo*, which was a Brecht play, and I was looking for a cast. And my girlfriend said, 'Oh, well, I have a friend who lives in the building who is a fireman, but he's also an actor and he's really great.' So I met Steve and got to know him really well. We did a bunch of rehearsals. But in the middle of that, he got a job, and I got a job, so the play kind of fell apart. And later, we would see each other on the street. And we were friends, so he asked me if I would shoot a short movie for him. I did that, and later we did *Animal Factory*, which was written by Eddie Bunker, who wrote *Straight Time*. That is one of my favorite films I've ever worked on, and for a lot of reasons. One is I love working with Steve. The second thing was my wife was the costume designer. The third one is that it was shot in Philadelphia, where my mother was living, so she could take care of my kid. Steve is just one of the greats; he's a real, genuine, incredible, amazing, lovely person. And I don't say that about many people. He's a real friend, which is unusual in this business because everything is so superficial, particularly in LA. So many relationships are superficial, so it's great when you find somebody you really connect with. New York is where I really started to get into the independent thing. But ultimately, I moved to California after my wife and I had a child, and there was a producer strike in New York. Then one thing after another started happening for me. I felt very lucky that I was able to earn a living working in the film business."

It is Parmet's dynamic handheld approach, which was well honed during his time shooting documentaries, that informs much of the film's energetic visual style and supports the frenetic moments of Michael's manic assaults. The cinematographer details some unlikely inspirations for his and Zombie's aesthetic:

"One of the reasons that I was hired to shoot *The Devil's Rejects* was that Rob Zombie wanted a style that was very loose and handheld and very realistic, but also classical in some ways. So the models for that film were Westerns, like *High Plains Drifter* and *The Outlaw Josey Wales*, and things like that. Rob was really looking for a loose style that sort of amalgamated those two things. And he was familiar with my work; he saw a bunch of my movies, particularly some documentaries that I had done. That's how I hooked up with Rob. And then when he asked me to do *Halloween*, he said he liked my style and asked if we can just up that a little bit. It's not much different than what we did in *The Devil's Rejects*, except that we shot it 35-millimeter. Most of *Halloween* is shot handheld, about 90% of the film. I've kind of mixed it up between handheld and a more polished style. I think really great handheld can be some of the most exciting photography that there is because you're in a direct relationship with the actors. It also has the kind of ancillary effect of the news, which has been handheld for years, and it gives you a sense of reality and immediacy. When it is used right in a horror film, it can be kind of scary. A lot of people have commented about cinematography, but rarely have people actually brought up the dynamics of the handheld aspect of the job, which is really important. The whole idea of handheld is it shouldn't look like handheld. It should be really controlled but always have the element of the unexpected, particularly in documentaries."

Despite the brutality of the film, Zombie is capable of emotionally effective moments, most excellently in the pre-massacre montage in which Zombie juxtaposes Deborah Myers pulling a shift at the strip club with Michael sitting alone outside his house, his trick-or-treating plans curtailed after being abandoned by Judith in favor of having sex with her boyfriend. Artistically constructed in sound and editing around the Nazareth song "Love Hurts," it is a briefly tender moment before the carnage ensues in earnest and elicits a genuine moment of sympathy for Michael as it offers yet another glimpse into the family dynamic that he endures.

Parmet considers his director's artistic tendencies and the early misinterpretation of Zombie's abilities by some of the crew: "A lot of people think of Rob as a rock and roller, but he went to art school and wanted to make movies from the time he started going to art school; then he got hooked up with his band, that sort of tangentially, and luckily, became very successful. But he always wanted to be a filmmaker. And he has great artistic impulses. I mean he's a real artist. He can draw, so he can storyboard his films; a lot of the ideas came out of his storyboards. He is really good, but he also has this kind of sensationalist quality, this image that he creates of himself. That isn't necessarily exactly who he is. He created this character that we know as Rob Zombie, but there is a lot more to the real Rob Zombie than just this pop musician. He found a way to make money by doing something that he likes doing, but he always wanted

Director Rob Zombie with his *Halloween* cast members Scout Taylor-Compton (left) and Dee Wallace (2007). Dimension Films/Photofest ©Dimension Films

to make movies. If you go to his house, there are just hundreds and hundreds of movies, just walls of DVDs, and he knows film history. It was really funny because when I first started working on *Halloween*, the crew in particular were like, 'Rob Zombie? Who is this guy?' And it took me a while to get to know who he really was. So the film started out with this kind of negative energy because everybody thought Rob was not a heavyweight, that he was this lightweight making a movie, and nobody really took him seriously. I had a couple of talks with the crew, and I said, 'Listen, this guy is super talented. What you see of him as a musician is very superficial. There's a lot more to him than this.'"

"I loved working with Malcolm McDowell. I grew up with *A Clockwork Orange*, so it was great to witness him working. We traded hats. It was wonderful. And there were some memorable moments; one night in particular stands out. It was the scene at the insane asylum; we were doing a crane shot that night, and

Director Rob Zombie on the set of *Halloween* (2007). Dimension Films/Photofest ©Dimension Films

we were at a Veterans Administration Hospital, which was doubling as this insane asylum. Across the street was a big fence that we couldn't see through. So we're here shooting the scene, and somebody says to me, 'There's a bunch of monkeys behind that screen!' I said, 'What do you mean?' So I walked over to this

Cinematographer Phil Parmet and director Rob Zombie with Daeg Faerch (front and center) and crew. Courtesy Phil Parmet

chain-link fence that had a screen behind it that we couldn't see past. So I peeled it back a little bit, and I saw a bunch of monkeys in there. We start shooting, and my gaffer climbs up on a ladder and looks over the top of the fence and said, 'There's thousands of monkeys in there!' So I said, 'Well, what are they doing with those monkeys? They're probably experimenting on them and taking their brains out; they're torturing monkeys.' And this guy walked by me and said, 'What did you say?' And I replied, 'They are probably torturing monkeys.' When I said that, this guy flipped out and started screaming, 'We never torture monkeys!' And then, five minutes later, a bunch of executives walked over to me and said they wanted me to leave the property. 'What do you mean, leave the property?' They said, 'You made a comment about experimenting on monkeys.' And I told them it was just a flippant remark; I didn't see the monkeys. And they said, 'Well, you have to leave the property.' And then a police car pulls up and everybody says, 'Phil has to leave the property.' So then all the executives get together and say, 'Well, we'll just have somebody else leave the property. So they fired like five people.'"

While the crew eventually came around to Parmet's respectful view of their director, his relationship with Bob and Harvey Weinstein was less cordial; they were questioning Zombie's auteur sensibilities and creating tension on the set. The cinematographer elaborates:

"Technically speaking, it was a straightforward shoot. I mean we worked long hours, and that was hard. But we had a fair amount of money, so it was a good experience in that sense; however, it was really hard for other reasons. What made it challenging was the way Harvey Weinstein jumped on Rob and was on his case every day. And Rob is not the kind of person who wants that kind of supervision; nobody wants it. But it became a very difficult shoot for Rob, and that kind of transferred to me. It wasn't like they were on the set every day, but they would comment on stuff. And Rob would come into work feeling not very good, and that would trickle down. *The Devil's Rejects* was a blast; we had such a great time on that, and we became great friends after it. But making *Halloween* was so full of tension. It was not a fun shoot; they were too much in our shit, as they say, and it's hard to be an artist when people are jumping on you and are looking at everything that you do and they don't understand where you're coming from. They didn't get the tone of the film that Rob was trying to achieve. And it wasn't horror in the traditional sense. I don't know about Bob, but Harvey Weinstein was a nasty guy, just horrible. I've heard things about them over the years, but I was never directly affected by anything that they did. But on *Halloween*, they put a dark curtain over the whole production. The worst part of it was the Miramax thing, and I have my personal things with Rob because of all that; after they came down on Rob, I felt like I was at the bottom of the pile and got kicked. So I don't want to say he is a great guy, but he is an amazing artist. And I think people underestimate him."

For all of the film's flaws, it is clearly evident that Zombie cared about the property; there is a sense of sincerity within its frames that sometimes felt lacking in the David Gordon Green trilogy, which felt calculatedly constructed to cash in on fan

Rob Zombie shot by Phil Parmet on the Smith's Grove Sanitarium set. Courtesy Phil Parmet

culture and nostalgia for the 1978 film. While there are certainly affectionate nods to Carpenter's *Halloween*, it is defiantly its own beast, with Zombie never attempting to ape the style of any of the filmmakers in the franchise before him. Parmet affirms: "We never talked about trying to emulate the style of the original film; what we did talk about was trying to re-create the feeling, something that would honor the history of what we were doing. It's not brain surgery. It's not the greatest movie in the world, but it has a history and has a lot of rabid fans who want you to stay true to the idea of the original. And we didn't mess with the idea of it; I mean it's a *Halloween* movie, so you work with the elements of that. But we didn't really use anything stylistically that came before it; we were interested in creating something original. It was a Rob Zombie movie that used *Halloween* as a template."

With Zombie's love of the genre, the director was more than aware of the importance of having an ally in a magazine like *Fangoria*, which could tantalize fans with images and articles on the films to come. Zombie was 14 years old when *Fangoria* first hit the newsstands in August 1979, the ideal age to engage in the monster-movie madness that filled its pages, and as a keen horror fan, he would have noticed the kind of coverage that the magazine offered the 1980's horror releases, particularly the front cover features on the *Halloween* movies. That changed in the 1990s, when Dimension Films took control of the property and failed to fully utilize horror-genre media in rallying the core fan base. Where the Weinsteins thwarted the magazine's chances of comprehensive coverage of the productions of the three previous movies in the franchise, Zombie wasn't going to take any chances, so he duly took the reins and collaborated with *Fangoria* directly, knowing the value of good coverage in such a fan-favorite genre specialist publication.

"The great thing about Rob Zombie," Tony Timpone said, "is he was a reader of the magazine from issue one. He knew the importance of the magazine and reaching the fans. So right from the get-go he says, 'I want *Fangoria*; give them whatever they want.' He was very cooperative. He made sure that you knew he was onboard with us. He personally selected the photo that he wanted on the *Fangoria* cover, and he personally photoshopped it and color corrected it. He did whatever it took to make it the perfect cover for both of his *Halloween* movies; he was that hands-on. And he gave our writers great interviews and gave us exclusives. Rob Zombie was the big boss; he made sure that the Weinsteins didn't force their marketing ideas or impose any restrictions on us. He made sure to say, 'This is *Fangoria*; give them what they want,' so he made coverage of his two *Halloween* movies very easy. His photos were great; his interviews were great. So we got everything we wanted, total cooperation, which was not the case with *Halloween 6* and *H20*."

For Parmet, the film remains one of his most-celebrated films despite his work with independent and arthouse auteurs and several works with a European martial arts star whose name once adorned marquees with his major studio hits but is now working predominantly in the straight-to-home-video market. Evidently, "The Muscles from Brussels" is no match for the horror icon of Haddonfield.

"*Halloween* is one of the best-known films that I've done," Parmet confirms. "I mean, I did a bunch of Van Damme movies in Romania, and it seemed like everybody in Europe knew about Van Damme. But if you mentioned Van Damme in the United States, he's considered kind of a joke. Saying you made some Van Damme movies doesn't have the same weight as saying you made a *Halloween* movie. Everybody knows *Halloween*. Rob is an original person, a one of a kind; there aren't many Rob Zombies around. He's extraordinarily talented, whether that's in the visual arts or in music. I know on a personal level how hard it is to make a movie, any type of movie. My daughter just made her first movie, and I just watched how hard it was. It's an amazing journey that's just very, very difficult. To make a feature film is a gigantic accomplishment, and the fact that Rob has made four or five of them puts him up there in the annals of some of the major filmmakers. But the thing is that horror doesn't get very much respect, even if it is made by very serious filmmakers. Whether its Cahiers du Cinéma or the Academy Awards, the chances of you getting nominated for a horror film, no matter how good it is, even if you're Roger Deakins, you won't get the kind of respect you would get from shooting other kinds of movies. But on the other hand, it's kind of fun to be an outsider in a way. Rob is one of the guys who says, 'I don't give a fuck. I'm going to make the movie that I want to make.' I have to say one of the things I really loved about Rob is that he loves to scare people. To make a really scary film is an accomplishment; a good horror film is like being on a really good roller-coaster ride. I didn't know very much about Rob before *The Devil's Rejects*, but when I saw the first cut, I was blown away by how powerful it was. Whether you like the movie or not, man, it has a great power and emotional energy. I would be really interested to see him get out of the horror genre and do other material, but he found a niche where he can make money and where he's accepted."

Initially reluctant to return to Haddonfield for a sequel, Rob Zombie was eventually convinced by Malek Akkad, who offered creative freedom to further explore the Michael Myers saga within his own vision. If audiences thought the 2007 version was brutal, they were in for a shock, as the sequel is one of the most

Halloween II (2009) poster art. Dimension Films/Photofest Artwork ©The Weinstein Company

viciously violent mainstream horror films of recent memory, containing a level of brutality that is only tempered by the beautifully surrealist visions of Michael as a younger man accompanied by his mother and the symbolic white horse, which is referenced in the film's opening quote: "White Horse—linked to instinct, purity, and the drive of the physical body to release powerful and emotional forces, like rage, with ensuing chaos and destruction." The line provides another source of motivation for Michael beyond the terribly tormented upbringing that he experienced in his early years. Whether the white horse was always part of his psyche or emerged from his subconscious as a result of that traumatic time is not clear, but it is quite obvious that the visions aroused the rage and inspired his course of action. At the end of the film, after Laurie has defeated Michael using his own weapon against him, she emerges wearing his mask, seemingly having suffered a mental breakdown, and so the final images of the film see her alone in a psychiatric ward envisioning her mother and the white horse. Her countenance turns from blank and expressionless to a slow, devious grin, suggesting Laurie's trauma and fight for survival have morphed into rage, as symbolized by the white horse. Perhaps this rage has been lying dormant in Laurie all this time, buried by the comfortable middle-class upbringing that the Strode family afforded her, but having been implanted by her mere presence in the Myers household during her infancy. Zombie's handling of these themes, through his deft flair for crafting striking imagery and finding emotion in the unlikeliest of places, takes the film (albeit fleetingly) out of the mire of morbid malaise that he places the viewer in right from the opening frames.

Tony Timpone recalls the feedback and divided opinions from the *Fangoria* readership: "I think Rob Zombie's films stand alone as interesting artistic works. The response from the fans was kind of split but mostly negative. The fans didn't like seeing the formula messed with in such a radical way, especially in terms of going into Michael's background and trying to explain what made him the way he is. If you're into the kind of social subtext of the Myers family background and all that, then it is a rich work to mine, but it's not for everybody."

Indeed, one of those that it wasn't for is Michael Myers himself, well, one of them. *Halloween: Resurrection* main man Brad Loree was not impressed with the extent to which Zombie took both the bloodletting and the backstory, as he reveals "I hated the fucking Zombie film; it so demystified him and humanized

The symbolic white horse appears before Michael. Author's Collection

him. It used to be that you were afraid of him and you weren't sure why because he is fairly normal-sized guy; he wasn't big, but he had a methodical pursuit about him. And there was a mystique about why he was so super strong and why he was the way he was, but then that was all answered in Zombie's film. And there's no suspense. He is seven feet tall, and you know all the people are going to die. Imagination is very important, but those movies go all out on the gore; the initial sequels relied more on suspense. Great films leave the mystery to the audience; that's where I think true filmmaking comes in. When you cross all the T's and dot all the I's, it is too much. I've never seen Rob Zombie's second *Halloween* film and probably never will."

"By the time it got to *Halloween II*, you could tell his heart wasn't in it," Timpone says. "He didn't really want to make that film, but he at least tried to do something incredibly different and radical and off the wall with the crazy dream sequences and things like that. His creative brain was very much in there, and he wanted to do something that wasn't a retread and that was scary and disturbing and violent and vicious, which it was. There were some great things about Rob's films, though, especially the look of Michael Myers, which is so good. Wayne Toth did a great job redesigning the mask, and Tyler Mane did a real fearsome job playing the character; he made Michael scary again. That's for sure. Malcolm McDowell was fun as Dr. Loomis. So it had a lot going for it. And I think the fans appreciated all the cameos throughout both movies; all the fan favorites show up in there, from Diane Thorne to Clint Howard, Bill Moseley, Sid Haig, you name it. He had everybody in those movies. And it's part of the fun of it because Rob Zombie always does a fan service that not only satisfies the fans but the fan in himself. He wants to work with people he admired and admires, and so you feel his love for movies."

Chapter Six

Evil Dies Tonight
Halloween *Lives Forever*

"Happy Halloween, Michael." —Laurie Strode

The announcement of a new *Halloween* film that would be released in 2018 and see the return of Jamie Lee Curtis to the franchise created much excitement in the horror community. With Curtis on board, the film instantly comes with a weight of authority, for she is the connection to John Carpenter's original text. She is Laurie Strode. And while that was cause for celebration, one must admit that it was a little deflating that not only would the Thorn Trilogy be retconned once again, but we would also have to pretend that *Halloween II* and its direct sequels, *Halloween H20* and *Halloween: Resurrection*, never existed. Such Hollywood amnesia underscores the industry's value of branding over storytelling. Forget the temporal and emotional investment that viewers have in remaining faithful and following story threads of characters such as Jamie Lloyd, for the studios want audiences to remain loyal to the logo. It's a curious thing, that after enjoying and enduring seven formal sequels (not counting Zombie's two), audiences are expected to consider that the only really important film in the entire franchise to date is the first one. That said, Green's trilogy provides many enjoyable moments for longtime followers and devotees of the *Halloween* franchise and do contain some humorous Easter eggs for fans of the sequels to spot, such as the appearance in *Halloween Kills* of the Silver Shamrock masks from *Halloween III*. It seems that the 1978 *Halloween* carries with it such a sense of integrity and importance, as does its association with John Carpenter, who remains one of the few auteur filmmakers whose name carries considerable credibility in both the Hollywood mainstream and alternative independent world, that to be connected directly to it gives the new sequels more meaning, and this has worked in the favor of Green's trilogy. That Jamie Lee Curtis has returned for the recent films also increases their chances of immediate acceptance by the fan base, and mainstream visibility. But it is the Carpenter connection that is mostly exploited for cultural capital.

Green's belated 2018 sequel to Carpenter's 1978 original is a well-produced piece of mainstream horror filmmaking made by Blumhouse Productions, a studio that has become something of a noted house of horror since the sleeper success of *Paranormal Activity* in 2009. The studio has been churning out an impressive array of original titles and many respective sequels to such, creating contemporary franchises that are keeping horror fans content—*Insidious*, *Purge*, *Sinister*, *Ouija*, and *Creep*—and have gained respectability with a selection of films that have managed to win over critics with their sociopolitical subtexts and contexts: *Get Out* (Jordan Peele [2017]) and *BlacKkKlansman* (Spike Lee [2018]). However, they are not infallible to missteps, particularly when reviving known properties. Blumhouse have served up various remakes, reboots, and legacy sequels, the kind of thing that must always reckon with the expectations of seasoned fans of the originals, including *Amityville: The Awakening* (Franck Khalfoun [2017]), *The Craft: Legacy* (Zoe Lister Jones [2020]), *Firestarter* (Keith Thomas [2022]), and *The Exorcist: Believer* (David Gordon Green [2023]). But what separates Green's *Halloween* from those mentioned above?

First, its confluence of creators is interesting. Green and his writing partner, Danny McBride, are an unlikely filmmaking duo for such a horror trilogy given their respective creative backgrounds. Green made some modest dramas in the early 2000s, such as *George Washington* (2000), *All the Real Girls* (2003), and *Snow Angels* (2007), before coming to more commercial prominence with the stoner comedy *Pineapple Express*. McBride's

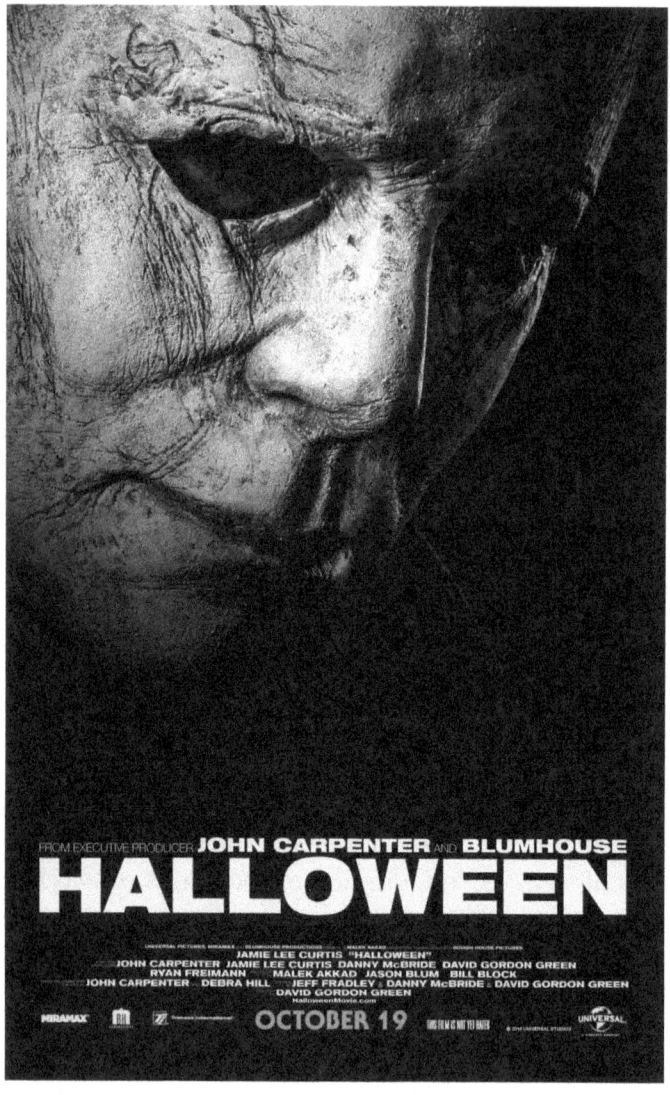

Halloween **(2018) poster art.** Miramax/Universal Pictures/Photofest ©Universal Studios

career has mostly been in the realm of mainstream studio comedies. Together, however, they revitalized the *Halloween* franchise, bringing it back into the pop-culture realm and into mainstream conversation with a solid piece of horror entertainment, an authentic and as well made a *Halloween* sequel as one could expect 40 years after the original, even if it peaks early, as its greatest scene occurs in the opening five minutes and which was featured almost in full in the film's trailer.

The most successful aspect of Green's film is in its depiction of something rarely seen: the traumatic life of a survivor. Most final girls of horror films survive to live another movie or two, or three . . . maybe four . . . so we may see them coming to terms with horrendous events of the recent past in sequels that take place only several years after the temporal setting of the original. But Green's *Halloween* is set 40 years after the night Michael came home to wreak havoc on Haddonfield, and the character of Laurie has had four decades of grief, trauma, paranoia, and addiction to grapple with. What makes the film interesting is to see how Laurie will face the monster as a woman in her 60s, another rarity, as most horror movie heroines are not that advanced in age. She is not a promiscuous wayward teen ripe for the slaughter; she is a woman with a life's worth of character building behind her and cannot and will not be dispatched in the flash of a knife. The way Green flips our expectations of Laurie is to be applauded. In the first third of the film, she is struggling with family and alcohol and is presented as fractured in a way we kind of expect, but she is soon revealed to have spent these past 40 years preparing for Michael's inevitable return. Her skill

Baiting Michael. Author's Collection

and efficiency with weapons and the network of traps and obstacles set up to ensnare him shows that while Laurie was battling more domestically oriented demons on the surface of things, she kept her survivalist tendencies sharpened for the severest of counterassaults. If the film wanted to tick some timely sociocultural boxes, Laurie's resurrection as a heroine of agency and resolve certainly speaks to female empowerment, but to reduce it to such would be to do it an injustice, for Laurie is much more than a token, a slogan, or a symbolic gesture. Taken as an entire four-film unit, from John Carpenter's *Halloween* to *Halloween Ends*, we are offered a multidimensional woman who bears the scars of violence inflicted upon her by a violent, unreasonable man.

While the Blumhouse trilogy trades on its connection and shared ideals with the original *Halloween*, one thing that betrays this is the level of unflinching violence that the films depict. Rob Zombie's two *Halloween* films have rightly been accused of being excessive, but something about the murky lower-class contexts of Zombie's films set them in a world that is already grimy and brutal. Green's films are slick in the manner of most contemporary horror films; the photography has a green-brown tone to it, the camera is restless, and the editing often postclassical (jump cuts, etc., not "invisible"). Carpenter's film—and the sequels of the formal franchise (up to *The Curse of Michael Myers*)—was made in an era when style and tone were informed

Laurie is ready for Michael's return. Author's Collection

more by physical setting, location, and lighting, without the reliance upon the digital aids and tools that are used by today's filmmakers to imply mood and atmosphere. To their credit and advantage, aesthetically the films are their own beast; they don't try to ape the Carpenter style, for that would be a fool's errand, as the director's style is so distinctive and unique to him that anyone even so much as trying to evoke the master is to not only be critiqued poorly in comparison but to also show a distinct lack of originality. Michael Simmonds's cinematography is interestingly organic, seeming to change tone with each film. The first is autumnal, warm and heavy in brown; the second is vibrant, colorful, almost garishly so; and the third is murky and washed out, bleak and grim, as the narrative draws to its bloody conclusion. Only in the final scene of *Halloween Ends*, with Laurie finding some peace with herself, does the film brighten up before sending us out of theaters feeling good with some nostalgic revelry as the familiar guitar riff of Blue Öyster Cult's "(Don't Fear) the Reaper" sounds the closing credits.

Unlike most horror reboots/remakes/sequels, David Gordon Green's *Halloween* was a massive hit with fans and critics alike, revitalizing the franchise and making it relevant and recognizable to a whole new generation of viewers. Tony Timpone, of *Fangoria*, was happy to see Green returning the franchise to its roots:

"I love *Halloween* 2018; I think it's one of the best of the series. Jamie Lee Curtis was terrific. As a matter of fact, I think she deserved an Oscar for her role in that movie over *Everything Everywhere All at Once*. I think she's better in *Halloween* 2018; she gave that film such vitality and strength and three dimensionality. You really felt her struggle and her pain. It did a great job picking up from the Carpenter film. And yeah, there was tons of fan service in there, such as going back to having Nick Castle play Michael in some scenes, and a lot of visual in-jokes and Easter eggs throughout the film, almost to a distracting effect. But you could tell their hearts were in the right place. I wasn't editing *Fangoria* when the last trilogy came out, but in terms of cooperation, I'm pretty sure they got everything they wanted because they did great covers on all three movies, though it wasn't like the old days when *Fangoria* was the only one on the set. Now, they were part of these junkets with all these web people and all these other fanzine-type magazines that were covering the

Halloween Kills **(2021) poster art.** Miramax/Universal Pictures/Photofest ©Universal Studios

Halloween Ends star Jamie Lee Curtis confers with director David Gordon Green (2022). Universal Pictures/Photofest ©Universal Pictures

movies. But they came up with some killer covers, and in terms of interview material, they got everything they needed, as far as I could tell from just being a reader. They had great access to David Gordon Green and Jamie Lee Curtis. So again, they realized the value of working with *Fangoria*, not ignoring that fan base, which has been so loyal to the franchise since 1978."

Much more in line with the less ambitious and more thrill-seeking franchise sequels of the 1980s and 1990s is *Halloween Kills*, which seems more focused on being an enjoyably silly slasher film and makes for perhaps the most entertaining film of the Blumhouse three. Knowing that *Halloween Kills* was the second film of a trilogy, there was always going to be the expectation of its being a holdover work, expanding the story but offering no true resolution to its drama, for that would be saved for the third and final entry. But *Halloween Kills* ended up being far more entertaining for these very reasons; it had no aspirations to say anything of thematic weight; the first film did that in spades. Nor did it have the burden and responsibility of wrapping up all the narrative strands to a satisfying conclusion. It was a simple and effective sequel that functions as the second act in a single-narrative arc of the overall trilogy, as Tony Timpone concurs:

"*Halloween Kills* is a good middle movie. It's a nonstop barrage of violence and the ultimate slasher film in terms of body count. It's just Michael in unstoppable monster mode. I cannot believe all the people who are killed in that film. David Gordon Green and Danny McBride as collaborators made a point of making you care for the characters, which we didn't see in a lot of the other sequels; when the characters get slaughtered, you kind of feel something for them. They made a point of building them up before they knocked them down. So you're not rooting for them to get killed, like in a *Friday the 13th* movie where you cheer when someone gets killed; in this film, you felt bad when somebody is slaughtered by Michael Myers. I thought they did a good job, and it was very well shot. I love how it all takes place in that one night and how it picks up from the events of the previous film. I liked it, though I didn't like it quite as much as the first of the trilogy. But as a middle film, it was pretty solid."

If *Halloween* brought sincerity to its depictions of a woman fighting ghosts of the past and demons of the present, and *Halloween Kills* put the fun back into the franchise when it seemed it may be getting bogged down in social subtexts and the huge weight of being an authorized sequel to a recognized classic,

"Evil dies tonight!" The mob emerges. Author's Collection

Halloween Ends was the anticlimactic denouement, which was neither intellectually stimulating nor generically exciting.

"I was kind of surprised with *Halloween Ends*," Timpone admits, "because I thought they were grooming that young,

Halloween Ends (2022) poster art. Miramax/Universal Pictures/Photofest ©Universal Studios

troubled boy to be the next Michael Myers hero. So I was surprised that they literally killed the golden goose and Michael's potential successor, but then I have to give David Gordon Green credit for trumping our expectations. They weren't leaving the door open for another one—Michael's done, he's finished, there's no successor to take his part. Time to move on. I mean, these guys have made enough money on this series. It's time to go do something fresh; there are plenty of books and novels on the shelf that they could adapt if they don't have any original ideas. I really don't think they will ever make a film as good as Carpenter's original. But there's too much money to be made, so eventually they'll get around to doing another one somehow, somewhere. I'm glad that it ended like it did. The fans hated *Halloween Ends*, but I liked it. I don't think it was as strong as the previous two entries, but I do admire the fact that they tried to do something different, especially with Jamie's character, Laurie Strode; she is a completely different character from the previous two films in that she has managed to deal with her grief and overcome it. Her rage is now at bay, and she literally conquered her demons. And I also liked the big Grand-Guignol finish to the movie where they put Michael in the trash compactors. There's no coming back from that. I think there was a lot of good stuff in that film, though it wasn't as bloody as the previous movie; thank God, I think that would have been total overkill. But the fans didn't support it like they had the previous two."

With the *Halloween* franchise nearing its fifth decade as a pop-culture institution, one that has left its mark on the history of American Cinema right out of the gate with its first film back in 1978, there isn't much left for it to do to make it any more beloved and appreciated as it is. The franchise as a single entity is a significant piece of film culture. And when broken down into the individual entries, we can appreciate the distinct styles, themes, and stories that each filmmaker brought to the franchise, and we can recognize the varying degrees of quality inherent. Some of the films have been justly recognized for their intent, for the skill of the respective directors, and for what they tried to do. Sometimes it takes the distance of time for boldness and deviation to be fully appreciated, and that is certainly the case

Facing the final girl. Author's Collection

with some of the *Halloween* films. In some cases, those films that were initially written off as ill-conceived or poorly executed have been reevaluated when viewed through the contemporary prism. Either through nostalgia or their themes' having greater meaning in today's culture and society, these films are finding new fans as each generation discovers the franchise. Some of the lesser films are still outliers, and while they do have some fans, in time, like the others, they will be reassessed and duly celebrated. What is next for the franchise is anyone's guess. Perhaps only the producer and heir to the hallowed *Halloween* throne, Malek Akkad, really knows, but in the meantime, cast, crew, and commentators can speculate upon and celebrate it all.

"I would like them to move on," Timpone admits, "but I doubt that's going to happen. *Halloween* fans really love to see the same formula repeated again and again. And they don't like to see any real deviation from that. Michael represents an evil that you cannot vanquish; you know, there's no way you could reason with this kind of killer. He's remorseless, he's unstoppable, and he's just like a blank slate. He's just a killing machine. It's the same when it comes to the shark in *Jaws*; you can't reason with it. He just has the mission to kill. And he's that force of nature that Carpenter is always talking about, it really is true. And I think the fans just like the familiarity of it too. It's like putting on a well-worn pair of shoes or jeans: you feel comfortable with it the way it is, you don't need to mess with the style or the look or anything, you take comfort in it. I think that's part of the appeal of the franchise.

"The last three films had a very big nostalgia factor that the fans, for the most part, enjoyed. And the fact that Michael has no personality is perhaps another attraction for the fans; he is just this blank robot from whom there is no escape, and they find that frightening, whereas Freddy cracks jokes and Jason is kind of larger than life. Jason is the closest thing to Michael. But *Friday the 13th* films do not have the same artistry involved as we saw in the *Halloween* movies. The *Elm Street* franchise brought in some imaginative filmmakers, but the *Friday the 13th* movies were just worried about making a quick buck and getting in and out as quick as possible. They really didn't care as much about putting quality on the screen, certainly not until they got to *Jason Goes to Hell* and *Freddy vs. Jason* and *Jason X*, with which they at least would try to do different things and have more fun with the franchise. *Jason Lives* at least had a sense of fun about it, but for the most part, they were just carbon copies of each other.

"The genre would be a lot less interesting without the *Halloween* movies," Timpone says, "because it inspired so many others, so many other slasher movies and other horror movies, and it inspired so many filmmakers who watched John Carpenter's original and wanted to do something just like what he was doing. So many modern horror directors say that they owe a lot to *Halloween* and what John Carpenter did with his early films, so Carpenter's film is a real landmark and has gone down in history as one of the most influential horror movies ever."

Cinematographer Daryn Okada considers *Halloween* to have opened doors for independent horror cinema and inspired aspiring filmmakers to try their hand at making movies. No doubt it did provide an alternative milieu for filmmakers to work exclusively but recurrently within that genre, while also offering the more ambitious and industrious a training ground for careers within the Hollywood studio establishment, as Okada expounds:

"The first *Halloween* was made when I started out in my movie career, and we were all doing small horror films. And you can learn a lot by doing those kinds of films; it's all cinematic. Debra Hill started out on low-budget films and made *Halloween*, and then I met her when she was at Disney as one of their contract producers; they wanted me to look at some small movies they were considering making. So the two of us came out of low-budget horror movies, and there we were making movies at a big studio like Disney. When I shot *H20*, I wanted it to feel like it was a part of John Carpenter's original vision, or to have the feel that John would have brought to it. I just didn't want to fuck up that legacy. For me it was about really respecting the original, admiring and honoring it. Regardless of what movie it is, you put so much of yourself into it, and you hope that the people who came before you don't think that you've just plagiarized or wrecked their work. At the premiere of the movie, I saw Dean Cundey and Debra Hill: I ran into them in the lobby when the movie was over, and I asked them, 'How did we do?' and they were both elated. That was the greatest feeling, and especially coming from Debra; just to know that she appreciated it meant so much to me."

Daniel Farrands remembers the first time he experienced *Halloween* and knew then that he could no longer remain loyal to the other mega-franchise originator that had previously commanded his allegiance:

"I saw the first film on TV in 1981, and after that, everything was *Halloween* for me. I went from Mr. *Star Wars* to Mr. *Halloween*. And interestingly, the following Friday, *Halloween II* opened in theaters. So I double-dosed, and my life was changed forever. And we weren't allowed to see *Halloween II* because it wasn't on television, but we convinced some kind of hippie who was in line buying tickets to buy tickets for us because it was an R-rated film. So whoever that guy was, thanks a lot! In a way, I think *Halloween II* had an even bigger impact on me than the first one because I saw it on the big screen; the music was so much more effective in the theater coming out of these big, loudspeakers all around me. And I experienced it with an audience who were screaming and yelling at the characters, and I had honestly never experienced that kind of interactive thing that happens when you experience horror films with an audience in a theater.

So that was really the beginning of it all. To me, *Halloween II* was a continuation of the same movie. I mean, it's shot by Dean Cundey, who is a genius. And it had Jamie Lee, it had Donald Pleasence, and story-wise, it was literally a continuation of what I had seen the week before. So I didn't look at anything as being bad or inferior in any way, shape, or form. And I might have loved it even greater because it was more of it. In a way it scared me more because it just felt bigger.

"It's astounding to think that I was 12 years old when I was exposed to *Halloween* and *Halloween II* and then *Halloween III*, which we were all scratching our heads about, and then all these years after that I was making *Halloween 6*. Around the 20th anniversary of *Halloween 6* was when I noticed the tide started to sort of change a bit. That was when I started to get those emails and fan letters from all over the world and still get to this day. A lot of them tell me how *Halloween 6* was the first time they experienced a *Halloween* film in the theater, or it was the first *Halloween* that they saw. But it's great to me, and it is very flattering. It's a weird, full-circle thing, and I enjoy just seeing how it's kind of lived on. And now that it has been out for so long, it has become successful. The longevity of it is amazing."

Thanks to Farrands's fan worship of the franchise, the heroine of his film, Marianne Hagan, was more than aware of the importance and expectation of becoming part of the revered *Halloween* history:

"Dan made me very aware of how beloved the franchise was and so we wanted it to be a really good movie, not just a good horror movie. There hadn't been one in six years. I went and rented all the previous films, and it was then that I also realized just how important Donald Pleasence was to the whole thing. I was so nervous around Donald that I could barely talk. I get like that when I'm around people that I really admire. I come off as being cold because I'm just too nervous; I don't have the confidence. So I don't know what to say, and I don't want to say anything stupid. [adopts Old Hollywood mid-Atlantic accent] "Hello, Mr. Pleasence. Ms. Hagan. I look forward to working with you." I could never be like that; I just stand in the corner. It was especially wonderful to work with Donald Pleasence because

I come from the theater and Donald was Harold Pinter's muse for many of his characters, particularly the character of Davies in *The Caretaker*. I was so intimidated by Donald's presence. But on one of the working days where it was me, Paul [Rudd], and Donald running down the hallways, I was sitting in one of the directors' chairs and reading *Vanity Fair* magazine, and Donald came up and sat on the chair next to me and said, 'What are you reading?' And I said, 'Oh, *Vanity Fair*,' and I showed him the cover, which had some cheesy movie star on it. And he said, 'Ahhh, Thackeray's best!' And I howled with laughter because his wit was so sharp, even though he was not well physically, which was quite apparent right away. His wife was on the set with him, and he did not hang out between takes. She brought him straight back to his trailer. And he was also using a cane, and they added a line into the movie where he talks about using a cane to Mitch Ryan's character. But when you could get him, it was extraordinary. I can't think of another actor of that ilk that I could have worked with. The fact that I was able to work with Donald Pleasence on his last movie meant something. I've done a few conventions, and I've met fans who can recite the entire movie. They know all my lines! Some of them get hyper focused and obsessed, and they know everything. It has become part of my life; it comes up all the time. I got lucky so young that *Halloween: The Curse of Michael Myers* was my first major movie."

The *Halloween* franchise began with a modest independent film and became an industry, launching the careers of actors, directors, cinematographers, and others who never thought much of it other than being a very effective genre picture. Little did they realize that it would become a touchstone in their professional lives, that no matter what huge blockbusters they would go on to make, writers and film historians like me will be calling to ask them about the work they did on this humble horror movie they did back in 1978. Looking back on the legacy of *Halloween* and how it changed not only film history and horror cinema, but their very lives, some of those who were there in the very beginning reflect on what it all means to them.

Composer Alan Howarth considers the key to the longevity of the franchise and impact that it has had on culture to be one simple factor: "It's Michael Myers. The genius of the character, the faceless evil, it just worked. You could put anybody in those movies, but as long as you have Michael Myers, then the fans are happy because then you have a *Halloween* movie. It certainly wasn't designed to be this huge pop-culture thing; I'm sure John, Debra, and Tommy never thought it was going to be what it turned out to be. Back in the beginning, when they were making *Halloween* in 1978, they were all just in their mid-20s and were rolling up their sleeves and doing it on no budget. Jamie Lee Curtis was there on set and helped paint the house. They were all there working as a team. It wasn't as disciplined and regimented as the way it would become; they were just all there working together and being happy making a movie. They were kids, and never knew what it was going to become."

Dean Cundey, director of photography on the first three films, says, "I had done all these cheap, low-budget action movies prior to *Halloween*, but there's almost none of them that stick out in my mind as being anything different. They were made

Jamie Lee Curtis and director John Carpenter share a moment on the set of *Halloween* (1978). Album/Alamy Stock Photo

for a particular purpose, for the drive-in theater; they were made for a cheap price on a short schedule. None of them were exceptionally well written or well acted, but *Halloween* was the first one that stood out. And that is because I had a lot of input, so I'm proud of that. Nobody calls me up and says, 'Oh, I saw *Satan's Cheerleaders* the other day; what a fabulous film you made!' I'm sorry, but they don't; though with *Halloween*, people tell me that they have loved it since they were a kid or a teenager. It means something to them. It's interesting when I go to a fan convention. I have a couple one-sheets up of stuff I've done, and they'll say, 'Oh, *Halloween*! I remember seeing that when I was young and in high school, and now I'm showing it to my kids. Don't tell anyone!' And I think it's a good thing that they do because even though it's a horror film, it's a psychological experience . . . there's no blood! You never see a knife stabbing and slicing or repulsive, gruesome stuff; rather, it's all in your mind. I think that is what makes it a unique, stand-alone experience that has been popular through about three generations of audiences. So *Halloween* is a landmark movie in my life and career and, of course, in the world of low-budget independent filmmaking."

Production designer and editor Tommy Lee Wallace knew they had made a film that they would be forever proud of, but not something that would change lives and careers to the degree that it has for so many people. "We all knew by the time we'd finished it that we had a good movie on our hands and by the time John put the music in, which is extremely effective, we knew that not only did we have a good movie, but we had a scary movie. So we all felt that it would most likely find an audience. That's about as far as our imagination went. I don't think any of us could have dreamed of the phenomenal level that it rose to and, of course, to what it has spawned; we couldn't have predicted that. I have mixed feelings about its status as this iconic thing because I wish the movie had made me rich the way it did John and Debra and Irwin Yablans, but you know, that's the way the ball bounces. I feel very proud of it and very good about it, and I get a hell of a lot of respect because of it. So that's nice."

Brad Loree, the man behind the mask of *Halloween: Resurrection*, considers the impact that the franchise has had not only on pop culture and the fans but also on his own life: "Wayne, I had no idea what I was getting into when I took the *Halloween* job. Some people are so into it; I had one kid say to me [adopts ominous voice] 'You are the first Michael Myers with blue eyes.' If you can see Michael Myers's eye color, then you're not watching the movie! But I'm very humbled when fans want to meet me and ask for my autograph. I love horror fans because they are so loyal to their genre and they are just the nicest people—I don't get it, they all want to see blood, guts, and gore, but they are the nicest people that you will ever meet in your life. A writer buddy of mine once said to me that playing Michael Myers is like being a *Playboy* centerfold because that is all you are going to be known for in certain circles for the rest of your life. At 95 years of age, I'll be known as Michael Myers! So I hope the franchise isn't over with *Halloween Ends*. I don't know what that will do for its popularity if it is: will it get less popular or more popular? All I know is the demand for horror and the love for *Halloween* is alive and well. And now, because of that, I get to go to conventions, and I get to do interviews and talk about the film with people like you, Wayne, and make new friends all over the world. The whole thing of being involved in the *Halloween* franchise has been a lot of fun."

Index

Abbey Theatre, 49–50
Above the Law (film), 82
abstract psychology, 3
Academy Awards, 127, 211
acting, 24, 30–31, 38–39, *40*
Affleck, Ben, 188
After Darkness (film), 89–90, 110
AIDS panic, 114
Akkad, Malek: leadership of, 143, 181–82; reputation of, 84, 121, 227; Zombie and, 125, 211–12
Akkad, Moustapha: collaboration with, 61, 68, 75–76, 78–79, 92–93, 128; as executive producer, xiv–xv, 115–18, 120–21, 135; leadership of, 87–88, 90–92, 98–99, 134, 143, 152; Othenin-Girard and, 104, 112–13, 117–18, 124–25
All the Real Girls (film), 217–18
Almendros, Néstor, 66
Americana (film), 63
American International, 67
American Reunion (film), 157
Amityville (film), 217
The Amityville Horror (film), 71
The Amityville Horror (remake), 195

Anderson, Richard, 36
Animal Factory (film), 201, 203
Annaud, Jean-Jacques, 113
Apollo 13 (film), 18
Aquarius Releasing, 26
ARP Avatars, 79
Arriflex, 15
Assault on Precinct 13 (film), 2, 5, 8–9, 19–20
Atkins, Tom, 43, 49, *50*, 57
Atlantic City (film), 144
auteur theory, 2, 62, 99
Avenging Angel (film), 67

Babin, Paul, 73
Back to the Future Trilogy (films), 18
Badham, John, 165
Baker, Joe Don, 67
Banks, Tyra, 173–74
Battle in Outer Space (film), 6
The Bear (film), 113
Beck, Michael, 64
Beltrami, Marco, 168, 188–89
Berlin Film Festival, 90
Bertolucci, Bernardo, 62
Beverly Hills, 90210 (TV show), 176–77

235

Big Brother (TV show), 176
Big Trouble in Little China (film), 18, 79–80
Bitterman, Shem, 90, 93
BlacKkKlansman (film), 217
Black Shampoo (film), 13
The Blair Witch Project (film), 174–76
Bloodstone (film), 68
Blue Öyster Cult, 221
Blumhouse. *See specific films*
B-movies, 67
Bodhi Tree Bookstore, 134
Boorman, John, 194
Born on the Fourth of July (film), 118
Bornstein, Charles, 20
Boston Legal (TV show), 190
Bowie, David, 35
Brady, Jerry, 117–18
The Brady Bunch (TV show), 77
Braino, 35
Brandy, J. C., 132
Brecht, Bertolt, 202
Brown, Garrett, 202
budgets, 9–13, 20–22, 31–32, 48–49
Buechler, John Carl, 81
Bunker, Eddie, 203
Buñuel, Luis, 49–50, 62
"Burned Hills" project, 92
Buscemi, Steve, 201–3
Busta Rhymes, 173–74, 183–84, 193

The Cable Guy (film), 165
Cahiers du Cinéma, 211
California, sets in, 43–45, 53–55, 55
Cannes Film Festival, 127
Cannibal Holocaust (film), 174

Cannon Films, 82
Can't Buy Me Love (film), 67
Can't Stop the Music (film), 63
Capra, Frank, 3
The Caretaker (film), 231
Carpenter, John: Blumehouse trilogy for, 199; career of, 26, 34, 37, 49, *218*; collaboration with, 13–14, 16, 20–21; Cundey and, 18–19, 162–63; Curtis and, xiv–xv, 53, *232*; directing, *19*; in film school, 7–8; Hill and, 11, *15*, 21, 31, 47, 54, 232–33; for horror films, 216–17, 220–21, 226–29; Howarth and, 37–38, 46, 54–56, 58, 167; legacy of, 70, 83–85, 91–92, 102, 200–201; music and, 55–56, 70, 149, 167–69, 189–90; Othenin-Girard compared to, 115; Parmet on, 201; reputation of, 1–5, 27–28, 38–39, 41, 148, 151–52, 197; Steadicam for, 163; success of, xiv, 26, 93, 141–42, 147–48, 191, 217; at USC, 62; Wallace, T. L., and, 5–7, 16–17, 19–20; for Zombie, 198
Carr, Allan, 63
Caso, Alan, 73
Castle, Nick, 179, 192, 221
CGI effects, 72, 183
Chappelle, Joe, 140, 144
Children of the Corn II (film), 127
Children of the Corn: Revelation (film), 195
Child's Play (film), xiii
Churchill, Ted, 102–4
Cinderella Liberty (film), 62
Cinema Paradiso (film), 159
Citizen Kane (film), 3, 66
Clark, Bruce, 12

Clark, Greydon, 13, 31
A Clockwork Orange (film), 205
Close Encounters of the Third Kind (film), 20, 160
Cloverfield (film), 175
Clueless (film), 137–38, 145
Collister, Peter Lyons, 61, 65–67, 71–75, 77–78, 84, 177–78
Coppola, Francis Ford, 8, 62
Cop Trap (film), 89–90
Corea, Chick, 36
Corman, Roger, 11–12
Cornell, Ellie, 76, 78, 85–86
Coscarelli, Don, 159–60
Coto, Manny, 123
The Craft (film), 217
Craven, Wes, 2–3, 126
Crazy People (film), 136
Cream, 35
Creepshow (TV show), 123
The Crying Game (film), 126–27
Cundey, Dean: career of, xv, 12–13, 177–78, 230, 232–33; Carpenter and, 18–19, 162–63; cinematography by, 4–5, 32–34, 53–54; experience of, 11–12; on genres, 22–23; Hill and, 13–14, 229; Howarth and, 53–54; legacy of, 102; on lighting, 32–33; with Panaglide, 14–17; reputation of, 26, 31, 46, 72–73; Stella and, 14–15; Wallace, T. L., and, 2, 11, 48
Curtis, Jaime Lee: acting, 1, *24*, 30–31, *40*, 152; Carpenter and, xiv–xv, 53, *232*; Gifford and, 30–31; Green and, 221–23, *223*; in Hollywood, 74–75, 152–53, 161–62; return of, 153–54, *156*, 170, 173–74, 185–86, 221–22,

226; star power of, 172–73, 193, 216–17
Cyphers, Charles, 26–27, 31

Damien: Omen II (film), 195
Damon, Matt, 188
Dangertainment, 174, 176, 183
Dark Angel (TV show), 177
The Dark Side (film), 24
Dark Star (student film), 6–9
Daviau, Allen, 73
Davis, Miles, 36
Dawson's Creek (TV Show), 170
Days of Heaven (film), 66
The Dead (film), 50–51
Death of a Centerfold (TV movie), 30–31
Depardieu, Gérard, 161
The Devil's Rain (film), 64
The Devil's Rejects (film), 201, 203–4, 208, 211
Diary of the Dead (film), 175–76
DiCillo, Tom, 126–27, 197
Dickson, Billy, 147, 177–78
Dimension Films, 126, 127, 136, 156, 168–70, 187–88, 195–96, 210. *See also specific films*
Dirty Dancing (film), 102
Dirty Harry (film), 3
Disney, 161, 229
Dr. Giggles (TV show), 95–96, 123
Dog Day Afternoon (film), 62
Donner, Richard, 122
Don Post studios, 58
"(Don't Fear) the Reaper," 221
The Doors, 35
Double Indemnity (film), 52
Doyle, Tommy, 126
Dracula (film), 22–23
Draper, Rob: career of, xv, 122–24, 177–78; cinematography

238 / Index

by, 95–102, 107–9, 122–23; Othenin-Girard and, 102–5, 107–8; on Pleasence, 110–11; on violence, 108–9
Dune (film), 92
Durand, Chris, 162
DVDs, 82

East Los Angeles College, 159
Easy Rider (film), 33, 157
Eberlein, Bob, 12
Elvis (TV miniseries), 160–61
Emulator I, 79
Emulator II, 79
English, Bradford, 132, 140
Englund, Robert, 82
Escape from New York (film), 18, 34, 37–38, 49, 55, 79
Everything Everywhere All at Once (film), 221
The Evil Dead (film), 159
The Exorcist (film), 74, 131, 194
The Exorcist II (film), 194

Famous Monsters of Filmland (film), 24
Fangoria: for horror films, 23–25, 48–49, 213; leadership at, 25–26, 80–81, 83–84; legacy of, xiii–xiv, 221–23; press from, 119–20, 146, 169–70, 209–10
Farrands, Daniel: on cinematography, 141–42; Hagan and, 144–45, 147–48; on Hollywood, 140–41; horror films for, 129–31, 230–31; in meetings, 136; on sequels, 145, 229–30; on symbolism, 142–43; writing by, 128, 131–35, 138–39, 150–52

film schools: East Los Angeles College, 159; education in, 7–9; NYU, 65; UCLA, 12, 14, 159; USC, 6–8, 14, 62–66, 74, 166–67; Wallace, T. L., in, 7–8; workshops compared to, 96–97
film stock, 97–98
Flick, Stephen, 36
The Fog (film), 15, 18, 49, 75
Forbidden Planet (film), 200
Ford, John, 3
Forever Young (film), 157
formalism, 32–33
Forsythe, William, 198
Four Rooms (film), 201
Frankenstein (film), 22
Franklin, Richard, 60–61
Freddy's Dead (film), 46
Freddy vs. Jason (film), 193, 195, 228
Freeman, Paul, 119–20, 189
Free Willy (film), 123
Friday the 13th (film), xiii, 68, 83–84, 90–91, 142, 151
Friday the 13th (franchise), 224, 228
Friday the 13th (remake), 195
Friday the 13th Part II (film), 156
Friday the 13th Part III (film), 156
Friday the 13th Part VI (film), 60–61
Friday the 13th Part VII (film), xiii
Friday the 13th Part VIII (film), 115–16, 120
Friedkin, William, 194

Gate Theatre, 49
Geddes, David, 176–78, 183–86, *185*, 192
Geffen, David, 122
George Washington (film), 217–18

Get Out (film), 217
Getting Even (film), 66–67
Ghostbusters (film), 102
The Giant Gila Monster (film), 6
Gifford, Gloria, 29–31
Glaser, Milton, 6
Glynn, Tamara, 113–14
Goin' South (film), 66
Golan, Menahem, 82–83
Goldsmith, Jerry, 165–66, 188
The Good Wife (TV show), 190
The Goonies (film), 160
GoPro cameras, 174
The Great Escape (film), 77
Green, David Gordon: career of, 41, 170; criticism of, 219–21; Curtis and, 221–23, *223*; directing by, 200, 223–24, 226; for fans, 216–17; for reboot, xiv; reputation of, 191, 199, 208–9. *See also Halloween* Trilogy
Grey, Brad, 126
Grey's Anatomy (TV show), 190–91
Guare, John, 144
Gunsmoke (TV show), 63

Hagan, Marianne: acting by, 132, 136–40, *137*, *141*, 152–53; Farrands and, 144–45, 147–48; legacy of, xv, 230–31
Haig, Sid, 215
Hall, Conrad, 158
Halloween (film): characters in, xiii; as horror, 2–3, 4; influences of, 3–5, 17–18; legacy of, 131, 136, 138, 216–17; through lines in, 53–54; music in, 37–38; opening scene of, 102; poster for, 4, 135; pre-production of, 11–14; production design for, 9–10; reputation of, 23–24, 164–65, 229–30; scenes from, *5*, *23*; scholarship on, 1–2; script for, 28–29; success of, 18–21, 25–26, 41, 144, 191, 217, 230–34; viewers of, 16–17; voyeurism in, 141–42; Wallace, T. L., on, 5–7. *See also Halloween* franchise
Halloween (reboot, 2018): reception of, 216–23, *218–20*; success of, xiv; themes in, 39–41, 125. *See also Halloween* franchise
Halloween (remake): cast of, *205*, 205–8, *207*; cinematography for, 201–5; nostalgia and, 197–98; plot of, 198–200; poster for, *196*; reception of, 200–201, 210–11; success of, xiv; Zombie for, *206*, 208–10, *209*. *See also Halloween* franchise
Halloween II (film): cinematography in, 32–34; Curtis in, 30–31; directing for, 29–30; ending of, 59, 77; legacy of, 216, 229–30; through lines in, 53–54, 165; music for, 33–34, 38–39, 78–79; plot of, 26–27, 39–41; poster for, *28*, 135; reputation of, 26–29, 42, 58, 61, 146; as sequel, 31–32, 38–39, 136, 163, 176–77, 230. *See also Halloween* franchise
Halloween II (remake), 211–15, *212*, *214*
Halloween III (film): casting for, 49–51, *50*; cinematography in, 53–54; Ireland/Irish culture

in, 43–45, *51*, 51–53; legacy of, 216–17, 229–30; through lines in, 53–54; music in, 54–56, 78–79; plot of, 42–45; poster for, *44*, 135; reception of, xiv, 46, 56–58, 230; reputation of, 26, 45–46, 59, 84; screenplay for, 46–49. *See also Halloween* franchise

Halloween 4 (film): cast for, 74–78, *76*; cinematography in, 70–73; collaboration for, 66; crew for, 73–74, 179; ending of, 92; music in, 78–80; plot of, 59–61, 68–69; poster for, *60*, 135; press for, 80–82; reception of, xiii–xiv, 25, 82–86, 90; reputation of, 93, 127–28, 149; set locations for, 69–70; themes in, 39–40. *See also Halloween* franchise

Halloween 5 (film): cinematography in, 95–99; continuity in, 85–86, 109–11, 132–33, 146–47; directing, *105*, 100–109, 112–16; editing, 117–18; music in, 79, 118–19; plot of, 86–87, 116–17; poster for, *88*, 135; pre-production of, 88–95, *94*; press for, 81, 119–20; reception of, 120–25, 154–56; reputation of, 99–100, 127–28, 149; symbolism in, 70; writing, 87–89, 134. *See also Halloween* franchise

Halloween 6 (film): casting for, 136–38, *137*; continuity in, 87, 90–91, 111, 116, 146–47; filming issues with, 143–45; music in, 79; plot of, 131–33, *133*; poster for, *129*; pre-production of, 126–29; *Producer's Cut*, 132, 142–50; reception of, 146–53, 156, 170, 230–31; screenplay for, 134–35; themes of, 138–43, *141*. *See also Halloween* franchise

Halloween Ends (film), xv, 220–21, 223–25, 224–26, 234. *See also Halloween* franchise

Halloween franchise: cinematography in, 177–78; continuity in, 53–57, 59–60, 101–2, 111–12, 124–25, 127–28, 173–74; in culture, 150, 157, 230–34; fans of, 216–17, 229–30; heroines in, 74–75; as intellectual property, 143–44; legacy of, 226–27; Loree on, 192–93; Lux on, 191–92; music in, 34, 54–56, 200–201; Okada on, 162–64; Pleasence for, 76–77; point of view in, 177–78; press for, 216–17; producers of, 119–20; reception of, 57–58, 115–16, 131–32; reputation of, 83–84, 203–4, 211; sibling theme in, 39–40; staples of, 68–71, 94–95; success of, 152–53, 195–96; themes in, 154–55, 179–81; Zombie for, 197–201. *See also specific Halloween films*

Halloween H20 (film): cinematography in, 157–65; continuity in, 154–56, 174, 229; Curtis in, 153–54, *156*; directing, *162*; legacy of, 216; Miner for, 156–57; music in, 165–69, 186; plot of, 29, 40; poster for, *155*; press for, 169–70; reception of, 170–73; score

of, xv; success of, xiv, 127. *See also Halloween* franchise
Halloween Kills (film), xiii, 200, 216, 222, 223–25. *See also Halloween* franchise
Halloween: Resurrection (film): acting in, 178–82; cinematography in, 176–78; connectivity in, 41–42, 173; filming logistics of, 183–86, *185*; legacy of, 216; music in, 186–91; plot of, 173–74, 182–83; poster for, *175*; reception of, 191–93, 198; stylistics of, 174–76. *See also Halloween* franchise
Halloween Trilogy, 216–21, 222–25, 226–28, *227*. *See also specific films*
Hancock, Herbie, 36
Harders, Robert, 91–93
Hard to Kill (film), 82
Harlan County USA (documentary), 201–2
Harris, Danielle: acting by, 78, 84, 86, 102, 108–9, 113; casting, 59, 73–75, 76
Harris, Freddie, 173
Hartley, Hal, 197
Hartnett, Josh, 170
Hawks, Howard, 9, 19–20, 200
Heaven's Gate (film), 197
Heavy Weather (album), 35
Heckerling, Amy, 137
Hellbound (film), xiii
Hellraiser: Bloodline (film), 46
Hellraiser: Deader (film), 195
Hellraiser: Hellseeker (film), 195
Hellraiser: Hellworld (film), 195
Hellraiser III (film), 127
Hellraiser: Inferno (film), 195
Herrman, Bernard, 167–68, 171, 188

Higher Learning (film), 67
High Plains Drifter (film), 203
Hill, Debra: Carpenter and, 11, *15*, 21, 31, 47, 54, 232–33; casting by, 49; collaboration with, 93; Cundey and, 13–14, 229; leadership of, 38, 151–52; legacy of, 179, 229; networking with, 89–90; reputation of, 27–28; writing by, 2, 11, 13–15, 29–30
Hitchcock, Alfred, 3, 154
The Hitcher (remake), 195
Hollywood: B-movies in, 67–68; business in, 134; Curtis in, 74–75, 152–53, 161–62; Farrands on, 140–41; Golden Age of, 50–51, 99, 157; icons of, 52; independent filmmaking compared to, 21–22; music and, 34–38; New Hollywood movement, 6, 62–64, 157–58; in press, 121; studio system, 33, 230–31; USC and, 6–7
Hollywood Creative Directory, 134
The Hollywood Reporter (magazine), 121
Holst, Gustav, 166
Hopper, Dennis, 157
horror films: acting in, 38–39; Carpenter for, 216–17, 220–21, 226–29; cinematography in, 70–73; as comedies, 187–88; in culture, xiii–xv; by Dimension Films, 168–70, 210; documentaries on, 151; Englund in, 82–83; famous, 90; fans of, 192–93, 217; for Farrands, 129–31, 230–31; Hitchcock for, 154; Howarth on, 57, 148–49; independent,

157; low-budget strategies for, 48–49; in magazines, 23–25, 48–49, 213; for Miramax, 186–88; music and, 78–80, 118–19, 149–50, 200–201, 231–32; Othenin-Girard and, 113–14, 120–21; outliers in, 45–46; psychology of, 22–23; psychosexual experiences in, 114–15; science-fiction and, 46; sequels to, 59–61, 115–16, 127, 194–96, *196*; slasher films and, 83–84; Timpone on, 146, 172–73, 228; for Weinstein brothers, 126–27; writing for, 90–92, 150
House of 1000 Corpses (film), 197, 201
Howard, Clint, 215
Howard, Ron, 7, 18
Howard, Sandy, 64–65
Howarth, Alan: career of, 34–38; Carpenter and, 37–38, 46, 54–56, 58, 167; Cundey and, 53–54; on horror films, 57, 148–49; legacy of, 231–32; Othenin-Girard and, 119; replacement of, 165; reputation of, 78–79, 149–50
Hurt, John, 90, 110
Huston, John, 50

Incognito (film), 165
independent filmmaking, 21–22, 25–26
In Our Hands (documentary), 201
In the Soup (film), 201–2
Invasion of the Body Snatchers (film), 46–47
Ireland/Irish culture, 43–45, 49–53, *51*, 56
The Island of Dr. Moreau (film), 64

It (film), 11
It's a Wonderful Life (film), 3

Jackson, Michael, 67
Jacobs, Michael, 93
Jason Goes to Hell (film), 228
Jason X (film), 228
Jaws (film), 72
Jaws 2 (film), 195
Jefferson Airplane, 35
Jenner, Caitlyn, 64
Jesus Christ Superstar (film), 129–30
Johnny Suede (film), 126
Jordan, Neil, 126
Joston, Darwin, 9
Jurassic Park (film), 18, 161
Just Like Heaven (film), 157

Kennedy, John F., 200
KGB (film), 65–67
King, Stephen, 11
Kirzinger, Ken, 180, 193
KISS, 35
Kleiser, Randal, 62, 66
Kneale, Nigel, 46–49, 52–53
Kodak, 159
Kopple, Barbara, 201–2
Kovács, László, 33, 158
Kramer vs. Kramer (film), 66
Kurzweil K250, 79
Kyes/Loomis, Nancy, 25, 53

Lady in White (film), 157
Lake Placid (film), 161, 172
Lang, Fritz, 99
Lawrence, Peter, 126
Lee, Spike, 217
Leigh, Janet, 154, *156*
lens flares, 32–33

Leroux, Gaston, 82
Life of Galileo (Brecht), 202
Lions Gate Entertainment, 197–98
Little, Dwight: casting by, 75–77, 76; collaboration with, 75–76; Collister and, 65–67, 71–74, 84; directing by, 68–71, 78, 84–86; early career of, 61–65; legacy of, 94–95; Othenin-Girard and, xv; reputation of, 93; Seagal and, 82–83; at USC, 62–64
Lloyd, Jaime, 78, 86
Lonesome Jim (film), 201
Lookinland, Mike, 77–78
Loomis, Samuel, 1, 26–27, 59, 87, 109, 111, *133*
Loree, Brad, xv, 174–84, *182*, *185*, 192–93, 213–14, 234
"Love Hurts," 204
Lucas, George, 7, 8, 62
Los Luchadores (TV show), 180–81
Lumet, Sidney, 62
Lux, Danny, 186–92
Lynch, David, 50–51, 92

Macbeth (film), 49
MacMurray, Fred, 52
MacNeil, Regan, 194
Malick, Terrence, 66
Malle, Louis, 144
Malmuth, Bruce, 82–83
Mane, Tyler, 214–15
Man in the Wilderness (film), 64
Marked for Death (film), 83, 86
Mastorakis, Nico, 67–68
Max, Peter, 6
Maylam, Tony, 126
Mazursky, Paul, 62
McBride, Danny, 217–19, 224
McCullough, Jim, Sr., 12
McDowell, Malcolm, 205–7, 215

McElroy, Alan B., 68, 85–86
McLean, Nick, 160–61
McLoughlin, Tom, 60–61
Mean Girls (film), 157
Memoirs of an Invisible Man (film), 197
MGM studios, 81
Microwave Massacre (film), 157
MIDI, 79–80, 166
Midnight Cowboy (film), 157
Milius, John, 62
Mimic (film), 168–69
Miner, Steve: career of, 153; directing by, 156–57, 164; Durand and, *162*; McLean and, 160–61; Okada and, 160–62; Ottman and, 165, 167–68, 172; vision of, 167
Miramax: horror films for, 186–88; leadership at, 152, 163, 208; success at, 126–27, 136, 149–50
de Mol, John, Jr., 176
Monsters (TV show), 95
Moore, Dudley, 136
Morelli, Tony, 179–80
Morga, Tom, 179
Moseley, Bill, 215
Motion Picture Association of America (MPAA), 107
Moviolas, 36, 63, 118
MPAA. *See* Motion Picture Association of America
MTV, 197
Murnau, F. W., 99
Murphy, Eddie, 67
Murray, Andy, 52–53
music: Carpenter and, 55–56, 70, 149, 167–69, 189–90; characters and, 54–56; for *Halloween* films, 33–39, 54–56, 78–80, 118–19, 165–69, 186–91, 200–201;

Hollywood and, 34–38; horror films and, 78–80, 118–19, 149–50, 200–201, 231–32; by Lux, 186–91; making, 6; by Ottman, 165–69, 171–72, 186, 188–89
My Father the Hero (film), 157
My Name Is Earl (TV show), 190
Myrick, Daniel, 174
My Three Sons (TV show), 52

Narelle, Brian, 8
National Geographic (magazine), 65
Nazareth, 204
Nelkin, Stacey, 43, *50*
The Neptune Factor (film), 64
New Hollywood movement, 6, 62–64, 157–58
New Line Cinema, 67
New York University (NYU), 65
Nicholson, Jack, 66
Nicotero, Greg, 115
Nighthawks (film), 82
A Nightmare on Elm Street (film), xiii, 2–3, 83, 90–91, 151, 228
A Nightmare on Elm Street (remake), 195
A Nightmare on Elm Street 3 (film), 60–61
A Nightmare on Elm Street 4 (film), xiii
A Nightmare on Elm Street 5 (film), 120
NYU. *See* New York University

O'Bannon, Dan, 6–8
Odd Man Out (film), 49
O'Herlihy, Dan, 49–52, *51*, 57
Ohio Arts Council, 62
Okada, Daryn: career of, 177–78; cinematography by, 157–65; on criticism, 172; on franchise, 162–64, 228–29; Miner and, 160–62
The Omen (film), 194
Omen II (film), 131
Ondříček, Miroslav, 104
Ordinary People (film), 140
Othenin-Girard, Dolminique: Akkad, Moustapha, and, 104, 112–13, 117, 124–25; Brady and, 117–18; career of, 87–91; criticism of, 112–13, 121, 123–24; directing by, 94–95 *94*, 100–109, *105*, 112–16; Draper and, 102–5, 107–8; for Hill, 151–52; horror films and, 113–14, 120–21; Howarth and, 119; leadership of, 99–100, 102–3; Little and, xv; on MPAA, 107–8; on Pleasence, 109–11, 120; reputation of, 70, 133; writing for, 87–89, 91–93
Ottman, John: career of, xv; on criticism, 170–71; Miner and, 165, 167–68, 172; music by, 165–69, 171–72, 186, 188–89
The Outlaw Josey Wales (film), 203

Panaglide, 14–17. *See also* Steadicam
Panavision lens, 54, 164
The Parallax View (film), 62
Paramount (studio), 11, 197
Paranormal Activity (film), 174–75, 217
Parmet, Phil, 201–11, *207*, *209*
Pastorious, Jaco, 35–36
Paul Revere & the Raiders, 35
Peele, Jordan, 217
Peeping Tom (film), 3
Pepperman, Paul, 159–60

Phantasm (film), 157, 159–60
Phantasm II (film), 160
The Phantom of the Opera, 82–83, 86
Phillips, Todd, 176
Pi Keyboards and Audio store, 35
Pineapple Express (film), 217
Pink Floyd, 79
Pinter, Harold, 231
The Planets (symphony), 166
Platinum Dunes productions, 196
Pleasence, Donald: acting by, 1, 26, 31, *40*; collaboration with, 101; Collister on, 77–78; continuity with, 76–77, 84; Hagan and, 230–31; legacy of, 69, 87, 109–11, 150, 230; in makeup, 81; with press, 120; Ryan and, 132–33, *133*
Poetic Justice (film), 67
Pollack, Sydney, 62
Post, Mike, 186–87
Powell, Michael, 3
Project Greenlight (TV show), 188
Project X (film), 176
Prom Night (film), 41, 75
Propaganda Films, 67
Prophet 5, 79
Prophet 10, 79
Psycho (film), 3, 154, 171
Psycho II (film), 60–61
psychosexual experiences, 3–5, 114–15
Public Access (film), 165
Pulp Fiction (film), 127
Push Pin Studios, 6

Quatermass and the Pit (film), 46, 48

Raimi, Sam, 159
Ramsay, Todd, 37

Rapid Fire (film), 86
Read, Theron, 116
Reed, Carol, 49
The Return of a Man Called Horse (film), 64
Return to Forever, 35
Richter, Robert, 201
The Right Stuff (film), 102
Rio Bravo (film), 9, 20
Risner, Brian, 35–36
Robinson Crusoe (film), 49–50
RoboCop (film), 50
Rockwell, Alexandre, 201–2
Rockwell Downey plant, 158
Romero, George, 97, 175
Rosemary's Baby (film), 138, 142
Rosenthal, Rick, 29–31, 38–39, 176–77, 179, 182, 189, 193
Rudd, Paul, 132, 136–38, *137*, 145, 152–53, 231
Rue Morgue (film), 24–25
Rune Magic (Tyson), 134
Russell, Chuck, 60–61
Ryan, Mitchell, 132–33, *133*, 231

Sanchez, Eduardo, 174
Sands, Julian, 90
Sandy Howard Productions, 67
Satan's Cheerleaders (film), 233
Sayer, Jack, 59
Scalia, Pietro, 118
Scary Movie 2 (film), 187–88
Scheider, Roy, 136
Schlesinger, John, 157
science-fiction, 46
Scissors (film), 71
Scorsese, Martin, 62
Scream (film), 126, 155–56, 163, 168–69, 172–73, 189
Scream 2 (film), 168
Scream Factory, 151

Screen Actors Guild, 136
Seagal, Steven, 82–83
SeaQuest DSV (TV show), 136
The Searchers (film), 3
Season of the Witch. See Halloween III (film)
Série noire (TV show), 89–90
Serpico (film), 62
Sex, Lies, and Videotape (film), 126
Shanks, Don, 101, 105–8, 111
Shapiro, Marc, 80
The Shining (film), 102
Shorter, Wayne, 35–36
siblings, 39–40
Siegel, Don, 3, 46–47
Silence of the Lambs (film), 68
Silk, 35
Silver, Joel, 122
Simmonds, Michael, 221
Sinfonia antarica (symphony), 166
Singer, Bryan, 165–66
Singleton, John, 67
slasher films, xiii–xv, 22, 83–84
Smiling Dog Saloon (nightclub), 35
Snow Angels (film), 217
sociology, 3
Soderbergh, Steven, 126
Soul Man (film), 157
Spendlove, Randy, 186
Spielberg, Steven, 8, 18, 33, 136
Stallone, Sylvester, 82
Starr, Beau, 86
Star Trek (film), 36, 37, 166
Star Trek (TV show), 165–66
Star Wars (film), 130, 150, 197, 229
Steadicam: with 16-millimeter film, 73; for Carpenter, 163; for filmmaking, 14–17; reputation of, 22, 102–3; subjectivity with, 114–15

Stella, Raymond, 14–15, 17
Stoker, Austin, 9
Stolen Summer (film), 188
Stone, Oliver, 118
Straight Time (Bunker), 203
stunt doubles, 179–81
subjectivity, 14–17, 32–33
The Sugarland Express (film), 33
Sundance Film Festival, 87
Super 8 films, 65
Super 35 film, 164
Swift, Brent, 116
Synclavier, 80
synthesizers, 79–80

Tales from the Crypt (TV show), 95–96, 122–23
Tales from the Darkside (TV show/film series), 95–98, 122
Tarantino, Quentin, 127, 155
Taylor-Compton, Taylor, 205
Technicolor, 159
Terror Train (film), 41, 75
The Texas Chainsaw Massacre (film), 195
The Texas Chainsaw Massacre (remake), 195
Texas Chainsaw Massacre: The Next Generation (film), 46
The Thing (film), 14, 37–38, 192
The Thing from Another World (film), 200
Thomas, Ramsey, 90, 134
Thorne, Diane, 215
Three Days of the Condor (film), 62
Timpone, Tony: on horror films, 146, 172–73, 228; on Othenin-Girard, 121; press with, 25–26, 48–49, 57–58, 80–81, 83–84; on promotion, 119–20, 169–70; on reboot, 221–23, 225–26;

on remake, 213; on Zombie, 200–201, 210, 214–15
To Have and Have Not (film), 20
Toth, Wayne, 214
Touch of Evil (film), xv, 14, 101, 108
Tree Stumps, 35
Triumphs of a Man Called Horse (film), 64–66
Truffaut, François, 62
Tucci, Stanley, 202
TV movies, 20, 30–31
20th Century Fox, 83
21 Jump Street (TV show), 176, 186
Twin Peaks (TV show), 50–51
Tyson, Donald, 134

U2, 35
UCLA. *See* University of California Los Angeles
United Artists/MGM, 197
United States culture, 48, 114, 194–96, *196*
unit photography, 80–81
Universal Studios, 130
University of California Los Angeles (UCLA), 12, 14, 159
University of Southern California (USC), 6–8, 14, 62–66, 74, 166
The Usual Suspects (film), 165

Van Damme, Jean-Claude, 211
Vanity Fair (magazine), 231
Variety (magazine), 120–21
Verhoeven, Paul, 50
Vertigo (film), 72
VHS, 65, 82, 84
The Village People, 63–64
voyeurism, 141–42

Walker, Matthew, 113–14
Wallace, Dee, *205*
Wallace, Tommy Lee: on audience reception, 58; career of, 42, 47, 232–33; Carpenter and, 5–7, 16–17, 19–20; on casting, 52; on continuity, 56–57; Cundey and, 2, 11, 48; on directing, 27–28, 47–48; editing by, 20–21; in film school, 7–8; Kneale and, 52–53; on production design, 9–11; reputation of, 61; on screenplays, 49; on success, 22; writing by, 51–52
Warlock, Dick, 53, 179, 192
Warner Brothers, 82, 176, 197
Warnow, Stanley, 201
Weather Report, 35–36
Webcams, 174
Weinstein, Bob: horror films for, 126–27; leadership of, 208; marketing for, 210; reputation of, 136, 144–46, 149, 152–53, 168–70
Weinstein, Harvey: horror films for, 126–27; leadership of, 208; marketing for, 210; reputation of, 136, 144–46, 149, 152–53, 168–70
Welles, Orson, xv, 3, 14, 49, 101, 108
When A Stranger Calls (film), 131
The Who, 35
Who's the Boss (TV show), 136
Wiene, Robert, 99
Wilbur, George, 78, 150
Wilde, Oscar, 125
Wilder, Billy, 52

Wild Hearts Can't Be Broken (film), 161
Williams, John, 165, 188
Williams, Michelle, 170
Williamson, Kevin, 153, 156
Willis, Gordon, 158
Winston, Stan, 161

Yablans, Irwin, 233
Yeager, Kevin, 122

Zawinul, Joe, 35–36
Zemeckis, Robert, 18, 62, 122
Zombie, Rob: aesthetics of, 203–5; Akkad, Malek, and, 125, 211–12; directing by, 197–201, 203–5, *206*, *207*, 208–10, *209*; Green compared to, 220–21; reputation of, xiv, 41, 148, 191, *205*, 205–8, 211–15; Timpone on, 200–201, 210, 214–15
Zsigmond, Vilmos, 33, 158